Cruising Attitude

Cruising

Tales of Crashpads, Crew Drama,
and Crazy Passengers at 35,000 Feet

Attitude

HEATHER POOLE

wm

WILLIAM MORROW
An Imprint of HarperCollins*Publishers*

I have changed the name of some individuals, and in some instances also modified or changed their identifying features, to preserve their anonymity. In some cases, composite characters have been created or timelines have been compressed, in order to further preserve privacy and to maintain narrative flow. The goal was to maintain people's privacy without damaging the integity of the story, as well as to capture certain qualities in people that I felt best defined what life as a flight attendant is really like

FIRST EDITION

Designed by Cassandra J. Pappas

Library of Congress Cataloging-in-Publication Data is available upon request.

ISBN 978-0-06-198646-8

12 13 14 15 16   OV/RRD   10 9 8 7 6 5 4 3 2 1

For Cosmo

there.) I was explaining to one of those passengers that yes, his seat really did recline, even in the last row of coach, when another passenger, a woman wearing hip-hugger jeans and a yellow halter top that exposed a belly ring, walked up, handed me a boarding pass, and said, "Someone is sitting in my seat."

I looked at the seat in question, 35E, and saw that Belly Ring Girl was right. Someone was in her seat. What made this particular situation a little crazy was not the fact that she had just yelled, "This sucks!"—I actually hear that phrase all the time, which, in itself, does kind of suck—but the fact that 35E just happened to be the second worst seat on the aircraft, the seat located directly in front of the hands-down worst seat, the middle seat in the last row.

"Excuse me, miss," I said to the seated woman in 35E with the pink cardigan sweater tied loosely around her neck. "May I see your boarding pass?'

Handing me a boarding pass for another seat, a very good seat, an aisle seat at the front of the aircraft, Pink Cardigan snapped, "I'm not moving!"

Okay. I forced a smile at her. "Please, do you mind taking *your* seat, ma'am, so this young lady can sit in *her* seat? The flight is full."

"I told you, I'm not moving!"

Well, at least I found Crazy, I thought to myself, as she explained in detail why she wasn't moving. It had something to do with the movie screen.

"But there's a movie screen right near your actual seat," I pointed out.

That didn't matter. What did matter was that a tall man sporting a handlebar mustache now stood a little too close to me. Pink Cardigan continued to go on and on about the seat she refused to move to.

"Ma'am, you're in my seat," the man interrupted.

How he knew this, I do not know. Because when I asked to see his boarding pass he couldn't find it.

Plane Crazy

OKAY, WHERE'S CRAZY? That's what I'm wondering every time I board a flight in my flammable navy blue polyester. In flight, I've seen passengers get naked, attempt to open an emergency door in order to get off the "bus," reach inside a first-class meal cart and eat leftover food from a dirty plate, and get hit on the head by luggage—then threaten to sue the airline because the injury had affected their psychic abilities. Once I watched an entire group of passengers traveling to Haiti put a voodoo curse on a coworker in the middle of the beverage service. I've seen a woman try to store her baby inside an overhead bin. Not too long ago a drunken passenger grabbed a flight attendant's butt—right in front of his wife! All the newspapers wrote about it. One paper even posed the question, "What is with people going crazy on flights?" That's exactly what I want to know!

Just how crazy can it get? Well, not long ago, I was at the rear of the aircraft, welcoming passengers aboard while keeping an eye on rolling bags and overhead bins. As is not uncommon, a couple of passengers walking down the aisle looked upset as soon as they realized they were seated in the last row, otherwise known as the worst seats on the plane. (Hey, someone has to sit

Contents

Perhaps this is Crazy, I thought to myself. It was a little crazy, three people vying for the same crappy seat, was it not?

I sighed, turned to the half-naked woman who actually held the ticket for 35E and asked if she'd be willing to take the other woman's seat.

"Whatever. But you owe me a drink," Belly Ring Girl said to me.

Okay. One down, two to go. That's when Mr. Sweet Stache walked to the back of the airplane and plopped down on the floor, placing an overstuffed backpack between his spidery long legs.

"Don't worry," he called out. "I'll just camp out here during the flight."

I turned around. He smiled. I didn't smile back. He'd said it like he meant it and that worried me. Did he actually believe he could sit there? On the floor. In front of the lav. Beside my jump seat.

"That's not going to work," I said. It had a little something to do with that metal thing we like to call a seat belt. I was pointing to the illuminated seat belt sign, trying my best to get through to this guy, when his eyes glazed over, he got to his feet, and he began walking up the aisle like he knew exactly where he was going. Briskly he made his way from the back of the plane right through business class and all the way up to first class, where I'm told he stopped in the middle of the cabin and announced very loudly, "Fine, I'll eat your crappy first-class food!"

It was official. We'd found Crazy.

Later on during the flight, after the service was over and everything had calmed down, I sat on a homemade bench (two empty beverage inserts connected by an oven rack) in the business-class galley and began to eat a sandwich I'd brought from home. A passenger from coach whipped back the stiff blue curtain.

"Can I buy a business-class entrée?" She held up a wad of cash.

Wiping my mouth, I quickly got to my feet. "We don't sell business-class food because passengers who travel in business have already paid for the food, and actually eat the food—"

"Can't I just buy a roll or something?"

I couldn't respond. Because right at that moment, as she stood there waving a crumpled bill to pay for the roll or something, Sweet Stache walked out of the lav with his pants undone.

Oh boy. I gulped, turned around, and prayed he'd keep walking. *Please keep walking!*

He stopped.

"Water," he said, pushing the hungry passenger out of the way. In the galley, right next to me, is where he decided to zip up his pants.

Of course, I did what any other flight attendant would do—I quickly reached for a plastic cup. Anything to make him go away! That's when I saw, out of the corner of my eye, a brown leather belt whip into the air with a SNAP! The woman who wanted the roll or something quickly disappeared.

Oh God, I prayed, *please don't let him be too crazy! Please say he's just a little crazy.* Because I really didn't want to be strangled by a belt over the second worst seat on the plane or the crappy-ass first-class food he did not eat.

"Here ya go." I handed him a glass of water without ice, not once taking my eye off the belt, now stretched tightly between his hands.

"Thanks." The belt slackened. He placed it on the counter, next to my sandwich.

"You're welcome." I let out a sigh of relief. I had not been strangled.

"Coffee." A statement, not a question.

I peeked into the coffee pot. Great. An empty pot. "I'm going to have to brew a new pot. I'll bring it to you as soon as it's ready." And I guess crazy was catching, because then I did something totally insane. I asked a question I shouldn't have asked, the one question capable of making this crazy person even crazier. "Where's your seat?"

"Forget it!" He grabbed the belt.

I gasped. "Sorry!"

Forcefully, he jabbed the leather through the belt loops. "Damn right you are." And with that he took a bite of my half-eaten sandwich and disappeared back to wherever he had decided to camp out for the flight.

"Yeah, umm, can I get that roll?" asked a familiar voice behind me.

Of course, that's not as crazy as what had happened just a few months earlier. I had been standing between business class and coach during boarding, greeting passengers and hanging coats, when a woman in her early twenties pulled me aside and said she didn't feel well and had a fever. I was about to tell her she might want to deplane and take a later flight, when she glanced at my name tag, looked me earnestly in the eye, and added, "Do you know if there's a first-class seat available, Heather?"

The warning bell immediately rang in my head. Whenever someone uses my name, it almost always means a special request is coming.

"I'm sorry, but there aren't any open seats in first class available." Just as I was about to tell her that even if there had been an open seat we still would not have been able to accommodate her up front, she waved me away with a flick of the wrist and continued down the aisle to a coach seat.

On a 767, the business-class galley is located behind business class in coach. Coach passengers seated on either side of it in the exit row are normally frequent fliers who didn't qualify for an upgrade now hoping to score free handouts. So when the sick woman sat down right behind the exit row, I knew it wasn't my lucky day.

She rang her call light thirty minutes into the flight. I turned around holding a linen-lined tray with four drinks balancing on top—Diet Coke with lime, water no ice, vodka tonic, chardonnay—and asked, "Can I get you something?"

"I don't feel well. I'm nauseous."

"Would you like a glass of ginger ale?"

"I'd prefer tea. Herbal tea. But not in a Styrofoam cup, a mug—a real mug," she said, eyeing the oven-warmed business-class porcelain mugs lining the chrome counter.

"All we have is plain black Lipton tea."

"Fine. Can I get something to eat?"

As my partner continued working his side (and only his side) of the business-class cabin, I called my coworkers in coach who were just about to pull the carts into the aisle to do the service to get a rundown of snacks that were available for purchase. When I hung up the phone, she said, "Do you have any uncooked vegetables?"

"Uncooked vegetables?" I repeated. I wanted to make sure I'd heard that right.

"That's all I can eat."

"How about a roll or cheese and crackers?" offered my colleague. As a rule, we never offer business-class food to coach passengers, but she did look a little pale and we didn't want to divert the flight.

But this sick passenger couldn't eat rolls. She couldn't eat cheese. She couldn't eat salad. She couldn't eat nuts. She couldn't even eat chocolate! Nor could she eat the delicious homemade combination fried rice the passenger sitting directly in front her kindly offered. (But I did and it was delicious! Thank you, Kwan.)

The only thing she *could* eat were uncooked veggies, and if she didn't eat them now, as in *right now*, she would get violently ill—or so she said.

As soon as the flight attendants working in first class were done with their service, I went up to see if there were any leftovers available. There rarely ever are. Well, not only did I find a bowl of green peas sitting on the salad cart but the lead flight attendant actually allowed me to take the first-class peas to the princess in coach!

"It's your lucky day," I said, handing her the silver bowl along with a silver spoon.

Not a word was said. No thank-you. No nothing. Just two bites, an ugly face, and the bowl was handed back to me. The passenger seated beside her rolled his eyes.

No sooner did I turn my back than a call light rang. I didn't have to walk far to turn it off.

"I need your help to get to the bathroom," she mumbled.

Taking her elbow, I helped her to stand. As she got to her feet, she moaned, "I'm going to be violently ill." Then she quickly took four steps to the business lav. I handed her a barf bag, shut the door, and told her I'd return to check on her in a minute.

"I'm not going to make it," I barely heard her say from behind the locked door.

On the other side of the closed door, I yelled, "What do you mean you're not going to make it? Do I need to page for a doctor?"

"No. I just need . . ." I leaned in closer and cupped my ears against the door. The OCCUPIED sign turned to VACANT and I almost fell inside. "Potatoes," she mumbled. "Do you have any potatoes?"

"We have potato chips, but not potatoes." With all ninety-nine pounds of her weight leaning into me, I helped her walk back to her seat. "Are you sure you don't want a cup of club soda and a roll? It might make you feel better."

"I'm sure. Are *you* sure there aren't any potatoes on board?"

The only thing I was more sure about were my passengers in business class. They had to be wondering where the heck I'd disappeared to again.

I shook my head. We had no potatoes. And that was when the "ill" passenger, the one who may or may not have thrown up in the bathroom (depending on who you asked), which may or may not have been the reason why the sink was now overflowing with what may or may not have been water, brown water, looked at me angrily and hissed, "I haven't asked for much on this flight!"

Okay, it's important to point out here—at least it's important to me that I point out—that I'm really a nice person. I am. I love my job. I do. And I'll do pretty much anything for the passengers, within reason, whether they're sick or not. I will. Still, this passenger had gotten on my last nerve. But I kept my mouth shut and got down on one knee, the way we're instructed to do in training, and looked her in her red eyes and listened as she not so very nicely said, "And I've been pretty nice on this flight, considering the circumstances."

I inhaled deeply and nodded my head in agreement. It took all my strength not to remind her of all she had, in fact, asked for—a first-class seat, herbal tea, a business-class mug, uncooked vegetables, help to the bathroom, potatoes, and now this, to deplane first, that's it and nothing more. In fact, she had asked me for more than any other passenger in fifteen years of flying!

To be fair, it's not always the passengers who are crazy. Sometimes, it's my colleagues. Years ago, I knew there might be a problem when four out of the nine flight attendants working my trip stopped me before I could even get my crew bags into the overhead bin to say, "You'll be working the drink cart on the left-hand side of coach."

"Okay," I said, even though it was not okay. I'm not big on confrontation.

I'd been awarded this trip on reserve, which meant I didn't

know the crew. Not that that mattered. What mattered was they were based in San Francisco, one of the most senior bases in the system. I am New York–based, which is and has always been the most junior base in the system at my airline. It's where most new hires end up. At some airlines, flight attendant positions on the plane are determined before each flight based on seniority. Just because a flight attendant works the galley position on one leg of the trip doesn't mean they will automatically get to work the same position on the next leg of the trip. If a more senior flight attendant wants to trade positions, the junior flight attendant will do so. Not at my airline. We know where we're working long before we leave the house for the airport, and we don't have to trade if we don't want to. Even so, the rest of the crew felt superior enough to tell me where, exactly, I'd be working that day, even though I already knew where to work, which was not the drink cart on the left-hand side of coach.

After I stowed my bags in the crew-designated area for my position, a bin in the middle of coach on the right hand side, I walked to the very back of the plane to introduce myself to three flight attendants hanging out in the galley. The crazy look in his piercing blue eyes immediately gave him away as the problem colleague. I smiled anyway.

"I think I'll be working with you today. I'm Heather."

"Mike." Mike sat down on his jump seat. He crossed his legs and smoothed his thick black mustache, not once making eye contact. "I'll be working the beverage cart alone, if you don't mind."

Not sure of what to make of this, I looked to my fellow colleagues for support. There was none to be found. They were too busy counting meals and loading the ovens, a job that normally requires one person, not two.

"Umm . . . okay . . . but what am I supposed to do while you're working the cart alone?"

He shrugged and walked away. My noncrazy colleagues glanced at each other without saying a word as they continued to busy themselves in the galley. I was on my own here.

Looking back, I should have just listened to Crazy-Eyes Mike and let him work the cart alone. Why didn't I just twiddle my thumbs in the back of the airplane and watch? Instead, when it was time to start the service, I hopped on the other side and practically sprinted backward up the aisle as he pushed the cart with way too much force.

"Whoa, cowboy." I laughed, hoping he'd get the hint. He didn't.

Cowboy didn't stop there. It got worse, much worse. Unfortunately there is nothing in our training manual about what to do when a fellow crew member purposefully rams a cart into a passenger's seat and yells, "Bitch!"

"Oh my God, are you okay? I'm so sorry," I stammered to the woman now doubled over in pain. I looked at Mike. "What are you doing?"

As soon as the words were out of my mouth, his eyes bugged out of his head and his face turned red. In the middle of the aisle, surrounded by 123 passengers, he screamed out another, worse word. At me. I think.

The rest of the trip was spent frantically trying to calm down a few passengers, reassuring them that yes, something would be done about Mike. One passenger wanted to press charges. Mike had scared them all so much that not one person on the left-hand side of the airplane ordered a drink. Now I was stuck dealing with the mess. After everything calmed down, I began hand-running drinks back and forth alone while the flight attendants working the other aisle calmly maintained the flow of service. Mike sat on his jump seat and read the paper.

Ten minutes after Mike's outburst, the captain called and asked me to come up for a chat. Behind the comfortingly locked cockpit door, I told him exactly what had occurred. Choosing his words carefully, he asked whether or not *I* felt we should divert. I told him I didn't feel authorized to make such a decision. Because I was *afraid* to make such a decision! Who was I to take responsibility for an airplane making an unscheduled landing? The pilot should make that call. We did not divert. I spent the rest of the flight in the cock*less*pit.

When we did finally land, authorities met the flight. After all the passengers had deplaned, Crazy Eyes was escorted off by two cops. The crew scattered, all in a hurry to get home, and I slowly followed behind what I assumed would become an ex-coworker, a blue uniform sandwiched between black and white, as I walked alone to baggage claim to catch a courtesy van to my layover hotel.

We met up again later that night, as we would many nights to come, in a now recurring dream. I find myself wearing nothing but a navy blue feather boa, combat boots, and a baton on my hip while boarding a flight back to New York. My heart stops when I come face-to-face with Crazy-Eyes Mike. He grunts. I step out of his way to allow him to pass, and as he does, I notice his hands are locked in silver cuffs behind his back. Of course, I do what any normal naked flight attendant would do: I toss the feather boa over my shoulder and tell a smiling flight attendant I've never met before that she'll be working the beverage cart on the left-hand side of the airplane. Immediately she stops smiling and rams me with her suitcase, causing me to double over in pain. Then, just as I'm about to yell out a word I never use, regardless of how appropriately it might describe the other flight attendants or passengers, the alarm clock wakes me up. It's 5:00 a.m. and I'm working a flight to Seattle or San Diego or Santa Barbara. Doesn't matter where I'm going, really. All that matters is it's time to do it again.

So where's Crazy?

Or am I crazy?

You tell me.

I Never Wanted to Be
a Flight Attendant

IN ORDER TO be a flight attendant in the 1950s, women were required to be attractive—"just below Hollywood standards." No wonder many a hopeful starlet became a flight attendant as part of a backup plan.

Rumor has it Tom Berenger and Richard Gere once worked as flight attendants. I don't believe it, either, but I *have* dreamt about it. Several times. Richard looked amazing wearing nothing but a navy blue pinstriped apron serving me chocolate chip cookies in bed. Dennis Miller, on the other hand, really did work as a flight attendant for Continental, or so I've been told. Still trying to figure out how true that is. But what a snarky flight attendant he must have been! Actress Kate Linder, who has been on *The Young and the Restless* for more than twenty years, is *still* a flight attendant for United Airlines. You'll only find her behind a cart on the weekends. Kim Kardashian's mother, Kris, was a flight attendant for American Airlines when she met Robert Kardashian, O. J. Simpson's attorney. What's funny about that is Kris's second husband, Bruce Jenner, an Olympic gold medalist, was married first to a flight attendant who supported him while he trained for the decathlon. Bruce later went on to purchase a private plane, which he learned to pilot in order to make it on time to public appearances.

But flying is not for everyone. Ant, the comedian, was a flight attendant for American Airlines before he became a TV personality. Evangeline Lilly, who starred as a plane crash survivor on the television show *Lost*, hated her brief stint as a flight attendant, calling it the "worst job ever" thanks to short layovers and swollen feet.

Men who don't have a problem with swollen flight attendant feet include Robert De Niro, George Best, David Caruso, Wayne Newton, Lou Rawls, Montel Williams, Russian Prime Minister Vladimir Putin, Greece Prime Minister George Papandreou, Israeli Prime Minister Benjamin Netanyahu, and *American Idol* winner Ruben Studdard. They all married flight attendants. And let's not forget the most recent person to join the flight attendant wife club, Kelsey Grammer, who ditched his wife Camille, from *The Real Housewives of Beverly Hills*, to wed Kayte Walsh, a Virgin Airlines air hostess. Bill Maher, a self-proclaimed bachelor, dated fly girl Coco Johnsen for a couple of years until they wound up in court. And there are all the famous affairs . . . but I probably shouldn't go there.

The prime minister of Iceland and the world's first openly gay female leader, Johanna Sigurdardottir, once worked as a flight attendant for Loftleidir, a predecessor of Icelandair. Wife of rogue trader Nick Leeson (Barings Bank), Lisa Leeson, became a flight attendant for Virgin. Virgin's very own Richard Branson was actually born to a flight attendant. Prince William's wife, Catherine, Duchess of Cambridge, was born Catherine Elizabeth Middleton to parents who both worked as airline crew before going into the party supply business.

While times (and requirements) have changed, the job is still a desirable one. Thousands of people apply each year. At my airline, the average age of a flight attendant is now forty years old. For the first time in history, being a flight attendant is considered a profession, not just a job. Fewer are quitting, turnover is not as high as it once was, and competition has gotten fierce. Ninety-six percent of people who apply to become flight attendants do not get a call-back. In December 2010, Delta Airlines received more than one hundred thousand applications after announcing they had openings for one thousand flight attendants. Only the most qualified applicants are hired. Even though a college degree is not a requirement, there are very few flight attendants who do not possess one. Lawyers and doctors have been known to apply. This should tell you a lot about me, and anyone else you encounter in navy polyester. Think about that the next time you're on a plane.

Of course, the first time I tried to become a flight attendant I wasn't part of the lucky 4 percent.

In college, I went to my first airline interview in order to get away from a roommate who had more than her fair share of issues. She'd bring guys back to our dorm room and leave them behind. Try studying Japanese culture when your roomie is throwing up all over your clothes, the ones you'd specifically and repeatedly forbidden her to wear! So when my mother, a woman who had *always* dreamed of becoming a flight attendant, mailed me a newspaper clipping with an ad circled four times in red for an open house with a major U.S. carrier, I decided to apply. Not so much because I wanted to become a flight attendant, but because the airline provided a free ticket to a city out of state where the interviews were being conducted. Broke and tired, with a laundry hamper full of vomit and a disheveled man locked in the bathroom using my Q-tips, I just wanted to get away. I also wanted to fly on an airplane, something I'd only done three times before in my life.

Two weeks after I received a letter from the airline telling me where to go and what to say to the ticket agent to get a seat on the flight (not all airlines cover the travel expense), I stepped off the aircraft, sashayed down the jet bridge in four-inch beige pumps, a little black bag rolling behind, and made my way to a non-descript door clear on the other side of the busy airport terminal. There I found a giant room filled with hundreds of happy, smiling women. I stopped in my tracks. The banquet room was lined with neat little rows of applicants, knees held tightly together, ankles crossed delicately off to the side, dressed head to toe in blue and black. My brand-new canary yellow suit and suntan hose screamed LOOK AT ME! And not in a good way. Right then and there I wanted to die.

The women, all with their hair pulled tightly back, looked me up and down, then quickly turned their attention back to the front of the room. With my blond locks falling halfway down my back, they could see I was zero competition. Nonchalantly I wiped the frosted pink stain off my lips with the back of my hand, twirled my unruly hair into a loose bun, and took a seat in the back of the room. I wanted to hide, but hiding at an airline interview is not an option. Not if you want to get hired. Also not if you're the only person in sight wearing a shade of the rainbow.

After a brief introduction from the people conducting the interviews, we were divided into what looked like fifty groups of five. While I waited for my turn to be called, I made friends with the girl seated beside me. She had worked for a competitive carrier for five years but quit after she had a baby—the biggest mistake she ever made, she said. Now divorced, she really needed this job. I couldn't decide if her history with a different airline would be an advantage or a disadvantage over someone like me. When my group was finally called, we were taken to a private room and asked a number of fairly easy questions regarding our past work experience. Playing it safe, I made an effort to raise my hand second or third since I had overheard others talking earlier and knew not to be the last person to answer a question. We had been in the room for about ten minutes when a peppy women with red lips got down to business.

"Besides travel and meeting new people, why do you want to be a flight attendant?"

Silence all around. Finally I spoke up. Glamour! Excitement! Free passes! She smiled real big and said, "If you don't hear from us in two weeks feel free to apply again" and then dismissed us all.

On my way out I spotted the former flight attendant through the glass of another door as she was stepping onto a giant scale. When we made eye contact, she smiled real big and gave me a thumbs-up. My heart dropped a little as I gave her one back. Turns out, "free passes" wasn't the right answer.

Three years later I applied again. I had graduated from college and found an exciting job designing watches for a well-known company. But the pay was miserable, and when a promotion didn't lead to a raise, I quit. Once again my mother cut out an ad in the help wanted section of the *Dallas Morning News*. An airline I'd never heard of was looking for flight attendants. At $14 an hour, why not? I could travel around the world and meet new people while I looked for another job, a good job, the kind that pays well, that people have respect for—maybe something in marketing. And two days later, I was officially a flight attendant for Sun Jet International Airlines!

Sun Jet International, a charter airline based in Dallas, never once flew anywhere you'd call "international." They didn't even fly anywhere that might require a layover. It was 100 percent "turns," which meant I never had to pack underwear. There were only three airplanes, all leased, and Sun Jet flew the ancient birds twice a day to Newark, Fort Lauderdale, and Long Beach for just $69 a flight. At the time, other airlines charged eight times that amount for the same ticket, which should tell you a lot about our passengers. We quickly became known as the "Dancer Express" for all the go-go dancers from Dallas who flew to New York to make money. After their flight, all these bleach blondes could be found at baggage claim teetering on six-inch stripper heels waiting for giant tubs full of costumes to come jingling down the luggage chute.

It didn't take me long to notice that other flight attendants—*real* flight attendants, the kind who traveled to exciting destinations and had layovers in hotels—rarely returned my greeting whenever we passed each other in the terminal. It might have been the Sun Jet uniforms: white button-down blouses, two silver stripes adorning each shoulder, tucked into pleated, navy blue Bermuda shorts with navy blue hose and heels. I loved the ridiculous getup—after all, it showed I was a flight attendant! That is, until one day, when we landed at the Newark airport and I ran off the airplane to find something quick to eat before heading back to Dallas. As I impatiently waited in line at Nathan's hot dog stand, I saw it. The woman plopping the sausage into a stale bun wore a navy blue snap-on tie that looked exactly like mine. After that I refused to wear the tie.

Of course, it's possible the other flight attendants weren't snickering at our ties—it might have had something to do with our passengers. They were a class act, notorious for causing disturbances in airports. But why wouldn't they? I worked for an airline that made no qualms about using duct tape to repair broken armrests, seat backs, and overhead bins. No apologies were made to passengers forced to sit on soiled seat cushions that had been covered with a black trash bag in order to hide the vomit or pee from one of the dozens of unaccompanied minors who traveled with us regularly. Other airlines had limits on the number of unaccompanied minors. Not us. We were the airline of broken homes. Once I counted twelve UMs on a single flight. (This is unheard of with larger airlines.) Weight and balance issues were simply solved by removing luggage—*all of the luggage*, not just passengers with luggage—without informing anyone what had been done until the aircraft had landed. Passengers were often greeted by an announcement stating they could pick up their bags the following day. Of course, chaos always ensued, which meant security would have to escort the crew off the airplane. Once we were safe and sound behind a locked metal door emblazoned with an EMPLOYEES ONLY sign, we'd sneak out a back door and take the sky train to the employee parking lot, knowing full well we'd be dodging spit balls and loogies all over again in less than twenty-four hours.

Late one night on the sky train, I noticed a homeless-looking gentleman sitting in the corner and squinting at me. He looked me up and down and hissed, "Something wicked this way comes." I sat there in silence clutching the handle of my bag, too afraid to speak or even move, when it dawned on me. He must have flown Sun Jet before.

Our mechanical delays were legendary. We never canceled flights—ever! Why would we, when under the charter system, we could not collect revenue until a flight had flown? We were allowed to delay a flight up to forty-eight hours. It was printed on the back of the ticket in small print that no one ever read. Once, in the middle of a long, creeping delay that would eventually result in the nonunionized crew "laying over" on the airplane, each of us sleeping three seats across, an angry male passenger followed me into the ladies' room in the terminal. I had no idea he'd done so until I'd already sat down, which is the moment he chose to lay into me. The man gave me a piece of his mind through the stall door! I was too afraid to exit, let alone flush, so I just stayed there—literally, not going—until he disappeared. To this day, fifteen years later, I am reluctant to get off an airplane to use a public restroom during a ground delay.

But it's not like we hadn't been warned. During two weeks

of training at a three-star hotel that the airline didn't pay for but required us to stay at, our one and only instructor informed our class of twenty: "Our passengers do not always communicate the same way you and I might in the same situation." There was a pause, a really long pause, before she added, "You're going to hear a lot of words you probably don't hear throughout the course of a regular day." A pilot who was sitting in to answer questions about how airplanes fly began to laugh so long and hard that the instructor ordered him out. Immediately she moved on to the next subject.

But I don't mean to make it sound all bad! At the time I found myself on the line, Sun Jet was a small airline with only sixty flight attendants. Because of that, we got to know each other well and formed a tight bond that flight attendants at larger airlines rarely experience. We were there for one another, all of us, including the pilots. Every day it was us against them—the passengers, the company, you name it, we fought it.

Despite everything, we had a great time. The rules were simple. Last crew back to base had to buy the other two crews a round of drinks after work. Each afternoon three crews would fly out of the Dallas–Fort Worth airport between the hours of four and five o'clock. Newark, then Long Beach, then Fort Lauderdale, all scheduled to land at midnight back in Dallas. As soon as we touched ground at our destination, we'd rush the passengers off as politely as possible, pray the cleaners would be quick (they always were, which explained why the aircraft was never quite clean), reboard another full flight as quickly as we could, and race back to base, keeping tabs on each other through an air traffic controller in on the joke. At the end of the night we'd all meet up, pilots included, at a restaurant bar a few miles away to share stories about passengers who had been taken off in handcuffs. Until one night, a passenger who'd been escorted off by police—and who I assumed had been arrested—actually beat us to the bar and ended up sitting in a neighboring booth. Talk about an eye-opener. I learned a lot about how airlines work that night. Kick 'em off one flight, throw 'em on the very next flight. Depending on the airline, they might even get an upgrade.

At Sun Jet a week didn't go by when passengers weren't being kicked off our flights. One such fool locked himself inside the lavatory seconds prior to departure.

"Sir, are you okay in there?" a colleague asked, knocking on the bathroom door. "You need to come out now! We're about to depart!"

When the passenger refused to exit or respond to our calls, my colleague did exactly what we had been taught in training and unlocked it from the outside. As she pushed open the door, a guy jumped five feet into the air, causing the needle shoved into his arm to pop out, blood splattering everywhere, including all over my colleague, who immediately ran off the airplane. I'm surprised she didn't quit her job right then and there. The airplane got pulled out of service—and the passenger probably wound up enjoying a beer with the inbound crew, I'm sure.

A few days later, while helping to clean the airplane, a flight attendant stuck her hand deep inside a seat back pocket and discovered a used and haphazardly discarded needle. I shudder to think what would have happened if one of our unaccompanied minors had found it. I wondered if the needle had belonged to the infamous porn star who came on board scantily dressed with bruises all over her malnourished body, the one who had draped herself all over every overly excited male passenger who recognized her, and they all did, including the two old geezers in the cockpit who wouldn't release her from their grip until she agreed to say "cheese" for their camera.

Drug addicts and porn stars weren't our only problems. The elderly were out of control as well. While prepping the cabin for an emergency landing—*an emergency landing!*—an elderly woman screamed, "Where's my muffin? I want my muffin! I don't care what the hell is going on with this damn plane!" After the aircraft was safe and sound on the ground, I turned the TV on at home and witnessed the old bat still making a stink about her damn muffin to a local news reporter.

And then there was the eighty-something-year-old woman who decided to disrobe after takeoff because she "wanted to get off the bus." I don't make the connection, either. But she attempted to do this by wrapping her wrinkled fingers around an emergency exit door handle while screaming, "Let me off this thing!" I'm not sure which scared the passengers more, seeing someone so frail freaking out nekkid or watching a young male coworker wrap himself around her uncovered lady bits to try with all his might to unsuccessfully pry her fingers off the door—a door that cannot be opened in flight regardless of how badly an elderly nudist may want to get off.

After I grew accustomed to working with the traveling public, passengers became the least of my worries. Once, while taxiing to the gate, I'll never forget how scared I felt as smoke began to fill the cabin. Passengers quickly grabbed their bags and managed to exit the aircraft without further incident. The smoke dissipated before maintenance arrived. They never did figure out what could have caused it. But they did a great job of giving up on solving a "problem" they couldn't find.

"I am not flying a broken airplane!" the captain, an older guy with a couple of airlines under his belt, shouted to someone over the phone. Because he said it like he meant it, I gave him a thumbs-up. He gave me a wink. The company gave him an ultimatum. Cursing under his breath, he hung up the phone and growled, "Tell the agent we're ready to board." An hour later we were back in the air on our broken plane.

Things were run so badly at Sun Jet I'd actually get nervous when I didn't hear the computerized voice in the cockpit calling out, "Terrain, Terrain, pull up, pull up!" from the other side of the door when I was strapped in my jump seat on approach. Once a jump seat fell off the wall during descent. The two flight attendants sitting beside the cockpit door followed procedures and moved the first row of passengers to the floor. There was nowhere else to put them. Surprisingly, and without argument, the passengers did exactly as they were told. They lay down flat on their backs. The crew placed their legs over the passengers and manned the exit doors from the closest passenger seats.

Each Tuesday at the Long Beach airport, our airplanes were greeted by a middle-aged man in a dark suit. For most airlines, FAA inspectors check employees' flight manuals to make sure they're up to date and dole out hefty fines if they're not. At Sun Jet, we never once handed over our manuals; we usually handed over the plane. Well, just for a couple of hours until maintenance could come and change the white lights that led to red lights that did not lead to an emergency row, but instead led to a row two rows behind the exit.

The airline wasn't always to blame. Half the time it was our passengers keeping the FAA on their toes. Ten life vests had to be replaced after a group of high school teenagers decided to inflate them midflight during spring break weekend. Then there were the passengers who liked to take home souvenirs from the flight, things like fire extinguishers, ashtrays, first-aid kits, whatever they could get their sticky fingers on. These are all considered "no-go items." That means the flight cannot depart without them. Regular airlines might have replacements in stock. Not Sun Jet! We'd have to wait until one of the flights scheduled to land at midnight in Dallas could be sent to rescue us. At that point the drinking game would change. It became last flight back to Dallas wins.

But the craziest thing about working for Sun Jet had nothing to do with any of that. It wasn't even the time I had several passengers light up cigarettes because they thought it might be their last flight. No, the craziest thing about working for a charter airline was that I enjoyed it. I did! What's not to love about a job that allows you to sleep in every single morning? Who wouldn't love working twelve days a month—if that? Don't get me wrong, it's not that I *loved* serving drinks and picking up trash (and I'm not talking about my ex-boyfriends), but I did appreciate the flexibility, the freedom, the camaraderie, and the excitement of not knowing what the day would bring, as well as leaving that day behind as soon as I stepped off the plane. As for the drama, it always made for a great conversation piece at a party or over dinner with friends. So when I overheard two coworkers whispering about an upcoming airline interview for a major commercial carrier, I decided to throw my hat into the ring. It'd only be for a little while, until I found something else—maybe something in sales.

And that is how I came to walk into my third airline interview with grace and confidence, completely prepared for anything. I had experienced it all, and then some, in only three months at Sun Jet. My makeup had been professionally applied, my hair swept up into a conservative updo with absolutely no frizzies, a flight attendant no-no. During the group interview, I made sure to pepper my answers with the phrase "good customer service." I threw in the word "flexible" as often as possible. And I stressed that I wanted a career, not just a job, with an airline I could be proud of. That got me a real smile, not once but twice. When they handed me a PA card and asked me to read it out loud, I didn't for a moment remove what I imagined to be a first- and business-class smile. Then came The Question. Besides meeting new people and traveling, why did I want to become a flight attendant? I told them I found the flexible lifestyle appealing. When they asked how I prepared for the interview, I showed them my comfortable yet stylish navy blue heels and let them know where they could find them on sale. I even outwitted them with an answer to a trick question: "Answer the one question you thought we might ask but didn't."

One guy had actually confessed all his negative traits when posed the same question. Me, I said, "When can you start training is the question. The answer is today. But I'm flexible with whatever training date you have available."

With an answer like that, how could they resist?

During the psychological evaluation, I made a point of describing my character on the front side of the page the exact same way my family and friends would describe me on the flip side, whether or not I agreed. My sister didn't count. Seriously, besides her, I got along with everyone just fine!

Five minutes later I found myself sitting in an unmarked white van with two other wannabe flight attendants, currently a bartender and a nurse, all of us on our way to "medical" across the street. I knew for a fact that I had been hired.

"Medical" is the one and only word a hopeful flight attendant wants to hear at an airline interview. It means the airline is interested. It means there will be a scale to stand on in the near future. As long as the applicant can lift a required amount of weight, reach into an overhead bin to grab the emergency equipment, and pass an eye, ear, and drug test—and a background check—with flying colors, a training date will be assigned. Because of my brief experience at Sun Jet, I knew just how important it was to get the first training date possible.

At an airline, seniority is everything. Everything. It determines the type of trips you'll get and whether you'll be stuck on reserve or forced to work holidays for the rest of your life. It can make or break your career. And seniority is determined by class hire date, so it's absolutely essential to accept the earliest flight attendant training class you're offered. Unless the airline discovered something about me that I didn't know—like my being a felon or an illegal alien—I left medical knowing I'd been accepted to training. What I didn't know was when training would start. Most airlines will offer classes right away, with a new class starting each week. That's why I planned to give Sun Jet one week's notice. They weren't thrilled. Three of us were leaving for the same reason.

Little did I know that less than a year later, ValuJet would crash into the Everglades causing the flying public to lose confidence in low-cost carriers. In 1998, Sun Jet entered bankruptcy court, only to reemerge briefly as Southeast before going out of business forever. At the time I was thankful to work for an airline I could be proud of with the firm and comforting knowledge that the open sky was just a fun and temporary pit stop on the way to a real career, something in . . . oh, I don't know. I had a bachelor's in psychology, after all. I could figure it out later!

Barbie Boot Camp

3

"**Y**OU PACK IT,** you lift it." That's the mantra of flight attendants worldwide. One of the most common misconceptions about flight attendants is that it's our job to lift heavy passenger bags into overhead bins. This is not true. We have no problem finding a space for your bag. We'll happily turn a few bags around to make room. We may even *assist* in lifting the bag. Note the emphasis on the word "assist," as in we're not doing it for you. We're lifting it together. It's a team effort. Seriously, you are a key part of Operation Bag-in-the-Bin. I'm sorry—and I'm sorry I always have to say I'm sorry—but take a little responsibility here. You pack it, you lift it. And please stop yelling at me!

Here's the deal. What you pack and whether you check your bag or carry it on can drastically affect the outcome of your trip. Don't make travel more stressful than it has to be. Play it safe and do what flight attendants do. When it comes to preparing for a trip, we're experts. We travel light with just a roll-aboard and a tote bag, even when we're packing for days at a time. The secret is rolling. Rolling instead of folding leaves clothes wrinkle-free. Our other tricks? I always coordinate my outfits around footwear—a comfy kick-around pair for exploring the destination by day and something dressy for dinner and a show at night. Undies, socks, bikinis, whatever can be wadded up, are housed inside shoes. No space goes unused. To make things simple, pack black and be done with it. So what if you wear the same outfit over and over? That's what easy-to-pack accessories are for! Scarves and jewelry can completely change boring black into something fab. And whatever gets left behind becomes the perfect excuse to go shopping for something new! On vacation we get to know the locals at a Laundromat. What better place to read a guidebook or ask around for a great place to eat?

Of course, I did not know any of this in 1995 when I signed a clipboard and a FedEx guy handed over an official-looking letter from the airline. I'd been waiting for it since my interview two weeks earlier. I ripped open the envelope and read, "Congratulations!" My heart began to beat faster.

The letter welcomed class 23 to flight attendant training—round two in less than a year for me. Upon completing a seven-and-a-half-week course, I, along with two pieces of luggage—wait, did that say . . . two pieces? I read the sentence again. Two pieces. And it was written in big black bold print, so I knew the airline meant business. If that wasn't bad enough, neither bag could weigh more than eighty pounds, and they would both accompany me on an "exciting journey" to a new crew base the moment I completed training. No time to go home and repack. If you've ever had to pack two plus months' worth of clothing into two suitcases, you probably know the exact feeling I had in the pit of my stomach. How the heck could I possibly whittle my entire life down to 160 pounds? I read on. Did the airline really expect me to memorize more than five hundred airport city codes before training even began? How was I going to fit that in when I had so much—er, little—packing to do?

I sat down on my closet floor, staring up at my clothes. I couldn't decide what to take. I had no idea what I might need at a crew base. I didn't even know where in the country my base would be. So I ended up doing what any other twenty-four-year-old might do. I threw it all in: rubber flip-flops and furry snow boots, strapless sundresses and cashmere sweaters, a little black number and some workout clothes—you know, just in case. Who knew what kind of excitement awaited me? I threw in some costume jewelry for good measure, then plopped down on top of the first bag and tried . . . to zip . . . it shut! I couldn't get it closed. Frowning, I imagined myself passing through the pearly gates of the flight academy. A larger-than-life flight instructor would place my suitcases on an industrial-size scale and send me straight back home to Mom and Dad. Because that's exactly where I'd end up if I didn't make it through. I took out the snow boots and tried again. I removed the flip-flops and still I couldn't get the thing shut. One less sweater—make that two—and I was finally good to go. My mother promised to box up what I couldn't get inside and mail it to me later.

Three weeks after my flight attendant interview, with two thousand borrowed dollars in the bank (the amount suggested by the airline for incidentals, even though room and board were covered), I said good-bye to my old life and walked onto a small campus setting just five miles away from a major U.S. airport. I felt nervous and insecure, but my hair looked good, my makeup looked good, and I looked good. That's all that mattered.

Though my luggage toppled over every five steps, I somehow managed to pass through the flight academy's automatic doors without a hitch. Once inside, the place looked like nothing special, just a regular hotel lobby. A check-in counter was to my right, and sofas and wingback chairs were scattered about the open room. Straight ahead, through floor-to-ceiling windows, I made out a deserted swimming pool, a volleyball net, and a barbecue pit. To my left, I spotted a bar. A bar! Who knew training was going to be so much fun? A winding staircase on the right led to a landing overlooking the room, which was slowly beginning to fill with people.

"Excuse me," I whispered, my palms sweating, as I made my way through small cliques of future colleagues. At the desk, I checked in, then slapped a HELLO MY NAME IS HEATHER sticker across my chest. A shiny gold key and a packet full of papers slid across the counter, and I turned back to the room, not exactly sure what to do next. As I looked around, trying to play it cool, I realized everyone in the room looked amazing. A stunning black-haired, ruby-lipped, perfectly pale woman walked toward me, and suddenly I felt even less special.

"Hi," she said, flashing a cheerful smile. "I'm Georgia."

Georgia, it turned out, was a real-life beauty pageant runner-up from Louisiana who used words like "fixin'," as in, "I'm fixin' to get a drink. Ya want one?"

"Sure!" I parked my bags against the wall.

At the bar I ordered a Diet Coke. We moved back to the lobby to sit, and while we talked, we watched in awe as people continued to check in. It looked like there were at least fifty of us milling about. Like so many of my glamorous soon-to-be best friends, Georgia had always dreamed about becoming a flight attendant. She wouldn't let anything stop her from making that dream a reality, not even a jealous boyfriend, who, I quickly learned, had just moved to North Carolina.

"I told him I'd see him before he knew it, but he ain't happy, not one little bit. Men!" she snorted, and then took a sip of Diet Dr Pepper.

Georgia was not alone. All of us had left someone behind: family, friends, loved ones. I'd only been dating Paul for six months, and he'd actually been more than supportive of my new career choice. Probably because it gave him the opportunity to work around the clock in order to get both his landscaping and car-detailing businesses off the ground. To be perfectly honest, though, I had been looking for a way out of the relationship for a while now.

"It's just that he's really sweet and I don't want to hurt his feelings," I told Georgia. I made a face. "I'm not big on confrontation."

"And that, sweetie, is why the airline hired you!"

I didn't understand it then, but Georgia may have been on to something. At that moment, all I knew was that we were spilling our life stories and we'd only known each other for ten minutes! Already we were the best of friends.

"You know, we oughtta room together!" Georgia said.

I was thrilled and relieved. But it turned out that we weren't allowed to pick our roommates; they were preassigned. I promised to meet Georgia for dinner after we each dropped our bags in our rooms. I wasn't sure how long that would take her to accomplish. By the time I arrived, I'd thinned my luggage down to seventy-eight pounds even, but Georgia's version of packing light seemed to involve eight humongous bags that weighed about three tons. Each.

With a room key pressed firmly in the palm of my hand, I put on my brightest first-class smile and tried as best I could to roll my bags into the elevator without crashing into anyone— mission unaccomplished. Two floors up, I stood in front of my new home, slid the key into the keyhole, and took a deep breath. The moment I cracked the door open, I was blown away by one big, "Howdy! I'm Linda."

I stood speechless in the hallway, taking Linda in: teased bouffant, orange tan, turquoise jewelry, teensy-tiny blue-jean skirt, electric blue cowboy boots, matching blue eye shadow. My roommate, the person with whom I would spend the next two months in a space that looked to be the size of a small college dorm room, was a cowgirl. Well, the word "girl" might be a little misleading. Linda actually looked older than my mother. Yeehaw.

"Nice to meet you. I'm Heather," I finally got out as I reluctantly entered and plopped down on a hard twin bed. "Guess this one's mine."

Linda picked up the phone and I reminded myself not to judge a book by its cover. But it was just so hard not to as I noted cowboy boots in every color lining the closet floor. While I tried to make do with half of a tiny closet, I overheard Linda saying to someone that this was her second chance at life. That got me wondering, what went wrong the first time around? As I hung up seventy-eight pounds of casual business attire, the dress code for the flight academy, I listened to Linda telling at least ten different people she loved them. When she hung up the phone, I thought I saw her wipe away a tear.

"You okay?" I asked.

Nervously she laughed. "Sorry. Those were my grandkids. I miss them so."

Grandkids! No way. My cowgirl roommate was also a grandmother? Could we have had less in common?

On any good reality show, the first exciting event is the makeover episode. That first day of training was all about grooming. It's common knowledge that flight attendants must be willing to do two things: cut their hair and go anywhere. Well, I have crazy hair. It's half wavy and half frizzy. Weather, water, styling products, and the power level of the hair dryer all make a huge difference when it comes to looking presentable. Since I hadn't wanted to have any problems at training, I'd gotten my long blond locks chopped at a professional salon before an amateur hired by the airline could get a hold of me. The result, in my opinion, looked amazing. But because frizzies on a flight attendant are unacceptable, regardless of humidity, I was schooled on how to smooth and tame my unruly hair by creating a classic French twist with three hundred bobby pins and an entire can of hairspray. It looked pretty. My scalp hurt. I kept my mouth shut.

Georgia, of course, soared through Grooming 101 without having to change a thing. Our instructors used words like "beautiful, gorgeous, so graceful," to describe her, practically trailing her with a standing ovation. Flawless, a poster child for the airline, she had mastered the appearance of perfection early on in her pageant career. Why nobody hired her to run the grooming department, I don't know. The girl could work wonders with a bit of gloss, fake lashes, and a push-up bra. The instructors constantly instructed the rest of us to take note of the way she lined her lips, highlighted her cheeks, arched her brows, accented her eyes, and wore her hair. Some female classmates began to resent the adulation thrust upon Georgia, while others, particularly the men in class, adored her, taking each and every beauty tip to heart.

Linda, on the other hand, got a complete makeover. No one was surprised, not even Linda. We'd been divided into groups of ten and had been escorted to a salon on campus. Well, when I say "salon," I mean a room at the end of a long hallway that felt more like a mini cosmetology school than any salon I'd ever been to. Linda was the last one to take a seat in front of the brightly lit mirror. Though her jaw remained tense throughout the hour-long ordeal, she did not complain about the transformation, not once, not even when the frighteningly plastic grooming technician in charge wiped away the frosted blue coloring shellacked across her lids and demanded she never wear that horrid color again. Mauve replaced blue. Her hair was de-poofed. Glitzy earrings were exchanged for something more conservative, no bigger than a quarter in size. Because we were only allowed to wear two rings per hand, Linda removed four gaudy hunks of gold. As for shoes, cowboy boots don't work well with the uniform, so Linda took a taxi to a nearby mall and purchased something sensible, in leather, with at least an inch heel—no straps or buckles allowed.

"Don't forget that appearances are to be maintained at the flight academy from this day forth," announced the instructor before dismissing us at the end of the day.

"Even after hours and on weekends?" We all turned to see who dared ask such a question. Joseph, a big guy who looked like he might be more comfortable wearing sweats, smiled sheepishly.

"Even after hours and on weekends," stated the instructor, which would come to echo in my head late at night when I'd literally run to the gym, ducking in doorways whenever I thought I heard someone coming for fear I'd get caught wearing running shorts and a T-shirt outside the workout room. I had no idea how to get there without breaking the rules.

"Ladies!" one of our instructors would call out often whenever he'd enter the classroom. Back in the day he had probably been a catch. But the years had taken their toll, particularly where his head was concerned. He barely had any hair left. Khaki Dockers and a polo shirt with the company's logo embroidered across the pocket, the official flight instructor uniform, paired with white running sneakers didn't do him any justice, either. The first time we heard him say it, we sat staring blankly, eagerly awaiting his next word. It never came. He stood behind the podium slowly scanning the room, making eye contact with each and every one of us. He didn't look pleased. At one point I wondered if he'd forgotten what he wanted to say. But we quickly came to learn what it meant. We would frantically and in unison dig compact mirrors out of our purses, check our lips and reapply, even if we really didn't need to. If the guilty party did not make amends— now, as in right now—she'd get dismissed from class forever. Lipstick, at flight attendant training, was serious business. It had to be worn at all times.

"Why?" asked a classmate who had dared not to wear the color my airline had recommended that year, Clinique red. Instead she wore one that looked a lot like, well, no shade at all, a glossy nude. I liked it. But I knew better than to wear it.

"So passengers can read your lips during an emergency," said an instructor, matter-of-factly. None of us knew if he was serious.

The following day, Glossy Nude didn't show up for class. We weren't surprised by her sudden departure. We had no idea if she had quit or if she'd been kicked out. Most of us didn't even think twice about it. Well, except for Georgia, who came to the conclusion that women's lib had gotten the best of Glossy Nude. She made a group of us promise not to let it happen to us. I agreed, even if I disagreed about the unflattering shade of red that had been chosen for my pale skin.

Lipstick turned out to be the least of my worries. First off, living with my roommate was a challenge on its own. On top of all our obvious differences, I quickly discovered that Linda constantly apologized for everything. And I mean everything.

"Sorry," she'd whisper into the dark when the muffled buzz of her alarm clock beeped under the scratchy sheets. Class wouldn't start for another three hours, yet Linda was up and at 'em anyway, apologizing again for throwing back the covers too loudly. After hopping out of bed, she'd tiptoe across the worn carpet. Once inside the bathroom she'd shut the door, and then, and only then, would she dare flip on the florescent light, so as not to bother me—her words, not mine. Which were always followed by "sorry," whenever I told her not to worry about it.

Before my own alarm could jolt me out of bed, Linda would be long gone, already seated at a long table in the cafeteria with two other "mature" women from our class. They'd endlessly quiz each other over weak coffee, dry toast, and runny eggs, courtesy of the airline. Me, I rarely ate breakfast. There wasn't enough time to eat. Okay, the truth is, I couldn't drag myself out of bed early enough for breakfast. When it came to sleep, every second counted. God forbid any of us dozed off in class during a long, drawn-out monotone lecture over the correct way to organize a beverage cart or the importance of saying hello and good-bye to passengers using a different greeting each time. It became a game of who could go the longest without repeating. Hello, good morning, how are you, welcome aboard, nice to have you, thanks for joining us, good to see you, morning, hi, good-bye, see ya later, thanks for flying with us, looking forward to seeing you again, have a good evening, see you next time, bye-bye, good night. Get caught with your eyes closed during any of this, and you'd get sent packing. Thank God for the vending machine stocked full of Mountain Dew. I guzzled gallons of the stuff in order to stay awake.

Falling asleep in class wasn't the only way to obtain walking papers. Being late resulted in the same thing. This is why flight attendants have perfected the art of power walking. If for whatever reason we weren't in our seats come class time, no matter how good the excuse, we were instructed to leave our training manuals beside the locked classroom door and immediately return to wherever we'd originally come from. None of us wanted to go back home. We were all here to fly away! But because the airplane doesn't wait, neither would our instructors, who always smiled as they explained the dire consequences. I took notes. The way they treated us was an art form all to itself, and I figured the ability to be so politely condescending would come in handy at 30,000 feet. Or maybe it was 35,000 feet? I didn't know for sure yet, but it wouldn't be long before we'd all learn that cruising altitude depends on several factors, including weight of the aircraft, fuel, humidity, air temperature, winds, turbulence, and air traffic.

Given how crazy everything else at training seemed to be, I guess I shouldn't have been so surprised when our food service

procedure instructor turned to the chalkboard and started drawing out football plays. Well, it looked that way at first! Dumb-
founded, we just sat in our seats staring at the board as he drew
lines to represent aisles, boxes for carts, and arrows to show
movement. And every plane seemed to have at least two different "plays" for us to memorize.

The way in which we were instructed to serve passengers depended first on the airplane. There are "two-class" and "three-
class" flights, as well as three different services. A two-class flight
has a first class and coach cabin. (Imagine two big boxes with
several smaller boxes inside.) A three-class flight includes business class, but here's where it gets confusing. A three-class flight
might only provide a two-class service if the business-class seats
have been sold as coach seats. It happens. (Two sets of three small
boxes lined up side by side with six arrows pointing forward *and*
back.) First class isn't created equal, either. What a lot of passengers don't realize is on most two-class flights, passengers get a
business-class service in what is considered the first-class cabin.
And while first-class service on a long-haul, three-class flight is
exceptional, it often bears no resemblance, other than in name,
to its counterpart on a two-class flight to Oklahoma City where
the flying time is short and the ticket prices are cheap. (Five small
boxes inside one big box. No arrows.)

Many smaller airlines only fly one type of aircraft, so their
training, I imagine, is fairly simple. At my airline we work on
all different kinds of airplanes, so we had to be trained on each
one of them: F100, S80, 727, 757, 767, MD11, DC10, A300. We
took on a new airplane every week. Each aircraft type is a completely different configuration in terms of number of passengers,
lavatories, and galleys; the use and location of emergency and
medical equipment; the operation of window and door exits; and
how to command an evacuation. Over time an airline might retire
its aging fleet and replace one type of aircraft with something

newer. Flight attendants will then have to fly back to the academy on a day off to be trained. If flight attendants don't get qualified on a particular aircraft, they are not allowed to work it. And because they're unable to operate and command an evacuation if necessary, they are not considered "jump-seat qualified," which means they will not be allowed to take a jump seat on a flight that's full when they're trying to use their travel passes to go on vacation or get to work.

Each aircraft galley is completely different when it comes to size and storage, so the type of plane affects the service. The 737 first-class galley is so small that a can of soda can't stand up on the counter because an oven is located right over it. Some flight attendants might be inclined to pull out a cart, park it in front of the first-class entry door, and use the top as extra counter space. We didn't learn this technique in training because the airline didn't want us to block an exit, even in flight when it's physically impossible to open the door. I don't get it, either. The DC10 has the exact opposite problem. The airplane has a monster galley that first class, business, and coach all share. Carts are stored underneath the galley, so a flight attendant has to take a one-person elevator down to where the carts are kept and to spend the remainder of the flight sending up the correct cart at the appropriate time. You can imagine how popular this assignment is with new hires. Antisocial senior flight attendants love it.

The easiest way for a flight attendant to know which service to provide is to open up all the food carts and take a peek inside. A vegetable crudité after takeoff or salad toppings that include something other than a sprinkle of parmesan cheese and a choice of dressing is a sign it's a true first-class service. But during training, when we finally got to practice what we'd learned on a mocked-up section of an airplane galley, the cart was empty! There was no way to guess the service when no food or beverage was allowed on the trainer. With only a single empty cart, an empty coffee pot (to serve both decaf and regular coffee, as well as tea), an insert of empty soda cans, and half a stack of plastic and Styrofoam cups to work with, I placed a real napkin down on a real tray table and asked a couple of classmates with opened flight manuals resting in their laps if they'd like something to drink. The instructors scribbled notes down on their clipboards as we made small talk while I served a pretend vodka tonic with a twist of pretend lime. Nobody complained about the service, or even the food! In our minds it tasted delicious.

On long-haul and international flights the service in the premium cabins is elaborate. There are predeparture drinks, appetizers, hot towels, salads, entrees, an assortment of breads and wines, desserts, and more. In first class, we were taught to use a three-tiered cart for amenities such as magazines and newspapers, as well as for salad and dessert delivery. Imagine my surprise to learn that our tiny drink carts at Sun Jet were really three-tiered dessert carts at other airlines. No wonder it had taken forever to do a service! It turned out that at a normal airline, the dainty silver cart was supposed to be accompanied with the "horse shoe" method for serving appetizers and desserts to first-class passengers. This meant we served one side of the first-class cabin, pulled the cart up, and then served the other side. Drinks and entrees were to be hand-delivered. In business class, drinks and entrees were also hand-delivered, while salads and desserts were to be served from a regular cart, not the three-tiered cart.

In coach, regular carts were used for everything. On most flights in coach, we were taught to move the carts forward-aft (front to back), but sometimes an aft-forward service worked best. That is until the aft-forward service was cut out altogether a year or two later—in coach. In first and business classes it still remains. The direction of the service depends on the flight number (even or odd) and the direction we're flying (north-south or east-west). On shorter flights using larger aircraft, we learned to converge two carts if we wanted to finish the service. One cart would work aft-forward while the other worked forward-aft until they met in the middle in order to make the service quicker. (After 9/11 we stopped doing this, because having enough flight attendants on board to work two carts simultaneously in coach became so rare.) Then there were the "wide-body" (two-aisle) versus "narrow-body" (single-aisle) flights. On the wide-bodies—767s, MD11s, DC10s, and A300s—the instructors pounded into our brains that we must keep the carts as close together across the aisle from each other as possible. Not always an easy task to accomplish when some crew members were faster at serving than others.

Successfully passing a test on one aircraft didn't mean we had a clue what to do on another. Take, for instance, the emergency exits. There are single slides, double slides, tail cones, and wings. Even on a single aircraft the emergency doors and windows operate differently. The commands one classmate had to yell while at a window exit were completely different from the ones I yelled while at a door on the same plane. We were tested on a mocked-up section of a plane that looked exactly like it did in real life—except that the first-class entry doors were about eight rows from the window exits, which were about ten rows from the rear exit doors. This became even more confusing and difficult because there were always at least three of us being tested on evacuation drills at the same time, one of us positioned at each exit. We had to remain focused. The best way to do it was to outscream one another. To add to the stress, our instructors would throw in things like a fire or an exit door that wouldn't open or a slide that wouldn't inflate or a passenger who was too afraid to jump. Then we'd have to break into a whole new set of commands and procedures. We could score an A, B, C, or D on the computer tests that covered medical, safety, or security, but when it came to an evacuation, it was pretty much pass or fail. If we looked out an exit window in the wrong direction to make sure our pretend slide had indeed inflated, buh-bye! If we pointed to the back of the plane at the pretend engine and told passengers on the ground to run "that way," the wrong way, adios! Forgetting to position ourselves between the jump seat and the fuselage wall while the slide inflates with air and a pretend frantic passenger eager to escape a smoke-filled cabin might push us out to our death. One wrong word, one slip of the tongue, one teeny-tiny mistake and we were immediately told to stop without an explanation. After three strikes, we were out for good.

Linda would get so worked up before her drills she'd start to feel ill. But medical training is the only thing that frightened the heck out of me. I'll never forget the day our most laid-back instructor placed an infant doll on top of a table in front of the classroom and told us about the time a passenger rang her call light because her child was turning blue. Our instructor grabbed the naked plastic doll and checked for breathing. Resting its back on the length of her arm with her hand cradling the baby's head, she then flipped the doll over, balancing it on her other arm that rested on her thigh and began banging it with the palm of her hand—*whop, whop, whop!* Then she flipped the baby back over and using two fingers pushed hard on its scratched and discolored chest three times. We watched in silence while she flipped and banged, flipped and pushed, a long blond ponytail flipping along with it, until whatever the baby was choking on came out. Our instructor cradled the doll in her arms and told us that while she may have saved the doll's life, on her flight she hadn't been successful. Another instructor took over when it looked like she might cry. After we each took turns practicing the Heimlich maneuver on an infant, we learned what to do on children, adults, and pregnant women. Next up was CPR. Dozens of lifelike dummies lined the floor. Our classroom resembled a horror movie, or even worse, a morgue. With the heel of my hand I pushed as hard as I could on a plastic chest that barely moved and counted to sixty, my partner giving two breaths, for what seemed like hours.

It didn't matter how many times I went over the conscious and breathing versus unconscious and not breathing checklist, I just couldn't seem to grasp it. So I organized a study group with other classmates who were having trouble. We met after dinner in a hallway to role-play medical scenarios. Georgia played the unconscious woman. A purple hair scrunchie wrapped around her wrist represented a medical bracelet. She had diabetes. Linda became a nurse after someone suggested we page for a doctor— but we came to find out Linda wasn't really a medical professional, because when we asked to see her credentials she didn't have any. Sneaky! While Joseph ran to get oxygen and the medical kit, Linda, who had transformed back into a flight attendant, called the cockpit to report what was going on. I could handle nosebleeds, air sickness, diabetic comas, and seizures, but the thought of losing a passenger freaked me out. Just dragging Georgia's lifeless body over an armrest and into the aisle for CPR seemed daunting. And would I really be physically capable of dragging a grown man by the ankles to an emergency door to get him down a slide in the event of an evacuation? I'd take faulty hydraulics or an engine fire over a medical scenario any day.

Even though I knew we were only role-playing, it felt real and it always felt like we were about to run out of time. For me, flight attendant training was more difficult than four years of college because so much information was thrown at us in seven and a half weeks. What we were taught wasn't difficult, but the program had been specifically designed to wear us down. The airline needed to know how we might react in a number of less-than-perfect scenarios in order to give us a taste of what flying would really be like . . . and also as a way to get rid of those who couldn't hack it. So they pushed us to our limits, mentally and physically, filtering out the weak along the way. As we grew more and more exhausted, we were expected to absorb tons of information that had to be repeated verbatim. Procedures had to be done in step-by-step order. Late-night study groups were followed by early-morning drills. My adrenalin pumped nonstop for weeks. Imagine being on *American Idol* during Hollywood week, but instead of memorizing a song from the 1970s, you have to know the difference between dozens of weapons so that if you spot one in flight you can correctly communicate what it is with the cockpit. Instead of practicing Motown dance moves, we had to practice what to do in the event of ditching over water, a decompression, and planned and unplanned emergency landings. And just when we thought it couldn't get any worse, the paranoia set in.

It began the day we sat down to learn about the basics of first-class service. We were being shown the proper way to set a tray table, pour a fine bottle of wine using a drip cloth, balance six wineglasses on a linen-lined silver tray, and serve caviar without dinging the fine china with a silver spoon. At one point, someone noticed that Joseph had gone missing. I hoped he didn't have something contagious—that was the last thing I needed. During lunch break a few classmates went to check on him, but when they knocked on the door nobody answered. And when Joe's roommate entered their room that night, Joe's half was totally and completely empty. It was as if nobody had ever lived on the right-hand side!

We had questions. There were no answers. Initially, I wondered if Joseph's weight had done him in. He was a bit—okay, a lot—heavier than the rest of us. Georgia thought it had to be all his joking around. In class, Joe was always making us laugh. He was hilarious! Linda believed it had something to do with his sexuality. Joe did seem to enjoy showing off his feminine side. But I don't blame him—no one looked more glamorous in an evening gown than Joanne, his alter ego. We never did figure out what happened to him. Right then and there I made a mental note to begin collecting phone numbers of classmates I liked—just in case.

Slowly, slowly, bit by bit, we dwindled down from a class of sixty to forty-five. We never saw anyone leave—people were there one minute, gone the next. Is it any wonder that many of us came to the conclusion that our rooms, the bathroom stalls, and even the salt and pepper shakers were bugged? The instructors had to be watching our every move and listening to our every word. Why else did classmates suddenly disappear for no reason during a five-minute bathroom break? What made it even more disturbing was that the good ones, classmates who would make perfect flight attendants, were not immune. One minute we'd all be sitting together discussing the different types of hijackers or how to use an information card and a couple of soda-soaked blankets when encountering a bomb, and the next minute—*poof!* Another classmate was gone. Luggage and all. Not a word. Not a note. Not a mention of their name ever again. Of course we were too afraid to ask our instructors what happened for fear that we'd be next. Instead we silently sat in our seats, eyes darting in the direction of the empty chair as soon as we realized someone else had been booted out. Oh, sure, there were those who deserved to go, like the two who got caught fondling each other under the table during a what-to-do-during-a-hostage-situation movie, but for the most part none of it made sense. We never knew who would be next.

Four weeks into training I thought for sure it would be me. I had just exited the ladies' room with two minutes to spare when a stranger approached and asked for help. He said he was lost. I began to panic. Remember, the airplane doesn't wait for anyone. That includes me. On the other hand, customer service is extremely important to the airline. It had been drilled into our heads from day one that if we weren't able to assist a passenger, we were to find someone who could. The clock was ticking. I could try to help the lost soul find his way, but then I most certainly would have to leave my books by the locked classroom door. I also could apologize quickly, giving him the brush-off, which is exactly what I wanted to do, but what kind of customer service was that? It had to be a setup. Why else were there no right answers? I didn't know what to do!

But then, like a gift from above, a janitor appeared behind a cleaning cart. I sent her telepathic messages—look, over here, help, save me, please! Amazingly, she turned around and asked if everything was okay. Quickly I explained the situation, that the guy was lost and my class was about to begin and I couldn't be late—and then I just took off sprinting down the hall (which is, of course, another flight attendant no-no). I slid into my desk with about one second to spare . . . and spent the rest of the day looking over my shoulder, still not convinced that I'd escaped.

Just when we couldn't take it anymore, when it became apparent to those in charge that a mutiny was moments away, something amazing happened: our instructors ordered us to gather our belongings and meet in a room down the hall.

"What now?" I mumbled, grabbing my two-pound flight manual and standing up.

"I don't know how much more I can take," said Linda as a group of us walked down the hall together.

"Why do they have to torture us like this?" asked Georgia. The words were barely out of her mouth as we entered the room and spotted along the wall, lined up in neat little rows, brand-new black suitcases on wheels.

"Ohmahgawd," Georgia exclaimed.

Ohmahgawd was right, because the room had been sectioned off into four stations, and in each corner, right next to a full-length mirror, stood a woman with a tape measure around her neck. I swallowed hard. There was a long silver rack housing navy blue dresses, skirts, pants, jackets, and vests! What a wonderful sight to behold.

"Next week each of you will go on a work trip," the instructor announced. I could not believe my ears. I almost pinched myself just to make sure I wasn't dreaming. I nearly broke down and cried. I could have kissed each and every one of my instructors that very moment, calling to mind a psychological response known as Stockholm syndrome. Stockholm syndrome happens when abducted hostages (flight attendant trainees), begin to show signs of loyalty to the hostage-taker (flight instructors) regardless of the danger, risk, or torture in which they have been placed. The shift occurs in captives when they are shown simple acts of kindness. Take it from me, there is nothing in the world quite like viewing yourself in a flight attendant uniform for the very first time. This is the only possible explanation for why I actually thanked my instructors when we learned that the navy blue polyester getup, all $800 of it, would be deducted from our first couple of paychecks. (That included a black roll-aboard and tote, a navy blue Coach-style purse, a red sweater, a blue vest, a blazer, a trench coat, two skirts, six white blouses, a dress, and two pinstriped toppers, a.k.a. aprons. You had to order pants separately. It took twenty months to pay it off in $20 increments.)

Stockholm syndrome kicked in again on my first work trip, with just three weeks to go until graduation. The class had been divided into groups of three, and each group had been scheduled to work "a turn." That's a trip that leaves a city and returns to the same city on the same day. Really, we were just on board to observe. That is, our instructors informed us, unless the crew allowed us to help serve food and drinks or pick up trash. In the unlikely event that something went wrong in flight, we were told to take a seat and stay out of the way of the working crew.

Nashville, Kansas City, Fort Lauderdale, Detroit, Salt Lake City, I honestly do not recall where my training flight took us.

I was too excited about donning the uniform for the very first time to care. What I do remember is that we trainees were giddy with excitement, fresh from the charm farm, wearing uniform pieces that still needed tailoring. The hem of my skirt went past my knees. The working crew was a completely different story. They looked tired and frayed around the edges, and they seemed less than enthused when the gate agent escorted us down the jet bridge and announced our presence over the PA. Without discussing it with me, my two classmates decided they would assist the flight attendants working in coach and I would stay in first class. While I already had experience working for an airline, you may recall that it was nothing even close to first-class service, to put it politely. Even though I wasn't supposed to be doing anything, I was still scared I might screw it up.

"Don't be nervous," said the flight attendant whose job it was to show me the ropes. When she laughed it sounded more like a cackle. She popped open a can of club soda and poured. "The only way you're going to learn this job is by jumping in and doing it." After stabbing a slice of lime with a red stir stick, she balanced it across the glass and placed the drink on a silver tray. "This goes to 2B," she said, handing it to me.

When I came back to the galley and passed the empty tray to her, she said, "So what do you say you do the service by yourself?"

I gulped. "Really?" Because really, this did not sound like a good idea.

"Why not? Here's a list of drink orders and meal preferences. Inside the carts you'll find everything you need. I'll watch and make sure you do it right. If you need anything, just ask." She plopped down hard on the jump seat, fishing a book, *Smart Women/Foolish Choices*, out of her bag.

As she quietly read, I did things I'm not quite sure I should have been doing, like the entire service. I even "armed" and "disarmed" the door, which required me to get down on my hands and knees on a dirty wet floor to attach and detach the evacuation slide to the door. The other two trainees never came up to check on me. Maybe they were too afraid they'd have to do something other than assist with picking up trash—er, service items, as we have to say. After the flight I profusely thanked the smart woman who'd made the foolish choice, based solely on the book she read, for allowing me to do her job—a job I had not been paid to do—and raved about how nice she was to anyone who would listen, except my instructors, of course. I didn't want to get in trouble.

We had a total of two work trips during training, a narrow-body and a wide-body, so that we would be at least a little famil-iar with what to expect once on the line. Unfortunately for me, the wide-body is just a hazy blue memory because that week I came down with a terrible sinus infection. An instructor was kind enough to pull me aside before my flight and suggest I take cold medicine before, during, and after my trip. Drowsy from practically overdosing on Sudafed, I barely made it through the drink service before one of the flight attendants noticed how badly I felt and ordered me to take a seat in business class. I vaguely remember waking up in the dark between two well-dressed passengers and finding a slice of cheese cake on the tray table in front of me. I took a bite and fell back to sleep. When I woke up again the cake was gone and my table had been stowed for landing. Thankfully the crew was kind enough to give me an over-the-top rave review of a job well done. Otherwise that would have been the end of the line for me.

With just a week and a half before graduation an instructor walked into the classroom, picked up a piece of chalk, and wrote, "Atlanta, Boston, Chicago, Denver, San Francisco, New York, and Orlando" across the board. My stomach tightened. Then he turned to the class and said, "These are the crew bases that are now available and they'll be awarded in order of seniority."

As I've mentioned, seniority at an airline is everything, and it's determined first by class graduation date. But within each class, it is assigned by date of birth. This meant that Linda was the most senior person in our class, I fell somewhere in the middle, and Georgia ranked right behind me.

"Write down your name on a piece of paper," instructed our instructor. "Under your name write your seniority number. Under that, list the cities in order of preference—one being the city you most desire."

Linda, I knew, wanted to be based in Texas, but since that was not one of our options, I had no idea where she might request. Georgia's boyfriend lived in North Carolina, so I assumed she'd choose Orlando to be close. Whether or not she could "hold it" was an entirely different story, since there were only fourteen slots available for Orlando. San Francisco, one of the most senior bases in the system, where the average flight attendant had twenty-five years of experience, had only seven spots open. Those would mostly like go to our most senior classmates who already lived there. Boston, Chicago, and Denver were too cold to even consider. I kinda-sorta wanted to experience the Big Apple, just for the sake of experiencing it, even though I had no desire to live there long-term. Also, remember my boyfriend? I still hadn't gotten around to breaking up with him. I know, I know. So I made New York my first choice, a city located far, far away from Dallas, far, far away from him. Because New York was also a base with by far the most open spots available, I knew I'd be able to pair up with a few other new flight attendants. We could share an apartment and learn the ins and outs of the job together. It was also the most junior crew base in the system, so it offered the best trips for a new hire to work. Not to mention it had some of the best international flying systemwide. I couldn't wait to see Paris!

The very next day, nine days before graduation, we got our crew base assignments. I was headed to New York City! So was

Georgia. Not everyone was as excited as we were—an hour after the announcement, a couple of upset classmates who were not awarded their first choice quit. The day before graduation, five classmates were sent home. Five! Rumor has it they got caught partying in their room. That was the most we had ever lost in a week. Needless to say, it was an emotional time, which is why graduation is just a blur.

One thing I do remember well is what happened to Linda. Talk about a tear-jerker. In every flight attendant class there's one classmate who struggles the entire way through training. If they do actually manage to graduate and walk across the stage in front of an auditorium filled with family and friends there to witness the pinning of silver wings to a blue lapel, they do so by the skin of their teeth. But they also do so with the love and support of every single classmate bringing down the house with a standing ovation. That person in my class, the one with the clumpy Tammy Faye Bakker lashes, was the woman I had absolutely dreaded rooming with our first day. How could I have known she'd wind up working harder than anyone I'd ever meet to achieve a goal she refused to give up on no matter how many people called it ridiculous or how many years continued to pass by? And she would do so at a stage in life when too many women give up dreaming altogether! That alone was admirable. I was too young and immature at the time we met to realize how truly amazing she was. In the beginning all I'd seen were shoulder-length dangly earrings and hot pink frosted lipstick and wondered, *Why, why me? Why do I have to end up with the crazy old lady?* Crazy old lady wound up not being so crazy after all. In fact, she became my inspiration later on in life whenever I met an obstacle that seemed impossible to climb. Now it is I who must thank Linda for putting up with me!

When it was almost my turn to finally take the stage, an instructor took a ruler to my hair to make sure it was no longer than six inches from the collar. Close, she said, before moving on to the next person with questionable locks. I crossed the stage and an instructor pinned my wings on me. Then I joined the others who were standing off to the side and clapping. I looked at them proudly. We had made it through. Afterward I saw my mother, father, and sister for the first time in weeks. Together we laughed, cried, took a few pictures, and then, an hour later, it all came to an end. An instructor announced that it was time to go. The bus was waiting.

"Guess this is it," I said. My mother wiped her eyes. My dad gave me a hug. As I walked out the door my sister made me promise to call her as soon as I landed. It almost felt as if I were being sent off to war. I took a deep breath and climbed onto the airport bus behind Georgia. This was it.

Welcome to New York

4

ALL THOSE LIGHTS on the ground! That's what I remember most about flying over New York City the first time. I'd never seen anything like it. And off in the distance, next to a strip of blinking landing lights, the blackest of black: the Atlantic Ocean. The contrast was intense. I quickly snapped a few photographs from a scratched plastic window.

"Flight attendants prepare for landing," announced a man's deep, no-nonsense voice. The captain, I presumed. Suddenly the cabin lights were turned to bright. I blinked until my eyes adjusted.

"Ladies and gentleman," announced a woman's voice. "It is now time to . . ."

I knew exactly what time it was! Springing into action, I kicked my tote bag under the seat and pushed the silver button on the armrest. My seat popped back into place just as two attractive female flight attendants, whose skirts had been tailored so short that I could only assume they were single and looking, walked to the front of the aircraft. They sashayed down the aisle on navy blue stilettos, collecting cups, napkins, and newspapers while checking the status of seat belts, seat backs, and luggage. A passenger reached out and tugged the hem of a skirt on the move, simultaneously firing off a battery of questions about a missed flight connection and lost luggage. The flight attendant nodded and, smiling, pointed to a map inside the airline's magazine located in the angry passenger's seat back pocket. When she handed it to him, he immediately flung it on the seat beside him, determined to keep complaining for the remaining minutes before landing.

Georgia leaned across the empty middle seat between us and squeezed my hand. "Can you believe *that's* gonna be us in four days?"

It did seem surreal.

Four days. That's all the time we'd been given to find a place to live and settle in before working our first trip assignment as New York–based flight attendants. Talk about stress. There were a dozen of us on the flight, and most of us had no idea where to go, what to do, or just how much it would actually cost once we finally found a place. We certainly didn't know that tipping the super a few hundred bucks would greatly increase the odds of getting an apartment. The majority of us were from the Midwest where things like this didn't happen. We had come from cities where housing was, well, almost affordable for a person making less than $18,000 a year. (Of course, deduct $800 for our uniforms and we were left with about $17,000.) And to think I had actually turned down a merchandising job for a well-known men's line of clothing a few years ago because I didn't think I could survive in New York on just $30,000 a year! Now I would be making half that. No wonder so many apartment buildings flat out refused to house flight attendants. It took twenty of us living together to afford a one-bedroom.

In fact, as first-year flight attendants, we qualified for food stamps—that is, if the airline had allowed us to use them, which they didn't, so we didn't, which is how so many of us could fit into size 0 uniforms and why we never had to work out to keep our girlish figures. Lord knows we couldn't afford a membership to the gym those first few years on the job. It also explains why we were willing to accept dinner dates from men we might not have otherwise gone out with. I remember being so hungry at times that working a meal cart became torture! My stomach would rumble in the aisle as I silently prayed for passengers to refuse their meals. I even knew a few flight attendants who regularly hopped flights as passengers in order to eat what was being served on board for free. It's not as crazy as it sounds. Imagine being stuck in New York in the dead of winter and being able to fly to Miami just to get breakfast. We could spend a few hours lounging around the airport hotel pool, working on our tans and taking advantage of a 20 percent airline employee discount at the hotel restaurant bar, before flying back to New York in time for dinner. Hey, a flight attendant's gotta do what a flight attendant's gotta do!

But as our plane was landing in New York that first day, Georgia and I didn't know any of that. We grabbed our bags out of the bins, deplaned, and headed down to baggage claim, all giddy and full of excitement. Our instructors had told us to check the bulletin board at LaGuardia flight operations, wherever that might be, because that's where other flight attendants posted notices looking for roommates. Luckily, we wouldn't have to resort to that. I had a connection to a place in Queens, thanks to an old Sun Jet colleague who had once worked for Pan Am out of New York. We were lucky. We knew it, too. So did our envious classmates, who had already paired off into groups of four in order to save money on hotel rooms for the night. I have to say, for a group of people who were broke, homeless, and had no idea when our first paychecks might arrive, we were handling the situation beautifully. This, I'm sure, is exactly why we were hired.

I happily helped Georgia load several gigantic bags onto a Smarte Carte while our classmates waved good-bye from the Marriott hotel courtesy van. Georgia and I felt bad for them. Their first night in one of the most exciting cities in the world and they would spend it ordering overpriced room service at a chain hotel across the street from an airport.

Everyone had cleared out of baggage claim except for us and a family of four who seemed to be missing something like a car seat or a stroller—or maybe even a kid, based on the way they were frantically searching the premises. A group of men huddled together at the bottom of the stairs leading down to baggage claim. Dressed in black suits and holding little white signs, they leered at Georgia while they awaited passengers on incoming flights who had yet to recognize their names. We found a pay phone, and I dialed a number given to us by one of the attendants on our flight. I'd asked her about the cheapest way to get to Queens without taking a bus. The phone rang twice.

"Kew Gardens!" barked a raspy voice.

I told the man my name, where we were, and where we wanted to go.

"Fifteen minutes! Last set of doors upstairs!" he snapped and immediately hung up.

Georgia slowly pushed the rolling metal cart stacked so high with luggage she could barely see over the top, while I pulled two enormous suitcases on wheels, a smaller crew bag balancing across the top of one. Another group of men wearing jeans and bulky winter coats stood near the passenger arrivals exit. Their eyes lit up as soon as they spotted Georgia teetering along in high-heel boots.

"Need a ride!" they yelled across the room—a statement, not a question, that was repeated several times.

"No, thank you," we repeated, a dozen times, at least.

Normally I would have been freaked out by this aggressive behavior from a group of strange men at the airport, but we were in New York City. This was just how they did things. I knew this because my mother had made it her mission in life to warn me about all the things to avoid in New York. Gypsy cab drivers were one thing. After my mother had found out where I was going to be based, she bought a guide to the city and soon became the expert on all things New York, although she had yet to visit the city herself.

"Always take a yellow cab," she had told me out of the blue on several different occasions. "Make sure to look for a medallion," she'd insist, as if my life depended on it. (Of course, it took ending up in an empty parking lot in Harlem instead of at a theater on Broadway a few months later to actually learn this lesson so that I can in turn share it with you. Listen to my mother.)

Once Georgia and I had finally dragged our thousand pounds of luggage to the passenger arrival drop-off point, we found the area deserted. We stood there all alone, and cold, in the dark. LaGuardia Airport at night was creepy. Nervously I looked around, wondering if maybe we should go inside and wait. Instead, I put on a pair of black knit gloves. Georgia dug around inside of one of her smaller bags and pulled out a fluffy white muff. I'd never seen one before in real life, only in fairy tales.

"Ya think it's safe out here?" she asked.

"Sure," I lied. No need for both of us to freak out.

Just then, what looked like an old beat-up police sedan sped up to the curb, the horn honking nonstop, and came to a screeching halt in front of us. I took a step back. An old man wearing wire-rim glasses and a newsboy cap got out of the sedan and squinted at our bags.

"You're kidding, right?" he said.

"Are you with Kew Gardens Car Service?" I asked, hopeful that he was not, although KEW GARDENS was clearly printed in red-and-white cursive across the back window, the numbers 909 written below it.

The old guy reached into the car through the opened door and grabbed what looked like a CB radio handset. "Nine oh nine." He looked at us, looked at our bags again, and shook his head. "Nine oh nine."

"Is there a problem, sir?" Georgia popped her cinnamon gum.

"Is there a problem, she asks!" He laughed. "Where you from, sweetheart?"

She smiled a pageant queen smile. "Louisiana."

From inside the car came the scratchy voice of a man who sounded like he'd spent about twenty years chain-smoking in a coal mine: "Nine oh nine."

The driver pressed a black button and spoke into the handset. "We got a bit of a problem. It seems that Miss Louisiana here needs the wagon." Without another word, he got back inside the car, slammed the rickety door shut, and took off.

"Well, that was rude!" exclaimed Georgia. She glared at the two red taillights disappearing into the distance. "I'm in the right mind to report that guy!"

Georgia never did end up reporting him, and eventually a station wagon in desperate need of a paint job crawled to the curb. Without exiting the car, a long-haired driver popped the hatch, twirling a cigarette between his stained fingers. Georgia and I struggled to load our bags into the back. They barely fit. Once in the backseat, I sat on what looked like a blue blanket taken from an airplane. On further inspection, it was in fact a blue blanket taken from an airplane. It covered a rip in the leather seat.

"Where you ladies going?" Irish accent. Beady eyes darting back and forth between us in the rearview mirror.

"Beverly Road. Near Metro and Lefferts?" Shoot. It sounded more like a question, not the statement I had memorized and rehearsed in the bathroom mirror in the days before graduating from the flight academy in an attempt to sound like a real New Yorker. The driver nodded. Half a second later our heads snapped back and off we went to Kew Gardens.

Thanks to my mother's newfound knowledge of all things New York, I already knew that Kew Gardens, also known as Crew Gardens, is a residential area in Queens offering, for the most part, one-family homes in the million-dollar-plus range. There are also several apartment complexes and co-ops located in the area around Metropolitan Avenue and Lefferts Boulevard, a.k.a. Metro and Lefferts, two cross streets that run through the heart of the neighborhood. After World War II, a large population of Jewish refugees from Germany settled in the area, along with many Chinese and Russian immigrants. Dense and ethnically diverse, the neighborhood is popular with airline personnel because of its central location between LaGuardia Airport and John F. Kennedy International Airport. Because New York is considered a junior base for most airlines, there are a large number of flight attendants who commute to work. This is why so many crash pads are located in Kew Gardens, and why one can often see uniformed airline personnel at all hours of the day and night dragging luggage down cracked sidewalks past synagogues, nail salons, and Chinese food takeout joints on the way to and from the airport.

From the backseat of the car I stared out the window as neon signs whizzed by, a few of them in need of new lightbulbs. As we passed Jamaica Hospital, my heart sank. I didn't want to be anywhere near Jamaica, Queens, thanks to the movie *Coming to America* starring Eddie Murphy, a movie my sister forced me to rent before going to flight attendant training. Any moment now I expected to see dozens of homeless people warming their hands over burning cans of trash. When we exited the highway, there were gigantic black bags of garbage piled at least four bags high on the curb as far as the eye could see. Right before we turned into a neighborhood with tall, skinny houses sitting practically on top of one another, we passed by what looked like an abandoned bowling alley.

I couldn't hold it in any longer. "Ummm . . . excuse me, Mr. Driver, are we going the right way?"

I barely heard him say, "Yep." U2's "Sunday Bloody Sunday" blared from the speakers behind me.

When we stopped at a red light, a man bundled up in a ski

jacket with a matching ski mask approached the driver's side of the car holding a stack of magazines. He flashed the driver with whatever was hidden behind a lone copy of the *New York Post* while smiling at me. The driver didn't look, but waved him away with a flick of his cigarette.

"Is this neighborhood safe?" I asked.

"Yep," he said, and then he cranked up the stereo even louder.

The houses never did spread out, but eventually the trees grew taller and the restaurants began to look a little more inviting. When we stopped in front of a white wooden three-story house sitting behind a boarded-up fruit stand, the driver didn't say a word. He just popped the trunk and helped us get our bags out. The front light flicked on and a girl I would never see again opened the front door, told us her name, and invited us to come in.

Once inside Georgia and I stood on an Oriental rug in the dimly lit foyer, taking things in. Only a few steps away, a dark wooden staircase led up to the second floor. At the very top of the stairs I could see a bathroom. From where I stood below, it looked like the bathroom light was the only light on upstairs. To our right an archway opened up to a living room. A woman sat on the sofa watching television. Fashion, travel, and beauty magazines fanned out across a glass coffee table that now acted as a footrest.

The girl who'd let us in whispered, "I'd introduce you to her but I can't remember her name. I've only been here a few weeks myself and we just met today." As she buttoned up her black peacoat, she nodded at the two French doors to our left. "That's the room. Take the two beds by the window. Keys are on the dresser. Feel free to take two drawers each in the wooden dresser next to the closet." Then she was out the door and gone, off to meet a few friends and roommates at the local pizzeria, leaving Georgia and me all alone. Well, almost all alone.

Georgia peeked back into the living room. "Hi! I'm Georgia and this is Heather! We're moving in."

Staring straight ahead she said, "Marge." Georgia and I just looked at each other.

Not one to be easily deterred, Georgia sang, "Nice to meet you, Marge!"

"Likewise," she mumbled. That was our cue to go check out our room.

Twin beds lined the walls, six of them, which meant there would be six of us sharing a closet, one teeny-tiny closet, without a door.

Georgia sighed. "You've got to be kidding me. This just is not going to work!"

We had no choice but to make it work.

"Maybe we can purchase some cardboard drawers to place beside our beds," I suggested, after noting that's exactly what the others who were not there had done. After further inspection, I added, "What doesn't fit inside our two drawers we can keep packed away in our suitcases under the bed."

After we unpacked as much as we could, which wasn't much, we decided to take a look around the big, dark, creaky house. The first floor consisted of the large bedroom where Georgia and I now lived, a living room where Marge continued to camp out for the next twelve hours, and a pretty big kitchen. I peeked inside the fridge and noticed that everything had been labeled with different names. Same went for the pantry. Upstairs we found three other bedrooms. These were large rooms that looked more like army barracks than actual bedrooms. Two rows of unmade bunk beds stretched across the floor from one end of the room to the other. The occupants of these rooms were nowhere to be found, but a couple of suitcases were lying on the floor against the wall, unzipped, with clothes eager to escape.

The bathroom, located on the same floor, was shared by all of us. Each night from that night on I'd march upstairs and scribble my name on the piece of paper that allotted ten-minute shower times throughout the day. There were so many of us sharing that one bathroom that no one took responsibility for cleaning it. The black-and-white checkered floor had turned black and gray. A ring of dirt always surrounded the bottom of the tub. The drain was always clogged with hair, so showers consisted of standing ankle deep in water. At first the ten-minute shower rule seemed impossible, but the bathroom was so disgusting I did not dare linger any longer than necessary. Rubber shower shoes soon became my best friend.

Because so many of us slept in the same room, and because there was more time to shower if we skipped using the mirror in the bathroom, we all wound up using the living room downstairs as a kind of dressing room. Two dressing tables were pushed against the wall between the sofa and the giant TV. Flight attendants with early sign-ins would pack their bags the night before and leave them, along with makeup and curling irons, on the living room floor so as not to bother everyone else in the house while getting ready.

For all I know, there could have been sixty flight attendants living in that house. It was hard to tell because there was so much coming and going at all hours of the day and night. With so many people in one house, you'd think the place might feel crowded, but it was just the opposite. Many nights I found myself alone. And depressed. In the beginning I tried to introduce myself to each new face that walked through the front door, but then I eventually realized I rarely ever saw the same face twice. I'd just smile and say hello . . . until I finally just stopped smiling or saying hello, like Marge.

Now for a little Crash Pad 101.

A flight attendant's "base" is the city where his or her trips are scheduled to begin and end. "Commute, commuter, commuting" is the process of getting to work, in other words, flying to one's base city. Some New York–based commuters even live as far away as Europe and Hawaii. For the most part, commuters work "commutable trips," which are trips that depart late enough or return early enough that the flight attendant can get to work and home again on a single workday instead of wasting a precious "day off" commuting.

Flight attendant schedules average eighty hours per month— and by that I mean strictly flying hours. Time on the ground does not count toward a flight attendant's pay. And the clock doesn't officially start ticking until the aircraft door is shut and the airplane backs away from the gate; the flight attendant saying hello to you while you're boarding is not getting paid yet. Because of this, delays affect flight attendants just as much as they do passengers, maybe even more so. But this is also the reason that we can—and frequently do—trade, drop, and pick up trips from one another. This allows commuters to "back up" their trips (fly several trips in a row), which enables them to maximize time at work and get more days off at home. Commuters tend to work "high-time" trips. These are trips that are worth a lot of hours, enabling them to get their hours in as quickly as possible. For example, one four-hour trip takes less actual time than two two-hour trips, even though the paid flying time is exactly the same.

When it comes to finding a place to stay between trips, a commuter doesn't need much, since we spend very little time on the ground at our base cities. Enter the crash pad, a place where crew members literally crash between trips. These can be large apartments, a single room in a house, or even just a friend's couch. Some crash pads only allow men, others house only women, and some are mixed. In a crash pad with both men and women, usually the men will sleep in one room and women will take another, but not all the time. On top of that, there are crash pads for flight attendants and crash pads for pilots. Even these can be a mix of both flight attendants and pilots, but if so, usually the flight attendants will stick together in one room while the pilots stay in another.

The cost of a crash pad can range anywhere from $100 to $300 a month, depending on the size of the space and the number of people sharing it. A few flight attendants might be willing to fork over a little extra cash for their own room, but most of us prefer sharing with several other flight attendants to bring down the cost. Bunk beds make this possible. This is yet another aspect of flight attendant life ruled by seniority. The best beds, bottom bunks away from doors and light, are claimed by the most senior crash pad dwellers. The upper bunks tend to belong to the most junior crash pad residents. Rooms are also determined by seniority. In a house with more than one level, the top floor is the most senior since there's less traffic.

If you can believe it, there are even flight attendants who share beds to save even more money. These are called "hot beds." Because flight attendants are constantly coming and going, hot beds are literally kept warm because they're always in use. The way this works is simple. Before leaving for a trip, flight attendants will pack their pillows and sheets and store them in a tub with the rest of their belongings. Other flight attendants can use the bed on a first come, first served basis. There are sign-up sheets for hot beds at the house or apartment, so that flight attendants can sign up in advance on the nights they need them. This allows them to adjust their schedules accordingly.

Of course, a crash pad isn't the only option for a commuter. Some stay at airport hotels offering discounted rates and free shuttle service to airline employees. To cut costs, they will share these rooms with other flight attendants, even flight attendants they don't know. It doesn't matter if two flight attendants sharing a room work for the same company or have ever met before. Because the job is the same wherever you go, regardless of where you work or who you work for—and because we know that everyone who works for an airline has had a background check—we tend to have an automatic sense of trust and respect.

So when two flight attendants out of uniform discover each other during or after a flight, only to find out that neither of them has a crash pad, they very well might pair off and get a room together. The rules in this situation are simple: no small talk, set cell phones on vibrate, only take calls in the lobby, and be packed and ready to go before lights-out. It's all business when it comes to commuting—get in, go to sleep, get out! Sometimes I wonder: in what other occupation, besides prostitution, do two strangers trust each other enough to spend the night together in a hotel room five minutes after initial contact?

On the most budget-conscious (and in my opinion, least comfortable) level, there's even a small community of commuting flight attendants who have chosen to "live" at the airport between trips. Before 9/11 commuters could wander down to an empty plane to sleep in first class. Even though no one is "allowed" to live in flight operations, some flight attendants do, and have established a sorority-like environment. By day they take bus rides to Jamaica or Kew Gardens to get hair and nails done, or even better, trips to the city for fake designer bags in Chinatown. At night there are Chinese food takeout parties. The "quiet room" is where they sleep. It's a dark room with several recliners lining the walls, and it's normally meant as a resting area for crew members with a long sit time between flights.

There are many unwritten rules one must abide by when sleeping in flight operations. Most important is the chair located in the far right-hand corner of the room. It belongs to Kat. No one else is allowed to sit in it. God help the flight attendant who accidentally sits in Kat's special spot, a chair that looks just like all the other chairs except that right next to it sits a fan and a small wooden chest of drawers, topped by a dainty lamp that she lugged on a flight all the way from home. If a flight attendant is too loud at night, Kat will take care of the situation by flashing the guilty party with her FAA-required flashlight. If a flight attendant unfamiliar with the quiet room seating arrangement settles into the wrong recliner, that flight attendant could very well wake up shaking violently as two other flight attendants push the recliner across the room and out of the way. Despite the seeming convenience of a night at flight operations, if one of these flight attendants has enough time to jump on a flight home and still make it back to work in time the following day, even if that means she'll only spend five hours in her own bed, she will.

There are commuters, and even some noncommuters, who actually live in the employee parking lot at JFK. Their motor homes and campers line the back fence. If too many recreational vehicles begin to accumulate on the lot, the gods in charge of airport parking will intervene and run them off. No big deal. They're always packed and ready to go to a nearby airport where they'll set up camp again. The more adventurous, those without a permanent address, will drive across country and spend months at a time visiting new cities by day and sleeping in different airport parking lots at night.

And then there's Tom, the only commuter I know without a crash pad who manages to live the ultimate high-roller lifestyle. By gambling in Vegas he's acquired enough hotel comps to live for free in luxury on the strip for one week out of each month. He's been doing this for years now by flying high time and arranging his days off into blocks of three. When he's not living it up in Sin City, he'll either visit his parents for a few days or crash on an old friend's couch. Personal effects are stored in the trunk of a car he keeps parked in the employee lot or inside a gigantic suitcase that has yet to leave Ops. There's a reason the airline won't allow us into the frequent-flier lounges: We'd move in and never leave!

When we landed in Crew Gardens, Georgia and I were not "commuters." (Not yet anyway.) Because we were new hires, we were on probation for six months straight—if we did anything at all wrong, we were at risk of losing our jobs. Even worse, we didn't get travel benefits until our seventh month on the job! This is how Georgia and I came to actually live full-time in a crash pad. Now if we'd had our passes, we would have flown home as often as possible, that's how homesick we were. Instead we were stuck in New York, sharing a large bedroom in a three-story house with who knows how many commuters and six other new hires who also did not have travel benefits! And when we weren't flying, we were all there together 24/7.

Our crash pad on Beverly Road was owned and run by a man named Victor. He charged each of us $150 a bed. A retired TWA flight attendant from South America, he had a thick accent that was hard to understand. I figured he had to be in his midsixties, based on the handlebar mustache and two strands of greasy hair that covered his freckled head. He occupied the third floor, which consisted of a master bedroom bigger than most one-bedroom New York apartments, a tiny kitchen, and a bathroom large enough to house two chairs and a claw-foot bathtub. Victor, unlike most male flight attendants I've encountered, was not gay—although he did enjoy soaking naked underneath a mountain of bubbles. I know this because the night we arrived Georgia and I went upstairs to introduce ourselves and pay the rent. We knocked on his bedroom door and a voice from a door down the hall told us to come in. We did. That was the first time we encountered him in the tub. Victor also had a tendency to hang out around the house wearing nothing but a mankini or a long satin robe. The guy was pretty laid-back, considering he kept the thermostat under lock and key and didn't allow men inside the house (rule number 1: There were no other rules). Well, no men other than the two pilots who lived in the basement. I liked Victor.

Even though I had an idea of what life would be like living in a crash pad before I went to bed that first night in New York, it was still jarring to wake up and find Georgia missing from her bed, but two other women sleeping soundly nearby. How in the world did I not hear them come in? I threw on a robe and quietly tiptoed out of the bedroom, softly closing the doors behind me. In the living room I found Georgia sitting on the sofa drinking coffee. The television was off. There was no sign of Marge.

"I didn't think you were ever gonna wake up. Better hurry and get dressed or we're going to be late for flight attendant orientation!" Georgia chirped.

Flight attendant orientation was set up to familiarize us with the airports, all three of them: LaGuardia, Kennedy, and Newark. This way, before our first trip, we'd know how to get from the employee parking lot to the terminal, where to find flight operations, and how to go through airport security to get to the gates. Before running to get dressed, I offered to call for a cab.

A familiar scratchy voice answered the phone. "Kew Gardens!"

After I mentioned my name and address, the voice burst out laughing. "What's so funny?" I asked.

"Did Miss Louisiana sleep well last night?"

It was him, the crazy old driver who was not just a driver but in fact a dispatcher who had grabbed a set of keys because there weren't enough drivers on the road last night. His name was Eddie. I knew right away that Eddie and I weren't going to get along. Being from Texas, I wasn't accustomed to people who weren't polite, who said what they meant and meant what they said. Then again I wasn't accustomed to much of anything about life in New York, which Eddie was quick to point out.

"Just send a car!" I yelled, hanging up on him before he could hang up on me.

Wide-eyed Georgia said, "Listen to you, Miss New York."

I didn't know if that was a good thing or a bad thing. Only time would tell.

5

Prepare for Takeoff

RESERVE FLIGHT ATTENDANTS have no life. None. Zero. Zilch. We sit around in our pajamas half the day waiting for crew schedule to call, and complaining about being on reserve to anyone who will listen. The other half of the day is spent explaining that we are in fact working, even though we are not actually on an airplane, since we're stuck at home and unable to do what we'd really like to do. This explains why the sock and underwear drawer get a complete makeover—twice—each reserve month. And nothing goes better with reserve than the Weather Channel. We're always tuned in. When there's bad weather, crews go illegal, and when crews are unable to fly, reserve flight attendants get called out to cover their trips. The only thing good about being on reserve is we might get to work a trip we would otherwise never fly in a million years. Senior flight attendants hold the best trips, but when they call in sick, flight attendants on reserve fill in.

Here's how reserve works. Bidding is the act of requesting a line. A line is a sequence of trips in consecutive order flight attendants (well, those not on reserve) are offered to work each month. At my airline we are offered more than two hundred lines. Each line has anywhere from three to ten positions to work, depending on the aircraft type. Lines are awarded by company seniority. This is why the best trips, flights to Asia and Europe, are always staffed with the most senior crew, and why the ground staff in Honolulu have been known to ask if the wheelchairs meeting the flight are for passengers or flight attendants. If a flight attendant has a seniority number of 200, that flight attendant should bid for at least two hundred positions to make sure she doesn't get a "miss bid" and be awarded a line she didn't want.

While nonreserve flight attendants choose from lines of trips, reserve flight attendants choose from lines of days off. Line holders can get ten to twenty days off a month, depending on their seniority. Reserve flight attendants on average only get ten days off. Days off are grouped together in three or four blocks per month, and each block can range anywhere from one to five days. When you're on reserve, the airline can (and will) assign a trip at any time of day or night. Sleep, something most people take for granted, becomes a guessing game since you never know when you'll have to fly next—crack of dawn or all night long.

When crew schedule, also known just as scheduling, contacts a flight attendant, the flight attendant has fifteen minutes to return the call and accept the trip. Otherwise she is assigned a "missed trip." Missing an assignment more than once can result in company action. If you're on probation like Georgia and I were, it can lead directly to termination. After flight attendants are assigned a trip, they have at least two hours to get to the airport and sign in on a computer in flight operations. Sign-in must occur an hour before the flight departs. If it doesn't, a reserve flight attendant working airport standby will be sent to cover the trip. Standby flight attendants spend hours sitting at the airport waiting around in case a flight attendant, even another reserve flight attendant, doesn't make sign-in on time. Being paid to hang out might sound like fun, but it can be draining, especially after sitting standby for five hours and then getting called out to work a five-hour trip ten minutes before you thought you'd be heading home. And since flight attendants on standby (or reserve) never know where they're going or how long they'll be gone, packing is always difficult. Standby flight attendants are only used in emergency situations, such as keeping flights staffed with what the FAA calls "minimum crew." In other words, there must be a certain ratio of flight attendants to passengers on board each flight, as well as enough flight attendants to operate the door exits in case of an emergency evacuation.

Reserve is a lot like being an on-call doctor—we must be ready for duty at all times. There are no late nights, absolutely no alcohol, and no going outside a manageable radius of our base (ours included three airports: John F. Kennedy, LaGuardia, and Newark). We have to be packed and ready to go at a moment's notice. This is why some flight attendants who use Laundromats are reluctant to wash their clothes. No one wants to get the dreaded call during the middle of a wash cycle! Or even worse, during a shower. (Don't worry—we still shower. We just do it quickly.) It's not uncommon to order a pizza and then get a call to cover a late-night trip to London and be out the door and on our way to the airport before the food even arrives. There's no warning, no lead time, and no excuses.

Each day at a certain time, reserve flight attendants call in to see if they've been assigned a trip, also known as a sequence, for the following day. If we do not have a sequence on our schedule, we queue up with a number. This number is based on the hours already flown during the month. The flight attendant with the least amount of hours is assigned the lowest number and will most likely be called out to work first. Sounds simple enough, right? Wrong. This is where reserve gets confusing. Because the person with the lowest number may not be "legal" to work. This is why flight attendants on reserve are always on edge. A high number on the reserve list is always a relief to those looking forward to a full night of rest, but it does not mean a flight attendant can relax. Reserve is like Russian roulette. You never know who will be called out next.

What can make a flight attendant illegal to work a trip? Usually it has to do with hours, number of days on duty, and aircraft equipment. A flight attendant can remain on duty without a layover from fourteen to sixteen hours, depending on the airline and whether or not it's a domestic or an international trip. A flight attendant needs eleven hours off between the end of one trip and the beginning of another. Reserve flight attendants get twelve hours. The minimum number of hours a flight attendant has "behind the door" at a layover hotel is eight, and the maximum number of days a flight attendant can work or remain on call is six. When flight attendants go illegal—exceed one of these numbers—a reservist is called in to cover the trip. If this happens "down line" (at an airport that does not have a flight attendant base), flights are either delayed or canceled if FAA minimum crew cannot be met.

These very same legalities affect reserve flight attendants, as they determine who will get called out to work next. Say I'm first on the reserve list and a three-day trip pops up. It departs at 8:00 a.m. Because my trip the day before landed at 10:00 p.m., I am not legal for the trip. Since I cannot sign in until 10:00 a.m., I cannot work a trip that departs before 11:00 a.m. The trip is then passed to the second flight attendant on reserve. But that person is only good for two days before entering a block of days off. The three-day trip is then assigned to the third person. Number 3 has worked more than four days in a row, so he is unable to take the trip since it would total seven days in a row of being on duty. The fourth person isn't qualified on the aircraft equipment, so the fifth person gets the trip. But she has the same problem I have. And so on and so on and so on until the fifteenth person on the list gets woken up by crew schedule at four in the morning to work a three-day trip.

If you think that's confusing, you can get a sense of what

Georgia and I were going through, learning the ins and outs of an unusual job that practically has its own language, a language that is nearly impossible to explain to family and friends who will never understand it, regardless of how many times we try. Life sucked. And it had only just begun.

"Oh shoot!" cried Georgia when the phone rang. It was day 4 in New York and we were officially on reserve. Neither one of us moved. We just sat on our beds staring at each other all big-eyed listening to it ring.

"Pick it up!" she demanded.

I gulped. Then reluctantly I did as I was told. "Hello?"

The monotone voice on the other end said exactly what I'd been dreading all day. "Crew schedule calling for flight attendant Poole."

The next morning I stepped out of an old white Kew Gardens minivan in front of LaGuardia Airport feeling like a million bucks. I was dressed in sensible navy heels, JCPenney stockings in the shade of "airline" and a navy pencil skirt, hemmed a perfect half inch above the knee. I'd given myself an extra hour to get ready in order to properly pin my hair back into a sophisticated French twist the way they'd shown us at the flight training academy. (Somehow I wound up with a chic side-of-the-neck bun instead.) My white button-down blouse had been starched and ironed to crisp perfection. It hid under a fitted navy blue blazer with two silver stripes around the wrist. To keep warm, I wore a long blue trench coat. And, fluttering in the chilly breeze, a red silk scarf was tied loosely around my neck. I couldn't get over how a small piece of fabric made me feel so elegant and feminine compared to the crisscross, snap-on Nathan's neck tie I'd worn at Sun Jet. As I waited for my driver to get my bags out of the trunk, I couldn't help but notice that a small group of travelers waiting in line to curb-check their bags were looking at me. I don't know what it is about a uniform, but it does make people take notice. Smiling, I waved at a toddler. My flight instructors would have been proud.

I attached my black tote to my matching rolling bag, took a deep breath and thought to myself, *Show time!* Two seconds later, I sailed through the automatic doors armed with a couple of pens, $20 in singles in case I needed to make change in flight, and a little black tube of M·A·C Viva Glam lipstick inside my blazer pocket. I passed through the food court, where vendors doled out powdered eggs and bricks of sausage to their first customers in line, and made my way to flight operations. I was a nervous wreck. In a little less than an hour and a half I'd be working my first of three legs today, a flight to Chicago that continued on to Dallas and then Austin. Thank God I'd been assigned the "extra position." At least in coach I kind of knew what I was doing.

"The extra" or "the add" is just that, an extra flight attendant that has been added to the crew at the last minute. The FAA requires airlines to staff flights with one flight attendant per fifty passenger seats. This is called minimum crew. Extras are used in all kinds of situations, for example, on full flights with short flying times and long hauls offering elaborate services. Take, for instance, the New York–Chicago route. The average flying time is an hour and a half. Flying time does not include taxiing to or from the gate. There's no way a minimum crew can serve and pick up that many drinks and meals in coach before it's time to prepare the cabin for landing. For the Dallas–Austin route, an extra ensures that we can complete a single beverage service for 140 passengers aboard a thirty-minute flight with only fifteen minutes of flying time between takeoff and descent. And passengers wonder why flight attendants get snippy when they can't decide what they'd like to drink!

The great thing about being an extra is you have no responsibilities on the airplane in terms of checking aircraft equipment, setting up the galley, or briefing the exit rows. Basically all you do is walk on board, oversee the boarding process, perform a safety demo and float between cabins helping whoever needs it most. Because extras hop from one flight to another and work with a new crew each leg of their trip, they rarely get caught up in crew drama. Of course, that's also the bad thing about being an extra. You're pretty much on your own—on and off the flight. After a flight lands, a crew will stick together and work another flight or layover for the night, never to see the extra again. It's not uncommon for an extra to work with several different flight crews in a single day and then wind up at a hotel all alone. Many crews don't even bother to learn the extra's name. You're simply referred to as "the extra," as in, "Are you the extra?" "Where is the extra?" "Ask the extra to get some napkins from first class."

When the extra (me) stepped aboard the airplane and counted five flight attendants sitting in first class, I thought nothing of it. I figured someone must have been "deadheading." A deadhead is a crew member being repositioned to work another trip in a different city. Because it is a work assignment, deadheads are high on the priority list and are even paid to occupy a passenger seat throughout a flight. When I introduced myself as the extra to the crew, one of the flight attendants smirked at me.

"You're not on this trip anymore," he said. Before I could assure him that I was on the trip, he informed me that he'd been called out on reserve at the last minute to fill in for someone who never showed up.

Without another word, I ran back to the gate to use the computer and pull up my flight itinerary. Quickly I scanned the list of crew names and sure enough, Poole had been replaced with Edwards. Confused, I called crew tracking. When prompted, I punched in my employee number and then entered my three-letter base code. After a short beep a voice said, "Flight attendant Poole, you've been assigned a missed trip."

"A missed trip? But why? I'm here. At the gate!"

"You never signed in." My heart dropped. This was not good at all, not while I was on probation, not for my very first trip.

At my airline, a missed trip, a sick call, or even a late sign-in equates to one point on your record. Three points and you get a warning. Three warnings and company action is taken. But for me, a new hire on probation without union representation, a single point could easily get me fired, no questions asked. Horrified and embarrassed, I couldn't imagine what I would tell my family and friends. How do you explain losing your job before it even began?

Ignoring a couple of passengers who had mistaken me for the gate agent since they were all lining up in front of the counter, I told the scheduler what had happened, how I'd gotten to the airport half an hour early just so I *wouldn't* be late, and how I spent a majority of that time playing around on the computer seeing what I could pull up using as many different flight codes as I could remember from training. Well, every code, that is, except for the one to sign in, the most important one of all!

I did what any other new hire on probation who was about to lose her job would do. I begged and pleaded to be put back on the trip, apologizing profusely for screwing up, asking if there was anything I could do to make up for it until I realized I was probably only making it worse.

"I'm in big trouble, aren't I?" I held my breath.

Eventually, the voice sighed and then said, "Sit tight. Stay at the airport in case we need you later."

"Thank you so much! You have no idea how much I appreciate this." Stockholm syndrome had set in. "So . . . am I on, like, standby duty now?"

"You're, like, sitting at the airport in case we need you later." Click.

Okay. That didn't make sense. On standby duty I was officially on the clock. If I just sat around waiting, how would I get paid?

I had to remind myself that that didn't matter. Money was not important—at least not at the moment. The important thing, I told myself, was that I still had a job. At least, I was pretty sure I still had a job. I wouldn't know for sure until later that night when I called in to see if I had an assignment for tomorrow. Curious, I typed in the flight code to bring up my record. There it was spelled out in white letters on a blue screen—MISSED TRIP. Head hung low, I walked to flight operations, and sat there for hours. All day, actually. Until finally it was so late that I figured there couldn't be any more flights departing LaGuardia. After working up a little courage, I called crew schedule.

"Hi, this is flight attendant Poole. Can I be released?"

I could hear someone clicking away on the computer. "Released from what?"

"Oh. Umm. Nothing. Sorry," I heard myself say as my mind screamed *Hang up already!* Instead I added, "Thank you," just to be nice.

Why I wasn't fired right then and there, I don't know, but I thank God for it every day. Others had lost their jobs for doing less. Rumor had it that one new hire got canned for calling in sick when she actually was sick! Another had been asked to leave for wearing a non-company-issued backpack through the airport terminal. Of course, that same flight attendant had also gotten a slap on the wrist a week prior for wearing the uniform sweater around her waist, so really she should have known better. Then there was the girl who pretended to be deadheading on a flight just so she could go home. Maybe she did deserve to be let go. But did the guy who got busted for falling asleep on his jump seat on a red-eye flight deserve the same fate? Luckily for us, things would drastically change in six months' time. I knew this because as I sat there in Ops waiting around for crew schedule to call, I saw quite a few things I could not believe, like flight attendants wearing their hair down, with buckles on their shoes, chewing gum in front of supervisors! Everything we'd been taught we couldn't do. But until I officially joined their ranks, I'd just have to make sure I did everything else perfectly. Starting with remembering to sign in next time.

While I was not officially sitting standby, Georgia was called out to cover a trip to Kansas City. Upon discovering that the entire crew was on reserve, and from our training class, she almost had a heart attack. As soon as she hung up with the scheduler, she dialed me.

Like most new hires, Georgia wasn't concerned about an emergency situation—we had that part down pat. What worried her the most was the service. "How are we gonna know if we're doin' it right?"

"You'll be fine," I lied. Because I was sitting in the middle of flight operations and didn't want to alert anyone, I whispered, "Just make sure you have your flight manual out and ready to go in case you need it."

That first week on the job, right before making the dreaded call to find out what I'd been assigned to work the following day, I'd pray for four things to *not* happen.

1. I did not want to work on a wide-body aircraft. The 767, DC10, A300, and MD11 were all so big and scary compared to what I had worked in the past. And the flight attendants who could hold trips on this type of equipment were even scarier. They were super senior, very cliquey, and totally set in their ways. The last thing I needed on probation was to piss off some senior mama who would write me up for not doing something a certain way.

2. I did not want to work the galley position. Why would I when all I'd done at Sun Jet was throw a couple of sodas and a bucket of ice onto a cart? At training, sure, we pretended to serve beverages to classmates on mock

airplanes, but we didn't even have real food to use! And the galleys we practiced in were not lifelike. In all our time in training, we'd discussed the different services in great detail, but we never actually set up a galley for one!

3. I did not want a trip departing out of Newark Airport. The airport was located in another *state*—two and half hours from my crash pad in Queens. In order to get there I'd have to walk a couple of blocks to the Long Island Railroad Station to take the train to Manhattan to catch the bus to Newark—a $30 round-trip fare, which is a lot when you can barely afford to eat. Not to mention that the four-hour travel time to and from the airport is not calculated into our twelve-hour legal rest time.

4. I did not want to work a morning sign-in. One reason I became a flight attendant was to take advantage of the flexible schedule, preferably the night flying. I just don't do mornings well. I'd take a red-eye flight any day over a departure leaving at the crack of dawn.

Somehow all my wishes came true that week. Three trips in a row I got called out to work a narrow-body turn. I surprised myself by feeling right at home. The airplanes were all so clean and nice and the passengers always smiled and said hello, but in addition, it was work as usual—minus the delays, duct-taped armrests, and overflowing blue water leaking out of the lav, just a few of the things I'd grown accustomed to with my previous employer. The two big things that did stand out more from my old airline those first few days on the job were the quiet cockpits and all the short hemlines.

I'll never forget sitting on the first-class galley jump seat during my first descent, my back against the cockpit wall, hearing nothing but absolute silence. It made me a little nervous. Okay, fine, really nervous! Long ago I'd learned to trust my instincts, and I just *knew* something had to be wrong. Why couldn't I hear the computerized voice in the cockpit talking? Concerned, I looked at the flight attendant in charge who sat beside me, a senior gal who'd seen it all and then some based on the number of medical emergencies she'd told me she'd handled over the years. But she seemed as calm as could be, looking out the porthole window at the ground down below. Even so, I couldn't let it go. I mean, what the heck was going on in the cockpit? Were the pilots dead? At Sun Jet we could always hear a computer voice yelling out commands from behind the locked door just before touchdown, things like, "Pull up, pull up—terrain, terrain!" After growing accustomed to that, the silence felt like a scream. If the seasoned flight attendant sitting beside me had not been there, I might have picked up the phone in a panic and broken sterile cockpit to find out. That would have had me fired for sure. Flight attendants are not allowed to contact the cockpit during sterile cockpit so that pilots can focus on what's important—landing the plane. This was one thing I got used to pretty quickly!

As for the hemlines, this was the mid-1990s and everyone, passengers and flight attendants alike, wore skirts and dresses as short as Heather Locklear on the original *Melrose Place* television series. Compared to the majority of my passengers and colleagues, I looked like an Amish woman who'd gotten lost and stumbled onto an airplane. My uniform quickly began to embarrass me. It was like being a freshman nerd surrounded by cool senior cheerleaders. Forget the silver wings—gold wings at my airline are only worn by flight attendants with at least five years seniority—one glance at my dress and everyone knew I was on probation. Even frequent fliers seemed to get off on letting me know that they knew I was new. One first-class passenger decided to get up and help us in the galley as soon as he realized there were a couple of newbies working his cabin. At first we were annoyed by his know-it-all presence, but when we realized we might land with a couple of trays still out in the cabin, suddenly we were thankful for his assistance in not only collecting glassware that needed to be locked in the galley before landing, but also for helping us hand back sixteen first-class coats. In the aisle, before buckling into his seat, he took a bow. The passengers gave him a round of applause. We, the crew, slid him a bottle of wine.

The hemline had an effect on pilots, too. One look and they knew they could ask for food items they'd never in a million years get from a more seasoned flight attendant. When I told one such pilot we only had enough mixed nuts for first-class passengers, he suggested I take one or two nuts, whatever I felt comfortable with, from each passenger's bowl. "It'll be our little secret," he added.

Even worse were pilots known to prey on flight attendants right out of training. Because we were young and dumb and unaware of the reputation some of these guys had, most of us found it flattering to be at the receiving end of their attention. In fact, one of my roommates, a "Cockpit Connie," enjoyed it so much that when she finally got off probation she didn't run straight to a tailor like the majority of us did. She left her hemline as long as possible so she could entice even more pilots into her layover hotel room late at night. On the flip side, there were the pilots who would see our long skirts and immediately go into father mode, trying to protect us from anything that could possibly go wrong in flight.

"If you have any questions, don't be afraid to ask, and if the passengers give you a hard time, let me know and I'll have them taken off the flight. I don't care what the company says, I don't put up with that kind of bull," one told me. Those pilots were, and still are, my favorite kind, and I'd like to thank each and every one of them for giving us the support we don't always get.

My worst flight attendant nightmare came true during my second week on the job: I got called out to work what we affectionately call the Death Cruiser 10. The DC10 was a monster of an airplane. It held more than 250 passengers and a crew of fifteen. Thirty passengers sat in first class, with fifty in business class. I'd been assigned the extra position, but things went from bad to worse real quick when I got to the airport. The flight attendant working the galley position called in sick. Because we already had an extra (me!) and it was too late to call out another reserve, scheduling told us to work it out. And so, one by one, in order of seniority, each flight attendant picked a position. Since I was the most junior flight attendant on the crew, I didn't even have to wait until it was my turn to figure out that the lower lobe would be all mine. I offered fifty bucks I didn't have to anyone willing to switch positions. No one took the bait. I upped it to seventy-five. They all laughed at me.

"Sweetie," said a senior flight attendant with a beehive bun. "I haven't worked a galley in twenty years. None of us have. You're on your own." Everyone nodded in agreement.

It must have been the sick look on my face that caused another flight attendant to pipe up with, "Just do the best you can. The passengers will survive."

Actually, I wasn't too sure about that.

Part of me wanted to throw up, but another, admittedly smaller, part of me couldn't wait to check out the infamous lower lobe. It had a scandalous reputation, on par with Studio 54. Located *underneath* first and business class, it can only be reached by a one-person elevator. Completely out of sight from passengers and crew, flight attendants could do just about anything they wanted while working the galley position on DC10. Listen to music. Have a smoke. Join the mile-high club. I'd heard all kinds of crazy stories. One roommate even swore that she once opened a cart, looking for passenger leftovers to eat, and found a flight attendant fast asleep curled up inside.

The thing that freaked me out the most about the DC10 was that it only had one galley for all three cabins. On most aircraft each cabin—first class, business, and coach—has a galley. That means three flight attendants in charge of the flow of service. Now keep in mind that each cabin operates almost as if it's its own flight in that no two cabins are ever doing the same thing at the same time. This is why the person working the DC10 lower lobe galley really has to know what he's doing—there's just one person in charge of setting up every single cart for all three cabins. When coach is in the middle of serving meals, business class might be starting salads as first class finishes up appetizers. A good galley is always one step ahead, preparing for the next service in each cabin.

At this particular point in my career, I had yet to work the galley on any flight, let alone three simultaneous services on one of the largest airplanes in our fleet. I hadn't even seen how the service worked, and now I was in charge of it! Oh, I'd take working the aisle and all the accompanying drama any day over getting stuck in the galley with no idea of what's going on. But, like Georgia working with an all-new crew, I didn't have a choice. So I opened my flight manual to the page with all the diagrams showing how to set up different carts, and armed with a pair of company-issued galley gloves that were so long and silver they looked like they might belong on a space shuttle, I waved buh-bye to my crew and took the elevator down.

When the elevator reached the bottom, I turned the handle and opened the door slowly. Oh. My. God. I just stood there in the windowless room with my mouth wide open. I was surrounded by carts and compartments—bazillions of them, filled top to bottom with silverware and linens, condiments and food, so much food—and even more glassware. And the ice, there must have been fifty bags I'd have to break up before the flight even took off! I had no idea where to start or what to do first—figure out how to organize the beverage carts or count the meals. Suddenly I began to feel claustrophobic. I needed to get out of there and quick. What if a fire broke out and I got trapped down here? Would anyone come and save me? When I spotted what looked like a fire escape hatch on the ceiling, I wondered which cabin I would pop up into. And how would I know when to go up and strap into the jump seat for takeoff? Would I be able to hear the captain's PA? I tried not to hyperventilate as I began opening each and every single cart and compartment door. They were far from empty. This was bad, very bad. On the verge of tears, I felt sorry for the passengers who actually spent good money for the service we were about to provide.

There are two types of flight attendants, those who work the aisle and those who prefer to never set foot out of the galley. In the galley you get burned, break fingernails, and snag your hose, but many flight attendants prefer this to getting poked, prodded, pulled, and grabbed in the aisle. Trust me—there are quite a few touchy-feely passengers who will probably live a whole lot longer if certain flight attendants stay in the galley. Some of these same flight attendants have become so antisocial and set in their ways after years of working the same position, they won't even allow coworkers into the galley without their permission. A few are notorious for locking it off long before landing, as if they own it. Doesn't matter if 10B wants a Pepsi and there's still thirty minutes left in flight. The galley is closed! End of discussion. Galley rules.

Those who prefer the galley over the aisle aren't all bad. Most are organized, handy, and familiar with the tricks of the trade. They can cut through the paper surrounding a bottle of wine using a pair of salad tongs. They'll keep coffee warm by placing cookie plates over aluminum pots. Champagne corks unwilling to budge are placed upside down in a cup of hot water for just a few seconds and then—*pop!*—mimosas for first class. (The airline does not condone this as someone is bound to get shot in the eye with a flying cork if it's not done correctly.) If the balsamic salad dressing is a popular choice in business, a good galley will mix in a little orange juice to stretch it out for a few more rows, thwarting potential passenger meltdowns. Because there are only a few ovens that keep everything warm, we can't cook meals to order, so when a premium-class passenger requests the steak well done, the galley will either deny the request or dunk the piece of meat into a cup of hot water until it's the proper shade of brown and once again, possible passenger trouble avoided. Lumpy hot fudge becomes smooth once again with just a drop of hot coffee. These are the kinds of things a good galley employee knows, which is exactly why I had no business working the lower lobe—or any galley, for that matter.

That's when I heard it. It could have been God. I'm not joking. Or maybe it was the lead flight attendant, or purser, having a manly moment. Either way, a deep voice from above said, "The most important thing you can do, Heather, is familiarize yourself with the galley." So that's what I did. And I don't think it was the worst flight in the world, although, by the number of carts that were immediately returned with curt instructions as to how to make them right, I'm guessing it came pretty close. Oh well, everyone has to learn somehow.

While I was stressing out over the DC10 service, Georgia was dealing with something almost worse. She'd been called to cover a flight to Los Angeles working in first class as the purser. That meant she was in charge of the *entire airplane*. If something went wrong, Georgia would be the one to handle it. Pursers are only staffed on long-haul or overseas flights. She'd been assigned the position on reserve, a position crew schedule only gave to regular flight attendants when there weren't any qualified pursers available. To even be considered for the training class, they go through an extensive interview process. Once accepted, the two-week course is intense and not everyone makes it through.

Honestly, if it had been me, I might have called in sick. Avoiding all that responsibility during my second week of flying would have been more than worth a point on my record. But ignorance is bliss, and Georgia had never flown with a senior crew on a wide-body before, so she had no idea what she was up against.

When I pointed this out, she just laughed. "Come on, what are the odds something will go wrong?"

Georgia, I'd begun to notice, had become overly confident after working that trip with an entire crew of first-time flight attendants.

Sure enough, thirty minutes after takeoff, one of the senior flight attendants from the back called Georgia in first class to inform her that two passengers in coach were fighting over an armrest. "You need to come back here and deal with this!"

"Are you serious?" Georgia giggled.

"Hey, last I checked, you're the one who gets paid the big bucks!" And it was true—rookie Georgia was getting two extra dollars an hour for the reserve assignment she'd drawn. But I know for a fact she would have preferred her regular salary to purser pay and all that went along with it.

Never one to cower under pressure, Georgia fluffed her hair, straightened her navy blue vest, and walked down the aisle to the back of the aircraft as if it were a pageant stage. She got down on one knee in the aisle like we'd been instructed to do in training. Getting down to the passenger's level makes flight attendants less threatening and puts passengers at ease. Generally speaking, regardless of whether or not we can solve a problem, the majority of passengers just want to be heard. So Georgia smiled a beauty queen smile, introduced herself, and then patiently listened to each passenger's side of the story.

"I've got an idea," she said, eyeing first one passenger and then the other. "How 'bout you use the armrest the first three hours in flight and then you can use it the last three hours. I'll come back from time to time to check on y'all."

"Okay," they said in unison. Problem solved.

As soon as Georgia got back to the first-class galley the phone rang again. This time it had to do with a reclined seat back. And it didn't stop ringing for the rest of the flight, but Georgia made it through. I wasn't sure she was going to make it through the next challenge though: the holidays were right around the corner.

6

Unhappy Holidays

CHRISTMAS MEANT EVERYTHING to Georgia, and it killed her that she wouldn't be able to spend it with the one she loved. It was bad enough she was already homesick and had approximately 184.2 days until her travel benefits kicked in, but she'd been assigned an undesirable schedule of days off that had her on call Christmas Eve, Christmas Day, New Year's Eve, and New Year's Day! The two of us were completely broke, living with a bunch of freaks in what could only be described as a flophouse, freezing our butts off far, far, away from home, and we were new hires on probation, and on reserve during what should have been the most joyous time of the year. We had been in New York for only fourteen days and life couldn't get much worse.

But then something miraculous happened. The crew-scheduling gods must have been smiling down on us. Not only did Georgia get assigned an easy, quick trip to Albany, but she also got assigned to work the trip with me! How lucky were we to get to work a two-day trip together over Christmas Eve and Christmas Day? If we couldn't spend it with our families, at least we got to spend it with each other. And we qualified for holiday pay—time and a half! (This disappeared after 9/11.) We couldn't wait. Well, really, I couldn't wait.

Georgia just wanted to go home. While I practiced my PAs out loud on the bed, Georgia curled up under the covers with the phone. She wanted to see how much a ticket to North Carolina would cost so she could make a surprise visit to see her boyfriend—John, Jack, Jake, whatever his name was—on her days off as soon as we got back. My guy, on the other hand, was way too understanding about my absence, even though I kept hinting around that he'd probably be better off without me. Anyone else would have found that sweet. Me, I was starting to get annoyed. The time had come to move on.

If it hadn't been Christmas Eve, our flight would have been perfect. Our load was light, the passengers were all very nice, the service went smoothly, and best of all, there were tons of first-class leftovers to eat, so I took it upon myself to set up the dessert cart like a buffet line. Merry Christmas to us! Georgia and I were hanging out in the galley talking about who knows what when the senior flight attendant, who had chosen to work in order to avoid his in-laws, exclaimed, "Oh my God, we're landing!"

Usually when a flight attendant says "we're landing" it's a good thing. It means the flight is almost over, and we'll soon be on the ground relaxing by a pool at a layover hotel somewhere. But add the words "Oh my God" to the beginning of that phrase, and a good thing instantly becomes bad, very bad, as in "you don't want to know" bad, as in "FAA personal fine" bad, as in "Linda, my roommate from training's makeup" bad! It was that bad. Quickly the three of us began cramming food, dishes, glassware, half-full bottles of wine, anything we could get our hands on into inserts that were already full. I glanced out the window and saw rooftops and streetlights.

Folding the dessert cart and shoving it inside its compartment, I asked in a panic, "Did either one of you hear the captain make the prepare-for-landing announcement?" Because I didn't want to have to take the blame for this!

"He never made it. Just leave the racks inside of the oven!"

ordered the senior flight attendant. "Lock the carts and take your seat ASAP. I'll grab whatever's left out in first class and then stow it behind the last row." He pointed at Georgia who stood frozen with eyes open wide, "You pick up trash on your way back to your jump seat—now, go go go! We're going to be on the ground in a few seconds."

I didn't even have time to buckle my seat belt when I felt the wheels grind against the runway. As we rolled down the tarmac, I could see Georgia and her partner in crime still standing in the aisle. Sweating, I made the PA welcoming everyone to Buffalo.

"Albany!" a few passengers yell out. "We're in Albany!"

"I mean Albany," I corrected over the PA.

Our layover hotel was a motel, only worse. The rooms smelled musty, the television didn't come with a remote, and the bed was covered with something someone's grandmother crocheted twenty years ago. I bravely walked barefoot across the shag carpet, closed the floral curtains, and sneezed. I was just about to call Georgia to see if she wanted to come over and order room service, but I couldn't find the menu. That's because there was no menu. The hotel didn't offer room service. And the restaurant was closed.

"If you're hungry there's a vending machine down the hall," the hotel concierge told me over the phone.

I knew that eating peanut-butter crackers and Cheetos in a musty motel on Christmas Eve would definitely send Georgia over the edge and down the road to quitsville. I had to think of something quick, an alternative plan to take her mind off the situation. Before I could come up with anything, I heard a tap on my window. My heart lurched. There it was again! *Tap-tap-tap*—so subtle and soft and—*whomp!* I fell to the floor, crawled to the rotary phone, and dialed 0.

"Send security to my room right away!"

Airline crews take hotel security very seriously. We don't tell passengers where we're laying over. When we get to the hotel, we never say our room numbers out loud. We either jot them down on one another's room key covers or quickly flash the key card. We never know who's listening. Because hotels are known to issue the same rooms to crew members day after day, month after month, and year after year, hotel personnel are quite familiar with which rooms are ours. Chances are the occupant of one of these rooms, which is always located near an elevator and an ice machine, or at the end of a long hall, is going to be an attractive female. Who better to cut up with a hatchet than a flight attendant?

Think I'm joking? There's a layover hotel in Los Angeles where a flight attendant was found naked and hanging in her closet. This is why we use our luggage to prop the door to our room open before retiring for the night. While one coworker checks under the bed, inside the closet, and behind the shower curtain another coworker waits outside in the hallway. Then we switch. I heard of a flight attendant who got down on hands and knees, lifted the bed skirt, and spotted a head staring back at her. She ran out of the room screaming bloody murder later to find out it was her own mirrored reflection that scared her so.

Not all flight attendants are quite so lucky. A handful became the victims of the guy who wore a white jogging suit and carried a plastic cup while riding the elevators up and down early in the mornings looking for flight attendants on their way to the crew van for pickup. Once he found his prey, he'd toss a "sticky white substance" on their uniform and then run away. This went on for months.

Fifteen minutes after I called the hotel desk/operator/security guy, I finally heard a knock on my door. Chain still on, I cracked the door open and told him what happened. He promised to go outside and do a walk around the property.

Georgia came to my door about two seconds later, all bundled up with rosy cheeks. "You've got to come outside. The snow is absolutely gorgeous!"

I gulped. I didn't dare tell her about the madman running around outside, knowing how close she'd just come to death.

She tossed my sneakers at me. "I made a snowman. Come see! Hey, didn't you hear me throwing snowballs at your window?"

Snowballs, killers, whatever, sometimes things aren't always as they seem.

When Georgia called Jake, Jeff, Jack, whatever his name was, to wish him a Merry Christmas, he thanked her and then asked if he could call her right back, hanging up the phone before she could say good-bye. Half an hour later she called him back, but he didn't answer. While she waited for him to return her call, we ate dinner out of a vending machine located on the second floor of our three-star motel. Although we would have been much happier with turkey and dressing at home with our family and friends, we made the best of it with a couple packets of peanut-butter crackers and Diet Coke. It wasn't how I'd ever expected to spend Christmas, but hey—we had wished for a job with a flexible lifestyle, hadn't we? It was just that in my dreams I saw myself in Zurich, not Buffalo—I mean Albany!

After we returned from our Christmas trip, I decided I wanted to go home, too, and nothing would stop me. Like Georgia, I had a credit card and I was determined to use it. But instead of relaying my credit card numbers to the airline representative over the phone, I hung up.

"Eight hundred dollars! That's how much it costs for a one-way ticket from New York to Dallas! I can't believe it!" Actually I could believe it. I just didn't want to believe it. But free travel was one of the main reasons I'd decided to become a flight attendant in the first place. Lord knows I couldn't afford to do so otherwise.

"Don't worry! Your travel benefits will kick in about . . . oh, six months!" Mimi, one of the many flight attendants in our house, sat on a twin bed on the far side of the room, intently studying a copy of *Glamour* magazine that she'd found on her last flight to Los Angeles. Although she'd been in New York only three weeks longer than the rest of us, she seemed so much wiser. None of us wanted to admit it, especially Georgia, but we looked up to the girl with the chic blond bob who had worked a 767 in business class her very first day on the job and lived to tell about it! Oh, how I dreaded getting called out to work a 767 for the first time. My disastrous DC10 flight had scarred me for life. I didn't want anything to do with another wide-body again.

Georgia shook the hot rollers in her hair. "I'm sorry, but it just ain't right we can't travel for six months—six months! I don't know if I can make it that long."

"Get used to it, princess," Mimi said, without looking up.

Glaring at Mimi, Georgia bit into a scrumptious antidepressant: a Twinkie from the box hidden underneath her bed. She purchased the sugary treats, along with the rest of her groceries, from the 7-Eleven located directly behind our house. No way would Georgia schlep two blocks in the freezing cold to the supermarket when she could pay a little extra for convenience.

Mimi stood up, tossed the magazine onto Georgia's bed, and then slid into a long black coat with a belted waist and a fur hood, wrapping a gray cashmere scarf around her neck, a recent gift from some guy she had met on a plane. She turned side to side in front of a long skinny mirror tacked to the back of our bedroom door, puckered up, and painted her lips a deep dark red.

"Okay, ladies, I'm outta here." Mimi had yet to learn our names. Instead she used endearments like "honey," "sweetie," and "ladies." I didn't blame her, considering the high turnover rate in our crash pad. Each week a new group of flight attendants was shipped to New York. Even though we'd only been living there for four weeks, roommates had already come and gone. Sometimes they just moved up, as in upstairs, before officially moving on. The last roommate quit three days after her first trip because a passenger had screamed at her for ruining his vacation when they ran out of eggs in coach.

"Don't wait up!" Mimi sashayed out the front door.

"Don't have to worry about that," mumbled Georgia.

"Do you think she's going out with 2A?" I smiled mischievously.

"Who cares what she's doing?" Georgia had little patience for Mimi's "nonsense." That's because Georgia had a serious boyfriend and didn't take relationships lightly. My ex, on the other hand, was still refusing to let things go. He had yet to realize that a long-distance relationship might be more difficult than he had first imagined, no matter how many times I tried to help him imagine it. Why did he have to be such a nice guy—that got on my nerves?! So when it came to men, all I really had was Mimi's stories of 2A, a new obsession of mine. He sat in first class on a flight from San Francisco and only ate caviar. He lived in a penthouse apartment on Manhattan's Upper West Side. He paid for drinks, lots of them, at trendy upscale hotel bars on the other side of town, not just for Mimi, but for all of her flight attendant friends—the more the merrier. Because she never invited me out to meet him, I had no choice but to take Mimi's word for it. According to Mimi there was no hanky-panky going on between the two of them. It was a relationship of companions only. Georgia had a hard time believing that! What man bought a woman luxury gifts and expected nothing in return? I had to agree, especially when I peeped out the window to see Mimi climbing into a swanky black town car. I made a mental note to keep an eye out for a first-class "friend" of my own. Only I preferred mine single and under the age of fifty. Life just seemed so much easier that way.

"I'm freezing!" Georgia said, pulling tight a blue terrycloth bathrobe with little white clouds on it. Her bed was so close to mine I could practically reach out and touch her shivering hand. "Should we ask Victor to turn up the heat?"

"You can. He's still mad at me."

Victor had been giving me major attitude ever since we saw the first wad of cash lying on the floor in the foyer a few days after we'd moved in. I didn't think twice about it until Victor introduced me to his twenty-year-old spaced-out girlfriend who was beautiful but could barely form the word "hello." It didn't hit me what was really going on until a few days later, late one night, when the wind blew so hard outside something crashed loudly to the ground, causing Victor to come running down the steps paranoid and naked with a shotgun. Our landlord, it turned out, was moonlighting as a drug dealer. Or maybe it was the other way around. Making light of the situation, Georgia and I had joked around about taking the money and going shopping, but when no one laughed, we decided to leave the money by the door and ignore it, like everyone else in the house. But when large sums continued to make regular appearances, I decided to confront Victor. This was the plan: I'd pick up the cash, march right up the rickety old stairs, and hand it over to him face-to-face. Just to see what he might have to say for himself. That's it. Then I'd come right back down and report the news to Georgia. Based on his reaction, we'd figure out what to do next.

"Come in!" Victor yelled when I knocked on the door. That's exactly what I did. Then I screamed.

"What?" He said it as if I were the crazy one, not him, a naked old man standing in the middle of a bear-skin rug just staring at me. I looked away and laughed nervously, then apologized, which is what I have a tendency to do in awkward situations. Like, for example, bare-skinned landlords on bear-skin rugs. Turning my face to the door, I extended the arm holding the cash to him. He said something, but I have no idea what it was, since I was out the door and sprinting down the stairs the second he snatched it out of my hand.

Now I'm not exactly sure what it was that pissed Victor off: the fact that I had delivered the cash personally, thereby acknowledging I knew exactly what he was up to, or the fact that I had screamed bloody murder upon seeing him in the nude (shiver), indicating that I did not find him attractive. I guess it could have been a combination of the two. Whatever it was, I soon found myself paying the price. The evil stares were easy enough to ignore sometimes, but soon my roommates began accusing me of things I hadn't done, like eating their labeled food out of the fridge even though I hadn't even stepped into the kitchen! (It was filthier than the bathroom. And why cook when Dani's House of Pizza and Austin's Steak & Ale House were within walking distance and Golden Fountain Kitchen delivered the best spareribs and eggrolls in town?) But when a pilot I had just met for the first time confronted me about accusing him of sexual harassment to Victor—something that had never happened!—I knew something had to be done about my lying landlord, and quick!

Georgia and I had been hitting the pavement all month looking for someplace else to live, but other than an illegal basement apartment inside a house that should have been condemned, there was just nothing available that we could afford nearby. After chasing down yet another lead that had already been rented by the time we finally got there, we decided to call it a day and find someplace to eat. The sun was setting. We were hungry. On our way home, we stumbled into the first place we found, a hole-in-the-wall Mexican restaurant, to grab a bite to eat and study the subway map. That's when we spotted New York's finest seated at a tiny table for two against the wall. We had never been happier to see undercover cops in our lives. (Button-down shirts not exactly hiding their guns had given them away.) Right after our waitress had placed a basket of stale chips in front of us, the boys not in blue introduced themselves. It didn't take long before we were ratting out Victor. The cops agreed it couldn't be a safe situation for a house full of women and suggested that they stop by the following day to check things out. Well, check things out they did. But instead of investigating Victor, they made themselves comfortable on our beat-up couch nursing the last of Georgia's Dr. Brown diet cream sodas and gawking at our roommates. So that was a bust.

That's when I decided to take matters into my own hands. I called Kew Gardens.

Eddie answered the phone. "Going to work, sweetie?"

"Not today. But we do need a car to take us to LaGuardia Airport. Georgia's boyfriend is getting into town." Then I added innocently, "Think you can send over Kent?" EMT worker by day, cab driver by night, Kent was a nice guy with not-so-nice looks. He could have been Chewbacca's cousin. "And can you tell him to park the car and ring the bell . . . in case Georgia isn't ready. You know how she is!" I gave a fake laugh.

After an emphysema-like coughing fit, Eddie cleared his throat. "What the hell are you two up to now?"

"Nothing!" I'd have to work on my fake laugh.

When we first arrived in New York the significance of Eddie's job didn't mean much to us, but soon we discovered that drivers come and go. It's the dispatcher who sticks around. Much like gate agents, dispatchers have power. They make things happen— like cars come quicker to the airport when a dispatcher likes you! This is a huge deal when it's snowing outside, you've got an early sign-in the next morning, and you're eager to get home because it's been a long day and your feet are killing.

Always, always make friends with the dispatcher.

Little did we know that our awkward encounter with Eddie on our first night in town would become a life-changing event! Here's what happened. After he drove off he went back to base and reported what had happened to the other dispatchers, who got a good laugh at our expense. This is how Georgia and I came to be famous in dispatching circles around Queens. At first the dispatchers were on the lookout for us, wanting to meet us, but after meeting us they actually started to look out for us. If I couldn't find Georgia, I called Kew Gardens. They could always be counted on to know where she had flown to and how many days she'd be gone. If Kew Gardens wanted a case of beer from, say, Germany, they would call us. If we weren't flying there we'd find someone else who was and ask them to bring it back so we could pass it on. When we needed to know which subway line to take to the city in order to meet a date at a certain location, we asked Kew Gardens. If they wanted a duty-free bottle of vodka, they called us. When we wanted to know if it was safe to go to a certain place in the city to meet a date, we called them. It's no wonder they came to know our comings and goings better than we did. And when one of our favorite drivers, also a dispatcher on the weekends, went to prison for robbing a bank after writing a ransom note on the back of a Kew Gardens time sheet, Georgia and I were just as upset as the rest of the guys. For Christmas we gave each of them a pack of smokes and a gift card to Dunkin' Donuts. They gave us a free ride to the airport. We became one big happy, foul-mouthed, chain-smoking, coffee-drinking family, even though Georgia and I didn't curse, smoke, or drink coffee—yet.

Perhaps most important of all, Kew Gardens Car Service turned out to be all that stood between us and the Q10 bus stop. In our opinion, the Q10 was a nightmare. It was bad enough just trying to have exact change in quarters on hand at all times to ride the bus, let alone dealing with bus drivers who screamed at us to move our bags out of the way before we even had a chance to actually sit down and do so. To make matters worse, the driver with the bouffant hair would glare at us in the rearview mirror as she pressed the pedal to the metal, sending us stumbling down the aisle trying not to land on anyone. It didn't take us long to realize that work was stressful enough without the added stress of the Q10. So while the majority of our colleagues chose to take the bus in order to save money for more important things like manicures and alcohol, Georgia and I learned to paint our own nails and take advantage of places like Brother Jimmy's BBQ, a place in Manhattan that offered airline personnel with crew ID buy-one get-one-free drinks, so that we could afford the $8 Kew Gardens Car Service ride to the airport.

When Kent the driver knocked on the door, I quickly let him inside. We stood in the foyer making small talk while Georgia finished "fixin'" her hair. My plan was for Victor to see the kind of posse I ran with. That way he'd think twice before playing dirty with me. Two seconds later, a pair of gold silk slippers came padding down the stairs. Victor took one look at my friend and kept on walking.

By the time Georgia and I arrived at baggage claim, suitcases were already circling the carousel. I wouldn't normally have tagged along, but Georgia had demanded I meet the future father of her children before they checked into a hotel in the city. Jake, John, Jack, whatever his name was, was the manager of a bar— or maybe he owned a restaurant?—but, either way, as soon as he heard Georgia sobbing over the phone about how much she missed home he immediately decided to book a flight to New York and arrived the following day.

"Oh my gawd, I'm so nervous," purred Georgia as she eagerly scanned the lingering crowd. No sooner were the words out of her mouth than she let out a shriek and ran toward the baggage carousel. I craned my neck to see, but a skinny guy with long greasy hair was blocking my view of Mr. Wonderful. Only because he smiled at me, I smiled back at him, but I stopped smiling when Georgia jumped into his long, skinny arms.

I was doing a little better in the man department. My boy-friend finally got the hint and broke up with me. Thank God! It took him long enough to realize that we wouldn't see each other any time soon. I really had to emphasize the "any time soon" part quite a few times before he actually understood that it was me, not the airline, keeping us apart. Men!

A relationship with a flight attendant can be tricky, because being a flight attendant isn't just a job, it's a lifestyle. No matter how many times we try to explain it, most people have a hard time really grasping that the only thing consistent about our life-style is just how inconsistent it truly is. Our schedules are always changing, making it difficult to create long-term plans with loved ones. We work odd hours and rarely get holidays and weekends off. We're away from home for days at a time, and a lot of that time is spent at hotels with colleagues of the opposite sex. There aren't a lot of people who can handle that. This is especially true for those involved before their flight attendant career began. It's just too different for most men to deal with. Nine times out of ten, imaginations get the best of those left on the ground. They think all pilots look like Hugh Jackman instead of Danny DeVito, and that all the passengers seated in first class are trying to lure us onto their private islands with promises of champagne and caviar. Soon loneliness turns to jealousy and jealousy leads to frustration or anger. In the end, a person can only take so much and eventually someone will break up. It's either break up or quit flying.

This is why the people flight attendants get serious with must be confident, independent, and capable of making do for days at a time without their loved one. No one wants to spend an entire layover dealing with an insecure partner. What we really want is to be left alone—we've just spent the whole day taking care of needy passengers. A flight attendant also needs a partner who can make spur-of-the-moment plans, as well as deal with last-minute changes that involve backup plans A, B, and C, because when you work for an airline something is bound to go wrong. Jake, Jack, Jeff, whatever his name was, promised Georgia that he could do just that. He swore he'd be there for her through whatever tough times came their way. That he was in it for the long haul and that she had nothing to worry about, at least not when it came to him.

But she did worry—she wanted him to know he was still a priority.

A few weeks later, she walked through the front door of his apartment and yelled "Surprise!" Only it was Georgia who got the surprise of her life when a naked lady hiding in the closet sneezed. Jeff tried to distract her, but a woman knows another woman's sneeze! Devastated, Georgia flew right back to New York and cried on her twin bed for three days. I bought her endless pints of cookies-and-cream ice cream from 7-Eleven, and rented movies like *When Harry Met Sally* and *Thelma & Louise*. The last thing I wanted Georgia to do was quit. Not over a guy. A shitty flight, maybe I'd understand. But a dick, no way, not going to happen. I'd make sure it wouldn't happen. Especially because I didn't want to get stuck in New York by myself!

7

Cruising Altitude

YOU'RE ON A flight trying to get a little rest when the kid who's been kicking your seat for the last half hour suddenly begins to scream. Your head spins around like Linda Blair from *The Exorcist* and you give the parents an evil glare. When that doesn't work you ring your flight attendant call light and ask the attendant if perhaps she can help, all the while counting down the seconds to landing.

The likely culprit? It's not bad parenting—it's blocked ears. As the plane lowers, altitude changes increase air pressure, which pushes the eardrum inward. Because children have relatively narrow Eustachian tubes, they're especially susceptible, particularly if they're clogged by an inflammation or an ear infection. In the air, blocked ears can cause severe pain and dull hearing, and it can occasionally lead to hearing loss. What can parents do? Don't allow the child to sleep during descent, find something to suck on—a bottle, pacifier, gum, or hard candy—and postpone air travel if a cold, sinus infection, or allergy attack is present. Oh, and just ignore the jerk seated in front of you.

Blocked ears don't just affect kids. I've seen grown men get teary-eyed in flight. Most people know that chewing gum helps, as does constant swallowing or yawning during descent. This allows the muscles in the Eustachian tube to contract and open, equalizing the pressure. When you hear a clicking sound, you know it's working. Using a nasal spray or decongestant several hours before a flight is always a good idea when feeling congested. Steam can also help to ease the pain. Many passengers knew this and would ask for wads of hot wet paper towels stuffed inside Styrofoam cups to place over their ears. The steam seeped from the cloth through the cup and into the ear. (Unfortunately, because so many people have been burned using this technique we are no longer allowed to do it. Sorry!) But the best method for clearing ears is to use the Valsalva maneuver as soon as you begin to feel your ears starting to close. Pinch your nose, close your mouth, and gently exhale through your nostrils. Blowing too hard may damage the eardrum. Continue to do this periodically until landing. On the ground, try taking a hot steamy shower and drink plenty of hot tea. If you're frequently plagued with ear pressurization problems, invest in a pair of disposable ear plugs called EarPlanes. And don't leave home without them.

Blocked ears can ground a flight attendant for days, even weeks. We may feel okay on the ground, but once up in the air the pain can become excruciating, especially when working a trip that hops from city to city, taking off and landing several times in a day. One flight attendant I knew continued to fly instead of calling in sick, and ended up losing not just her hearing in one ear after her eardrum erupted in flight but also the job she loved. Crews must be able to communicate quickly in dangerous situations. If we can't hear a passenger calling for help, a coworker screaming for a fire extinguisher, or the captain giving us the secret code over the PA to initiate an evacuation we're useless. It's not all about serving drinks—we're also in charge of saving lives. So, no eardrum, no job.

Despite that risk, and because she was still on probation (with only three months to go), Georgia didn't want to call in sick for fear of losing her job. So when crew schedule assigned her a turn, a trip that leaves and returns back to base the very same day, she didn't think twice about accepting it.

"I'll be fine," she announced, and then blew her nose. She didn't sound fine, so I gave her what I had left of a box of extra strength Sudafed and a travel-size packet of Kleenex.

Because Georgia was scheduled to come back to New York later that night, she didn't bother taking her roll-aboard. She'd been able to pack the essentials inside her tote bag; flight manual, flashlight, makeup, galley gloves, wine opener, wallet, and a pocket mask in case, God forbid, someone needed mouth-to-mouth resuscitation in flight. In the air Georgia felt fine, all things considered, but thirty minutes before landing, as soon as the airplane began to make its descent into Chicago, that quickly changed. She chewed not one, but three pieces of Dentyne gum at a frantic pace. When that didn't work she yawned as wide as her mouth would go, a dozen of times, then swallowing hard over and over. As a last resort she took turns chewing, yawning, and swallowing, sometimes doing two of them at the same time, all the while preparing the cabin for landing. When that didn't work she pinched her nose and tried blowing, gently at first and then more forcefully, ignoring passengers who held up cups, napkins, and newspapers for her to dispose of. "I'm sorry, I can't help you!" she yelled at a passenger who had a question about a gate connection as she ran to the back and strapped in, doubling over in pain. Once on the ground things improved a little bit. Although Georgia could barely hear because both ears were closed, she wasn't about to let that stop her. After years of working the pageant circuit she was used to pushing her body to the limit, so if anyone knew pain, it was Georgia, and this was nothing compared to six months of hard-core dieting in preparation for swimsuit competition! Determined to suffer through it,

Georgia took more Sudafed and sipped hot tea while waiting for the next flight to board.

This is not an unusual scenario. Flight attendants are reluctant to call in sick for many reasons, the most important being that no one wants to get stuck on a layover far away from home, especially when there are kids involved. Many of us will push it until we get where we need to be before putting our name on the sick list. But once on the list, an employee is not allowed to travel, not even as a passenger on another airline. An employee who does, and gets caught, is no longer employed. Trip trades, drops, and pickups also go on hold when a flight attendant is on the sick list. In trip-trade world, if ya snooze, ya lose. If you're not able to manipulate your schedule within the first five days after bids have finalized, you can forget about getting time off for all those baby showers, graduations, weddings, vacations, holidays, or whatever important days you need off the following month.

At my airline if we call in sick three times we're issued a written warning. The only way around the warning, and a trip to the airport on a day off to speak with a manager about why we were sick and what we could have done to avoid it, is to see a doctor, even for a cold that can be managed with over-the-counter medication. With a doctor's note, a sick call will go from two points to one point. If we apply for a family leave, that point will disappear altogether. If we do not have enough working hours in a rolling twelve-month period to apply for a family leave (420 hours), the point stays. Three points and it's back to the written warning. Three warnings and it's buh-bye, airline. But, as a flight attendant, seeing a doctor isn't simple at all. For one, it's expensive when you make as little as many of us do. And we have to have the doctor fill out a packet of family leave paperwork so thick you'd think we were asking for a discharge from the military! One doctor, a family practitioner, actually dropped me as a patient when he tired of filling out these tedious forms.

Another doctor, an ob-gyn, refused to fill out the forms when I, many years later, became pregnant. She couldn't understand why I couldn't just do another job for the airline, like one on the ground.

"Because I'm a flight attendant," I told her. "We don't have other jobs. I can't just work as a ticket agent while I'm sick. They go through weeks of training too!" No matter how hard I tried to explain, the paperwork remained unsigned and I had to find another doctor.

It's important that flight attendants find doctors who understand what the job really entails. For instance, we don't just roll our bags gate to gate—we lift eighty pounds plus into the overhead bin each and every flight. We don't just serve drinks—we push and pull two-hundred-pound carts on an incline. We can't just handle the sniffles with a box of tissues—we have to worry about our eardrums exploding. Once I pleaded with a podiatrist not to release me back to work too soon after breaking my pinky toe. "You'll be fine," he assured me. I wasn't fine. Not fine working a ten-hour day at 35,000 feet inside a pressurized cabin. Not fine running gate-to-gate as quickly as possible in order to avoid a delay in some of the biggest and busiest airports in the world. When I went back in to his office to have him fill out a few more forms on top of the ones he'd already signed, because the airline had more questions about the nature of my injury, I told him my toe didn't just hurt, it throbbed. He suggested I take six Advil and relieve the pressure by cutting a hole in the side of my shoe. I just stared at him.

As per the flight attendant uniform guidebook, footwear may not have holes cut in the sides. Shoes must be conservative in style, plain black or navy blue, and have a covered toe, enclosed heel and enclosed sides. And there's more. Heels must be a minimum of one inch in height, width of heel should not exceed width of sole, heel and sole should be identical in color. Shoes must be polished and in good repair, and buckles, colored trims, lace-ups, loose straps, ties, bows, or other adornments are not permitted. Heels or flats (loafer style with one-inch heel) may be worn with pants, but heels must always be worn with a dress or skirt while in public view. Obviously the podiatrist had no idea what it was like, *really like*, to work for an airline. Imagine a first-class flight attendant's panty-hosed toes hanging out of a shoe with a hole cut in the side! There was no point in telling the doctor any of this, since the initial paperwork had already been signed, faxed, and approved by airline medical. I was already back on the line, practically OD'ing on Advil, while hobbling up and down the aisle.

If we choose not to see a doctor for something as minor as a cold, a manager will lecture us about what we're eating and whether or not we're taking our vitamins and working out. As if that's going to help when a passenger comes running up to first class from coach and, like a rotating sprinkler, barfs in a semicircle from the jump seat, all over a couple of commuting flight attendants, across the cockpit door and galley ovens and all over the galley floor. Think that's bad? Try watching a colleague bend over to clean it up with a shovel and a gel-like substance that turns vomit into a big foamy goop, his crew ID and cell phone falling out of his shirt pocket smack-dab into the mess. Seriously, what can one really do to avoid getting sick when a very large man traveling from an international destination walks out of the lav, looks at you funny, pats you on the head, and then yaks all over your tote bag on day one of a three-day trip and all you have to clean it up with is a wad of stiff paper towels and harsh generic soap from the bathroom?

No longer able to pretend she felt fine, tears streamed down Georgia's face as the plane descended into Detroit. It was the second leg of the day. There were two more to go. As the airplane taxied to the gate, Georgia noticed a little girl in the last row of coach peeking between the seats at her, giving her parents the play-by-play of what the sad flight attendant was doing.

"I didn't even try to hide it. I thought my head was going to explode. That's how bad it was!" Georgia would later cry to me over the phone.

After everyone deplaned, the flight attendant working with Georgia in coach told the first-class flight attendant what was going on. She in turn relayed the information to the captain. Without a word he went into action, sidestepping around cabin cleaners busy discarding trash from the seat back pockets, fluffing pillows, straightening seat belts, and lowering armrests. Georgia stood in the back folding a pile of wadded-up blue blankets she would stack neatly inside a bin for the next flight when the pilot called out from midcabin, "You're calling in sick!"

Wide-eyed, Georgia sat down on the armrest and nodded. Afraid to abandon her sequence, which would leave the crew in need of another flight attendant in a city that didn't have a crew base to pool from, she was just as nervous about disobeying the captain's orders. It's his plane. Everyone must do as he's told. Either that or walk off and suffer the consequences later.

One look into Georgia's big blue watery eyes and the captain added, "If the company gives you any grief, tell them I made you do it. Better yet, tell them to call me!" He handed her his business card. On thin white card stock a phone number was printed underneath his name. A cartoon drawing of an airplane decorated the bottom right-hand corner.

"Thank you, Captain," Georgia mumbled, tucking the card inside her pocket. Reluctantly she collected her things and walked off the plane, never to see or hear from the pilot again, even though he was cute and she would have been interested if she hadn't already sworn off all men. Georgia wasn't just down on men, she was down on love, down on life, and stuck on the ground in Detroit. Little did she know life was about to get even more stressful.

Never in her wildest dreams did Georgia think she'd ever spend a week in a hotel room with only a single pair of underwear and a hotel bathrobe and *not* be on her honeymoon. But an hour later that's exactly where she was, washing out undies in the bathroom sink and at the mercy of overpriced room service. The hotel did offer free shuttle bus rides to and from the airport, but that's it, so unless she wanted to fork over even more cash she didn't have in order to take a cab somewhere in her uniform, she was stuck. Oh, to be young, broke, and pantyless for seven days. She spent her time catching up on favorite soaps and racking up a phone bill so high it would make her teary-eyed come checkout time. Initially, Georgia and I spent our daily calls laughing about her predicament. How naïve we were.

"I don't know about this job," said Georgia over a pay phone late one night at a bus stop in a strange town neither one of us had ever heard of. Georgia was bound for Chicago in six-inch heels. When her ears still hadn't cleared up after a few days, she'd been instructed, as per company orders, to get to the nearest airline medical center located at a major airport to have her ears checked ASAP. "Things are gonna get better, right?"

"Right!" I said, and I meant it, too. "You're on a bus wearing a uniform that hasn't been cleaned for days and your one pair of undies are still damp after being washed out and hung to dry in the shower overnight." When I heard her giggle, I knew she'd be okay—at least for a little while. Hopefully, until she made it to the next town and could call me back. "Think of it as an adventure. You know this is going to make a great story to tell your grandkids."

Whenever passengers joke around and order the filet mignon medium in coach, I always laugh. Every. Single. Time. Who am I to spoil their fun? This turned out to be an extremely useful life skill, one that Georgia was able to put to good use on her bus adventure. She didn't want to upset anyone, particularly the guy wearing the baseball cap and Oakley shades who sat in the rear chewing tobacco and leering at her for hours on end. To make matters worse, each time a new group of passengers walked on board, the moment they saw Georgia's silver wings they'd laugh hysterically and say something pithy like, "If you ain't flying, we sure as hell ain't, either!" Followed by high-fives all around.

"I don't get it, whenever anyone gets on the bus they plop down right beside me, regardless of how many seats are open," Georgia complained from the next stop.

"It's the uniform," I explained. "Subconsciously they know they can trust you and maybe even count on you in case there's an emergency."

This was true. A friend of mine who lived in Manhattan took the subway before connecting to a bus to get to work. During a blackout one summer, the train broke down for two hours and was trapped underground, in total darkness.

"My emergency training just came flooding back," he confessed to me late one night over a few too many apple martinis. "I grabbed my FAA-required flashlight and began barking orders, mainly instructing everyone to remain calm. At one point I even dumped my lunch into my tote so that the pregnant lady who was hyperventilating could breathe into the brown paper bag. I didn't want to be the one in charge, but I had no choice. Everyone was looking at me! I blame the damn uniform for that."

"And they have questions, so many questions!" Georgia exclaimed thirty miles away from her final destination. "What's your route? Do you stay in five-star hotels? Do you share rooms? Does the airline pay for your food? Do you know so-and-so? Like we know every single flight attendant at every single airline!"

I'd experienced the same thing. Even after just a few months on the job, the main question I'd learned to dread was, "What do you do for a living?" The moment I smile and say I'm a flight attendant, I find myself holding my breath. Without fail, there's

a two-second pause, which is always followed by one of two re-
sponses. The good response is full of excitement and ends with an
exclamation mark: "I've always wanted to be a flight attendant!"
or "My sister is a flight attendant!" The good response leads to
a very nice conversation about travel, which then leads to other
interesting topics related to travel, and maybe even plans to meet
up for lunch next time I'm in town. That's what happens about 10
percent of the time. The rest of the time, it begins with the same
four words: "On my last flight . . ." Then I'll hear a very bad
story about a flight from hell. Needless to say, the conversation
never goes so well after the bad response. How can it? I've just
been linked to the worst flight this person has ever had. Flight attendants aren't alone. A Super 80 copilot once confessed he never
wore his uniform outside the house so the neighbors wouldn't
know what he did for a living. He didn't want to invite unwanted
conversation. As soon as he got to the airport he'd change into
his uniform. And this was a pilot! No one ever blames the pilot
for a bad flight.

"I wonder if anyone blames the bus driver for a bad ride?"
I asked Georgia. "They're like pilots, kind of, in that they're in
charge of getting people to their destination on time. But they're
also like flight attendants because they get trapped with so many
people in a confined space for long periods of time."

Georgia had no clue what it was like to be a bus driver, and she
had no desire to find out. The only thing Georgia wanted to do
was get off the bus and go home. At her last and final stop, Georgia
grabbed her belongings and exited the bus, vowing to never ride
another one ever again. "Not even to Newark!" she added, just in
case she hadn't made herself clear. I didn't believe that. At the time
Olympia Trails charged $14 to get from Manhattan to Newark Air-
port, a steal of a deal compared to what a yellow cab charged: over
$30. From our crash pad it was $60 minus tip and tolls.

While Georgia continued to wait for her ears to clear at yet another airport hotel located near an airline medical facility in Chicago, I dealt with passengers, angry passengers, in the air. It didn't take long to learn that some people just can't be pleased, no matter how hard you try. The strange thing was, for every group of passengers who deplaned raving about the flight, there'd be another swearing to never fly my airline again. On a flight from New York to Los Angeles, one of those very passengers glared at me when I placed a meal tray on her table.

"How dare you. This is garbage, nothing but garbage!" the woman said, practically spitting. (Actually it was grilled chicken with green beans and a potato.)

I didn't know what to say, other than "I'm sorry." But that can sometimes make things worse if a passenger doesn't believe I'm sorry enough, which in turn could cause them to write a letter explaining exactly why they felt that way. Still on probation, I didn't want that. So I stood in the aisle wide-eyed behind the meal cart, looking across the aisle at my coworker, praying she'd step in and take control of the situation. My colleague just shook her head and kept on serving meals. I followed her lead.

Later on in the flight, as we passed through the aisles collecting service items and refilling drinks, I couldn't help but notice as I picked up the unhappy passenger's tray that, in the end, she must have enjoyed her garbage. It was all gone. How else do you explain the empty tray?

Garbage Lady was just the beginning of my experience with bad passengers. Enter the jackass. On a flight to Atlanta he sat in first class with his massive legs spread wide, gigantic feet in the aisle, muscular arms folded behind his head, while I, entrée in hand, struggled to get his tray table out of the armrest. He didn't budge. Not even when I bumped into his knee, causing a side of tomato sauce to fall into his lap. Immediately I began apologizing.

"Clean it!" he barked.

I ran to the galley and grabbed a handful of napkins, towels, and a can of club soda. Back at his seat I apologized again as I held it all out for him to take. He didn't move.

"Sir," I started, because I wasn't about to start rubbing his crotch.

His eyes were the only thing that moved. "Didn't I tell you to clean it?!"

Other passengers turned around.

"I . . . I . . ." I turned and ran to the galley in tears. We had not been trained for this particular situation. My coworker took one look at me and demanded to know what the hell was going on. After I told him what had happened, he grabbed my silver tray and swished down the aisle, lips pursed.

"Excuse me, sir. I'd be more than happy to help you with that." The jackass stood up, snatched the towel and club soda, and headed straight for the lavatory.

Helping passengers is a huge part of our job. But some passengers take advantage of our kindness. It took a long time to learn that going above and beyond can actually make these types of passengers even worse. On a flight to Los Angeles one elderly woman had me running in circles all through the flight. I didn't complain. She reminded me of my grandma, only she was my grandma's difficult twin with an addiction to plastic surgery. When she told me to carry her bag to her seat—an order, not a question—I complied. No biggie. I placed it inside the overhead bin. She asked me to fold her sweater just so, complaining about the first two ways I folded the oh-so-delicate garment, and then I placed that right next to the bag—sorry, on top of the bag. As instructed, I placed her pocketbook under the seat, but not too far underneath. I even opened the window shade, closed the window shade, and opened it again as per her request during boarding. Whatever she needed I took care of, and I did so quickly, "no dillydallying." And near the end of the flight, when she asked for a piece of paper so she could write a letter, I obliged by ripping off the catering papers taped to the carts and gave them to her. When she asked to borrow a pen, I handed her my last one from the Marriott. And I thought nothing of it when she handed me a folded piece of paper and instructed me to give it to the one in charge.

Silently the lead flight attendant read the letter, looked at me, and folded it in half.

"So what does it say?" I asked, even though I was pretty sure it had to be a raving review of the wonderful service I'd provided her. Honestly, I couldn't do any better than that.

"She's not happy. The help isn't wearing a hairnet."

What? I was in shock. After all I'd done for her! And anyway, my hair was in a regulation ponytail; tied below the ear, hanging no longer than six inches from the neck.

A few of the crew members who were standing around the galley started to laugh, which led me to believe this had to be a joke, like some kind of trick-the-new-hire-on-probation initiation. It had happened before. On my last flight the captain asked me to walk through the cabin and collect air samples with a plastic bag. I probably would have done it if one of my roommates hadn't fallen for the same gag a few weeks ago and then come home to tell us all about it. Another roommate had been asked to jump up and down as hard as she could to get the breaks to lock into place. "On the count of three," the captain called from the cockpit. And soon all the new hires were up in the air.

Pilots go through the same type of thing. One victim fell for the advances of a sexy first-class flight attendant. While checking into a hotel, she slipped him her room key and told him to stop by at a certain time. When he opened the door to her room, he could hear the shower running. Come in and join me, she instructed from behind the bathroom door. Unable to believe his good luck, he quickly got undressed and did as he was told. Bare naked, he walked into the bathroom. That's when the entire crew whipped back the curtain and yelled "Surprise!"

But something about this joke didn't feel so funny, because the purser didn't toss the note into the trash. Instead, he stashed it in the outermost pocket of his bag.

"You're not going to turn that in, are you?" I asked. No way. Flight attendants don't rat each other out.

The purser shrugged. "I haven't decided."

"Dude, she's on probation," a coworker exclaimed.

"I'm on probation!" I agreed quickly.

That didn't matter to the one in charge. Thankfully, I never heard anything from the company about the hairnet letter, but not too long after I did find myself sitting across from my supervisors at a big wooden desk to address a different letter, this one from another passenger I couldn't actually remember.

Passenger letters, good and bad, take months before they're passed along to those involved in whatever incident made the flight wonderful or horrible enough for someone to take time out of their busy day to write about it. This is why when we find a copy of one in our mailbox at work it's always such a surprise. Many times I've received good letters only to wonder if I'd really done what the passenger raved about. I've even suspected that perhaps passengers have gotten me confused with someone else. That's how old these letters are. There have even been emergency situations that passengers have written about, congratulating the crew on a job well done, and I've just stood in Ops holding the letter and trying to remember anything about it. Maybe it just goes to show how much drama we deal with on a daily basis.

As my supervisor read the letter out loud, I kept my mouth shut, as all good flight attendants learn to do when it comes to management. Better a slap on the wrist than having someone on the other side out to get you for a bad attitude. Mine came from a passenger who was upset that I didn't do anything to help a crying baby, and not just any passenger's crying baby, but the crying baby belonging to the passenger who had written the letter. Perhaps I could have been a little more helpful if they'd asked me for assistance at the time, rather than writing a letter after the fact. Flight attendants can't read minds! This after one passenger had barked at me for touching her infant son's tiny bare foot without asking and washing my hands first. Another passenger became annoyed when I handed his crying child plastic cups for stacking and a puppet barf bag. Hearing my supervisor rehashing the details of a flight I couldn't remember about a baby I didn't take care of, reminded me of a totally different passenger situation: this passenger had come to the back galley with a baby cradled in her arms and asked in a thick accent where she could put it.

In the overhead bin, I'd wanted to say, but I was too new to joke around like that, so I politely asked, "What do you mean?"

"How you say . . . child care?" she said.

You don't. But I didn't say that. Instead I explained to her that she'd have to hold the baby throughout the eight-hour flight from New York to London. She looked shocked. But not as much as I did when she told me she didn't have any diapers or baby food with her. I wondered if my manager could blame it on me as well.

"Do you have anything to add?" my supervisor asked after he finished reading the letter, dropping the red folder marked Poole back into the metal filing cabinet behind his desk. I sure did! But instead I just smiled and kept my mouth shut. Sometimes it's best to have zero opinion about something, kind of like a Stepford wife at 35,000 feet.

Not every flight attendant keeps her mouth shut. Some of us actually do break. These flight attendants become folklore heroes to crew, nightmares to passengers, and their stories live longer than most of their careers. One of these flight attendants went by the name of Susan. In her midforties, quick-witted, kindhearted, and extremely attractive, she made pilots drop their kit bags in the terminal just to take a look. After six months of faking a smile while putting up with too many unruly passengers on probation, Susan finally hit a wall and dropped the good-girl act when a passenger walked on board complaining about something, dropping a few F-bombs along the way.

"Sir, I understand you're upset, but you can't talk like that on the airplane."

"Fuck you," he said under his breath.

Enough was enough. She crouched down on one knee in the aisle beside his seat, and whispered very quietly, "Fuck you."

He flew out of his seat. "What the hell did you just say!"

"I told you—you can't talk like that, sir!" Susan ran to the cockpit. "Captain, we have a belligerent passenger on board, and I refuse to work this flight as long as he's here."

The captain placed a large map in his lap, turned around in his seat, and squinted behind thick glasses at a man now stomping up the aisle ranting and raving about the bitchy flight attendant. "Call the agent. Have him taken off."

A large and nervous-looking gate agent came on board to escort the angry passenger off the aircraft and onto another one leaving an hour later. That's how things like this usually go. Susan stood in the entry doorway. When the passenger glared at her, she smiled and said, "Buh-bye!"

That set him off. "She said 'fuck you' to me! That bitch said 'fuck you' to me!" Unfazed the agent kept on walking him up the jet bridge. The jerk looked over his shoulder at Susan one last time before entering the terminal. Not one to miss a beat, she mouthed two little words: Fuck. You.

Nine days after Georgia left the crash pad to work the turn that led to blocked ears, a nurse employed at the airline medical facility in Chicago released her back to work. Her ears were clear. She could finally board a flight. When the agent handed her a first-class ticket bound for New York, Georgia couldn't contain the tears. She'd never been so happy to get on a plane in her life.

"Are you okay?" I cried when she walked through the crash pad door. Her eyes were red and her face was puffy.

"There's just nothin' like bein' home after bein' gone for so long."

Even though Georgia seemed happy about bein' "home," I couldn't help but wonder if that bus ride had done a number on her. I could see it by the way she now wore her unbrushed hair in a messy ponytail on top of her head, and by her preferred choice of outfit on days off, pink sweatpants paired with an oversized T-shirt. But her makeup still looked flawless, even when we were just hanging around doing laundry across the street, so I didn't worry too much.

While Georgia and I soldiered on, our classmates began dropping like flies. It seemed like almost every day we heard about someone else who couldn't hack the lifestyle. One classmate quit because passengers didn't respect her, she said. She went back to being a dental hygienist. Another left because she couldn't get off reserve for her own wedding. A third actually had plans from the very beginning to quit after she got her passes and could take that round-the-world trip she'd been dreaming about with her husband for years. Most of the time we had no idea someone had left until we noticed their names were missing on the reserve page of the bid sheet. We'd ask around to see if anyone had heard anything about them until we learned what exactly went wrong. It wasn't unusual to find out no one knew anything, not even their roommates. Just as in training, one day they were here and the next they were gone. Thankfully, Linda, my old roommate from training, wasn't one of them. We never talked or ran into each other, but I'd heard through the grapevine that she was still

on the line, not always picking up all the meal trays before landing, but doing the best she could, and passengers loved her for it.

It's funny, isn't it, what will actually break a person. I would've
thought for sure that the dead body might have just been the
very thing to push Georgia over the edge after the naked woman
in the closet incident, but I was wrong. Just the opposite happened. It's like it almost gave her life.

"I knew that man was dead the moment I saw him all gray
and slumped over in the wheelchair," she whispered to me late
one night in the dark while our roommates slept in twin beds
that lined the walls. "His wife said he'd been sick with the flu
all week, and then when his daughter piped in and said they
just wanted to get him home I thought to myself, if he's not dead
now he certainly will be soon. The captain agreed. We diverted
an hour after we took off." Before I could ask why in the world
someone would try and smuggle a dead body on board, Georgia
added, "Do you know how much it costs to transport a dead body
the proper way? It's insane! No wonder that passenger out of
Miami tried to get away with packing his mother in a garment
bag!" Honestly, I wouldn't believe it either if I hadn't read the
company email discussing the incident myself.

Before long, the beauty queen I'd met on day 1 of training
reappeared, better than ever.

"When a gay man calls you fierce, you know you've got it
goin' on!" she confessed over a container of sweet and sour pork
after returning from a trip. I had to agree.

The only thing that made me nervous was that, even though
Georgia and The Cheater had broken up, she continued to stay in
touch. Whenever something weird happened on a flight, Georgia
would call him right away. Most of these calls also ended with
her hanging up on him or slamming down the phone and, on at
least one occasion, ripping his letters to shreds. But despite everything, Georgia still wanted to make it work. I couldn't figure

out why. Before long she started questioning herself, wondering if maybe he was right, maybe if she hadn't taken the job to begin with, none of this would have happened.

"I can't blame him. He's a man. Men get lonely," she sighed.

Nothing annoyed me more than the lonely-man card. "Don't take the blame for his stupidity. You didn't do anything wrong! He's the one who—"

Georgia held up her left hand and there on her ring finger I saw a simple silver band.

"He proposed?"

She blushed. "Actually he promised to propose when the bar starts doing better. It's a promise ring."

Thank God I still had time to make her come to her senses and see the light.

Well, the light never came. Two days later the airline canceled service to the city in North Carolina where Georgia's soon-to-be fiancé lived. While I figured this was bad news, I didn't realize just how bad until I came home from a trip and spotted Georgia sitting outside on the stoop in the freezing cold smiling ear to ear. I hadn't seen Georgia smile like that since, well, ever. As much as I hated to admit it, the girl was glowing with happiness. I knew my worst fear was about to come true. I could feel it. In fact I didn't even want to get out of the cab, but when the driver who always seemed overly appreciative of his $2 tip—"Oh thank you, miss, thank you! That is very kind of you!"—got another call I quickly grabbed my belongings and began walking up the sidewalk very slowly.

Four months after graduation, two months shy of getting off probation, I sighed the longest sigh known to humanity. "Please tell me you didn't do it."

"I did. I quit. I turned in my manual and cockpit keys today."

8

Love Is in the Air. Sort Of.

I N THE 1970S, when flight attendants were stewardesses and traveling was glamorous and only for the wealthy, the average time spent on the job was eighteen months. Stewardesses were required to remain single and childless, which ensured that the position remained a job, not a career, and enabled the airlines to use their young, attractive, and somewhat mysterious work-force as a marketing tool. Today most flight attendants either last just a couple of months or hang in for a whole lifetime. It's that extreme. In that first few months the drastic lifestyle change coupled with the difficulties of juggling a home life from 35,000 feet almost always results in pressure from loved ones to make a choice—them or the job. Flight attendants fresh out of training will either quit or watch their relationships crash and burn.

The day Georgia greeted me with the bad news outside on the front stoop, I had a phone number written on a beverage napkin for a new crash pad crumpled up inside my blazer pocket, and I didn't believe in fate. I thought the idea of fate was for the weak of heart, the kind of person who sat around waiting for life to happen, which is how I came to the conclusion that this thing with Georgia was just a bad move on her part, something that could be rectified. That is, if I got involved. Certainly she wouldn't have quit if I'd been home that day. While I knew she was under a lot of pressure from Jack, Jake, Jason, whatever his name was, I refused to sit back and allow her to throw in the towel so easily. I honestly believed if she'd just give it a little time in order to accrue more seniority, things would get better. They had to! Why else would anyone keep the job? It was up to me to make her see that.

Easy enough, I thought, picking up the phone and dialing our supervisor's number at LaGuardia Airport. When I heard it ring, I handed the phone to Georgia.

"Just tell him you made a mistake," I said.

Gently she placed the receiver back in its cradle. "I didn't make a mistake, Heather. This is what I want. I've been thinking about it for a long time. I know it's hard for you to believe this, but the job isn't for everyone. I want to go home. I signed paperwork. It's over."

I took one look at Georgia's giddy, ruby red smile and knew she needed help, the professional kind. "You're delirious. You're not thinking straight." Quickly I dialed our supervisor's number again. "Tell him you were depressed, that you didn't know what you were doing. Do it now before it's too late and he leaves the office."

Without any sense of urgency, Georgia started tossing a few pairs of jeans and a couple of sweaters into an opened suitcase on the floor. "You don't understand. You've never been in love before."

"Excuse me!" I hung up the phone. Never been in love? I'd told her everything about Brent! Well, almost everything . . .

What I had accidentally-on-purpose forgotten to share was, well, Brent and I kinda-sorta hooked up last week. When crew scheduling assigned me my first trip to Austin, Texas, my heart dropped. That's where Brent, my ex-ex-boyfriend lived. You see we hadn't broken up once, but twice—both times on or around Valentine's Day. The significance of the day didn't matter to me.

At least that's what I'd been telling myself every day for a year and a half now. Which might be why as soon as I stepped off the airplane in Texas and found myself in familiar territory, feelings from the past came flooding back. It was torturous being there without him by my side. Looking out the window of the crew van on our way downtown to the hotel, I spotted all the same places I used to see while driving around with him in the passenger's seat of his beat-up Corolla. I couldn't stop myself from going down memory lane as Everything But The Girl blasted through my headphones. When the song "Missing" came to an end, I hit replay, quite a few times, until we pulled up to a hotel not too far from Sixth Street and I, too, could not move on, because I, too, missed him, Brent, *like the deserts miss the rain*. Hidden inside a drawer beside the bed in my hotel room, I found a phone book. All I initially wanted to do was see if his name was listed. That's it. I just wanted to know if he lived in the same apartment we once shared. He did. Without thinking it over, I decided to call and hang up. Just to hear his voice. Nothing more. What could be the harm?

When I heard his familiar voice say hello, I froze. I may have swallowed, I might have even said hi, and before I knew it we were sitting across from each other on bar stools at a chain hotel in the middle of the afternoon on a weekday. It almost felt like I'd taken a ride in a time machine. I kept telling myself not to fall for him again, that Mr. Wrong would not turn into Mr. Right, but one thing led to another and, well . . . let's just say I should have known better. But at the same time, when he leaned in for a kiss, I thought, *A little bit of something had to be better than a whole lot of nothing*. That's when I remembered something wise I overheard a first-class passenger say to her seatmate: "He's good enough for right now." Except the reality was Brent was more than good enough for right now. Six feet tall, tan, muscular, and unbelievably gorgeous in a Fabio kind of way (but better), Brent was an almost Olympic athlete who'd broken records in the pole vault and played in a band on Sixth Street on weekends. Women came from afar to see him rocking out with a red guitar on stage in a dimly lit bar. He was everything most women in Texas dreamed about in a one-night stand, which is why so many panties were always being tossed up on stage. And to think he'd been my boyfriend for two years. The boyfriend I never expected to have. The boyfriend I couldn't believe I'd lost.

After dating through both my junior and senior years of college, Brent and I broke up not long after I graduated—around the time I moved back in with my parents, who lived four hours away and were supporting me while I searched for a job. For three or four months we took turns making the long drive to visit each other, which is why I thought things were okay between us. But long-distance dating is not easy on anyone, including me. It's especially hard on a man, particularly one who has a hot little thing wearing shorty-shorts chasing after him at work. When he wasn't jumping over eighteen-foot high bars with a single pole or playing guitar, he was a personal trainer. Yeah, he had it going on. In a way, I'm kind of surprised it lasted as long as it did. Even so, I never thought I'd get over the guy. The job helped. That is, until crew schedule called me out to cover that trip to Austin last week. So for Georgia to say I didn't know about love and loss and loving someone who should probably get lost, well, that was absurd. I knew exactly what she was going through and I didn't like it, not one little bit!

"I'm going home tomorrow," said Georgia, snapping me back to reality. When she stood and gave me a big hug, I realized it was useless. Her mind was made up.

"I'm going to miss you." I wiped away a tear with the back of my hand. "Promise you'll keep in touch."

"Oh, honey, I don't promise, I pinky promise!" We locked our little fingers and shook on it. In Georgia's world, nothing was more sacred than the pinky promise—except marriage. "I sure do hope you'll come to our weddin'!"

I envisioned myself wearing a big poofy pastel dress and jumping up into the air to catch a bouquet of roses, and then I pictured my own wedding, walking down the aisle in a sleek simple dress, toward a nameless faceless groom. I sighed. "Wouldn't miss it for the world!"

That's when the one who didn't believe in fate wondered if God had put her in my life for a special reason. We were best friends. We didn't need to work the same job in order to remain close. The best thing about being a flight attendant (off probation) is we can fly for free and we're allowed to choose a few family and friends as travel companions. When the time came, all I had to do was list her as one and we could hang out all the time. It would almost be like she never left.

I'd only been working four months, so I wasn't used to so many people coming and going in and out of my life. It was the going part that always tripped me up. But saying good-bye is a big part of a flight attendant's life. Imagine saying it to *at least* 100 passengers per flight. If you're scheduled for four legs (flights) a day, that's more than 400 people to meet, greet, and serve, usually in less than twelve hours. Multiply that by fifteen, the average number of days we work each month, and we've connected with 6,000 people in thirty days. That's 72,000 passengers a year—at least! Even the best of us can't give it our all to each and every passenger we encounter in our career. It's just not possible. Not even for the most professional flight attendant. Sometimes there's just nothing left to give. In the beginning it's not easy learning to turn it on and off with little transition in between, but flight attendants quickly become experts at it. This affects us in many ways—not just saying good-bye quickly, but opening up quickly as well.

Conversations I've had in the galley can only be compared to those that take place in bars, but worse, only because there's nothing like alcohol to blame it on. I've learned things about co-workers and passengers that are shocking, to say the least. For instance, I may not remember her name, but on descent into New York she told me all about her ex-husband, a pilot who cheated on her numerous times with other flight attendants, and whose former mother-in-law is trying to get sole custody of the children by using her job against her. There was another man who never told me his name, but I do know his first sexual encounter took place with a man twenty years his senior and now he only has a thing for older men—with red hair. Just like the one sitting beside him in 22B. I couldn't tell you their names, but I do know they'll be spending the night in jail because he punched her after she scratched his face for daring to call his wife in her presence as soon as the flight touched ground. There's a lot coming at us at once, and just as quickly as it started it's over, buh-bye, see ya later, thanks for flying with us today.

I call it jump-seat syndrome, and almost all flight attendants suffer from it.

There's no avoiding it. We get used to quickly getting personal with strangers over short periods of time, and it ends up carrying over into our relationships on the ground. Because of the job, if I make eye contact with a stranger, it's not uncommon for me to automatically respond by saying "Hi!" or "How are you?" just like I do at the boarding door, which is a little over the top for someone shopping at the mall or riding the subway. In big cities people rarely speak to one another if they aren't acquainted. This is why they'll nervously avert their eyes and pick up the pace. In their eyes I'm crazy. To save face I'll keep walking, still smiling, in an attempt to pretend I was speaking to someone else. Maybe I am crazy. What's worse is when I see the panicked look in the eyes of a new acquaintance when out of nowhere I'll share something that, on reflection, might have been better shared at a different time or place. Health and sex are topics normal people don't usually discuss until they know each other well. Of course, in my life there is no right time or place for anything, and flight attendants end up talking about this kind of stuff all the time.

Even with passengers, we're more open. In the air, I might think nothing of coming right out and asking complete strangers hanging out in the galley or waiting in line to use the bathroom what they do for a living, since they know what I do and think nothing of asking me where I'm staying for the night or what I'm going to do on my layover. Of course these conversations always revolve around travel, so it's no big deal. Names of hotels and restaurants are jotted down and tucked away for later use.

On the ground, however, this kind of talk doesn't go over quite as well, particularly at bars, and especially with men. When I ask about a guy's job it's because I'm curious about his schedule, not about how much money he makes! As a junior flight attendant, I need someone who's free during the week or I'll never see him. Plus, when it comes to using my passes for non-revenue travel, it's always easier to non-rev with a person who can take time off during the middle of the week when the odds of getting an open seat are greater. Most normal men, though, assume the worst when conversations turn to work right away. Some will even walk away. It doesn't bother me. I'm used to it. But it's only natural that I want to know where they're going, regardless of what they think about me. Not because I'm a stalker, but because I might want to go there, too—another time. The more people I meet, the more places I want to go! It's the nature of the job.

To say flight attendants meet a lot of people is an understatement. On the days I get stuck working in coach, I'll find myself standing in front of the cockpit door saying good-bye and I won't even recognize 75 percent of the passengers I've served. Flight attendants aren't alone. From Vancouver to New York I struck up a conversation with a passenger on landing. He told me that on his flight out they were delayed three hours on the tarmac. I looked at him funny and asked if his flight had departed a week ago. It had. Were you on my flight, he asked. Indeed I was. How in the world could we have missed each other on a six-hour flight that turned into a nine-hour nightmare with a light passenger load? We were in the same place at the same time with nothing to do but stare at each other and, well, not see each other I guess. Story of my life.

Then there are the passengers I do remember. Like the frail little boy seeking cancer treatment with a well-renowned doctor on the other side of the world. His last hope, pretty much. He asked me to pray with him. The happy couple on their way to China to meet their adopted daughter for the first time. They waited years for this very day. And I was a part of it. The anxious mother of the bride who already felt excluded from the festivities before they had even begun. I tried to help her see the bigger picture. The somber comedian who actually got to know his father better after he'd passed away than while he was alive. The elderly man whose knobby fingers never stopped creating origami birds for all the children on the airplane. When he ran out of kids, he passed them out to adults. One of whom took a stack full to share with the elderly at her mother's nursing home. In the beginning, I had a hard time getting used to this, all the connections (and disconnections) that never went further than the flight, all the connections (and disconnections) that meant nothing at all, all the connections (and disconnections) that happened in a snap and lasted a lifetime.

One of the strangest things for me in the beginning was to really connect and work well with a flight attendant, only to part ways so quickly, so coldly, as if I'd imagined the whole thing. Before the flight would even touch ground, all that we'd shared had already been tucked away and zipped up like a passenger's discarded gossip magazine inside a flight attendant's tote bag for the next flight. I have no idea how many of these moments accumulated before it was I who took off without a proper good-bye. I started doing it on the phone, too. As soon as I hear we're heading down that road, I cut it off and hang it up—literally. Drives whoever is on the other end of the call nuts!

As for Georgia, I missed the wedding. At least I think I did. Because I never did get the invitation in the mail. To this day I have no idea whether or not Georgia and what's his name even tied the knot. I never would have thought the last time I'd ever see Georgia would be the morning she climbed into a Kew Gardens cab and waved good-bye through an open window. We spoke a few times over the phone after she left. She had begun working for a reputable makeup line at a mall in North Carolina. I'd tell her all about the crazy passengers, weird flight attendants, celebrities sitting in first class, hot pilots who didn't ask me out, long layovers in wonderful cities like Chicago, Boston, Denver, Miami, Salt Lake City, San Francisco, and Seattle, and she'd tell me about the latest lipstick shades and the best moisturizers for fair and dry skin. Our conversations became shorter as I found myself holding back, playing down my travel experiences because even to my own ears my life sounded so much more exciting than it actually was. I lived a lifetime in three days compared to Georgia. Whenever a trip would end I always felt like I'd been gone for weeks, not just for a couple of days. Though no one on the ground seemed to notice I'd even left. At work my life was on fast-forward, while at home it seemed to come to a complete stop. At the same time I had to figure out a way to not give Georgia the wrong impression. I didn't want to make her think that perhaps she'd made a mistake.

One day I dialed her number only to be greeted by a computerized voice informing me the number had been disconnected. At first I didn't think much of it. I assumed she had moved and would eventually be in touch. I never heard from her again.

It took a long time to realize Georgia had "broken up" with

me, but it's true what they say about one door closing and another opening. While Georgia packed up her things, I dialed the number scribbled across the beverage napkin. A flight attendant had given it to me on my last flight, even though I had told her I didn't know of anyone looking for a place to live. Imagine her surprise when I called her that very same day. I told her I didn't need to see the place to know I'd be moving in—I recognized an emergency situation when I saw one, and there was no way I could deal with Victor's antics without Georgia. So what if I couldn't afford the extra fifty bucks for my own room? If that meant starving into a smaller dress size to afford the $200-a-month room, so be it.

9

Life on the Ground

I HAD ONLY BEEN in my new crash pad for two days when I became Yakov's wife. My new roommates and I had no idea who called code enforcement about illegally rented rooms, tied-up street parking, and general neighborhood shoddiness, but someone thought we were a public nuisance and wanted us out. Yakov, the homeowner and our landlord, cheerfully informed the two enforcement officers standing on our doorstep that we were *not* renters; we were family. That's how I became the wife of Yakov, an overweight and frequently sweaty Russian cab driver. Lucky me. Yakov then pointed to my roommate Jane and said, "My sister." Jane's eyes bugged out of her head, but she forced a smile and nodded. Our five other roommates were working, but unbeknownst to them we were now cousins. The men in suits didn't blink an eye. Still, they wanted to see the place, so Yakov gave them a quick tour and like that they were gone. I could only wonder what I'd gotten myself into.

Yakov had bought the two-story foreclosure in Forest Hills, a prestigious section of Queens, for $200,000 ten years before I moved in. At least that's the story I heard. The home had five bedrooms, two of which were illegally constructed, and each went for $200 a month. At one time my bedroom had been the other half of the living room and Jane slept in what had once been a sunroom. Tricia, Grace, and Agnes had the three bedrooms on the second floor and two commuters, Dee Dee and Paula, split the attic, which wasn't half bad for $75 a person.

Yakov lived in the basement. None of us had ever seen the inside of the apartment he called home, nor did we want to. We were too afraid of what we might find—a dead body, a blowup doll, a closet full of women's clothing, or even worse, our clothing. We just didn't know. After my experience with Victor, I knew anything was possible. Every time I took the short flight of steps outside our house down to Yakov's door, where he'd hung a wooden box for us to drop off the rent, I worried that he might be walking out at the exact same time. I didn't want an accidental glimpse of whatever lurked inside!

There was no explanation for our fears except that Yakov did things a little differently. He used kerosene to remove the linoleum floor. He kept a carton of eggs and a block of cheese on a concrete wall outside in the backyard under the green-and-white-striped awning that hung above his door, just a few steps away from the back door of the house. He wore the same blue sweatpants, bunched up around his gigantic calves, with thin white socks and brown leather lace-up shoes that had seen better days. While he'd hole up in the basement avoiding us at all costs, we always knew when he was home because Lucy, the dog, would disappear. We even knew when he was on his way home because Lucy, the psychic dog, would start barking nonstop twenty minutes before his yellow cab would pull into the drive.

Despite all that, life with Yakov turned out to be pretty good. Except when he had late-night poker games down in his basement apartment with a group of cabbie friends we'd never see but always hear, their thick accents getting louder and louder while smoke grew thicker and thicker. Always the first to break was Jane. She believed in nipping things in the bud. At five-feet-two, she wasn't tall, but she wasn't afraid of anything, least of all Yakov. With her light brown, shoulder-length hair tied in a topknot, she'd hop out of bed, stand at the opened back door, and hiss into the night, "Yakov! Stop smoking! And keep it down, down there!" Then she'd stomp through the house in her Birkenstocks and a long white terry-cloth robe to let him know she meant business. Yakov never acknowledged Jane's weekly scolding, and things would actually quiet down for a little while until once again the cycle would repeat itself and Jane would toss aside a copy of *Runner's World*, slide her tiny feet into her man shoes and exclaim, "What's wrong with him, it's one o'clock in the morning!" as she passed through the living room where the rest of us sat watching late-night TV if we didn't have an early trip the following morning.

Jane had no problem letting all of us, including Yakov, know when we were out of line. Rules were meant to be followed.

"I don't mind your germs," Jane once said to me, holding a container of toilet bowl cleaner while still in uniform after having worked a trip. "But not theirs!" She glared at the ceiling. Apparently one of our roommates had walked out of *our* bathroom, not hers, and announced she'd been up all night scratching. Bed bugs, I assumed. "It's safe to use now," Jane said.

Flight attendants work with the public in confined spaces with recycled air for hours on end, so germs are a major concern. It's why so many of us are addicted to antibacterial hand lotion. No joke, flight attendants alone probably keep Purell in business. This is also why our work shoes were not allowed to enter the house—a Jane-enforced contamination-free zone. On layovers Jane wore flip-flops in the hotel rooms and always used a washcloth placed on the bathroom counter to protect her toiletries. A shower cap became the perfect buffer for the remote control. Comforters went straight to the floor, since it was common knowledge they were rarely, if ever, cleaned. Hotel tubs were doused with a sprinkle of Bon Ami Jane kept inside a Ziploc baggie and scrubbed with a sponge tucked inside her tote bag at all times (and replaced often). Because there were rumors of flight attendants using coffeepots to wash out their hose, and because I myself had once witnessed a housekeeper using the same rag on the toilet seat and the rim of a glass, coffeepots and glasses got dunked in scalding hot soapy water for a good ten minutes before being used.

A no-nonsense woman with a little-girl voice, Jane went green way before it became popular. She'd collect newspapers and empty cans on flights even if she were landing at an airport that did not recycle. In 1995, most did not. Ten years later things weren't much different. In 2006, the National Resources Defense Council (NRDC) reported after a yearlong study that the U.S. airline industry discarded enough aluminum cans each year to build fifty-eight Boeing 747 airplanes and discarded nine thousand tons of plastic and enough newspapers and magazines to fill a football field to a depth of more than 230 feet. Even today what flight attendants collect on board is not recycled at many airports, particularly the smaller ones, though most airports do have recycling stations available throughout the terminals. And while you may see flight attendants collecting aluminum cans and newspapers on most of your flights, many are doing this of their own accord in hopes that somehow the neatly sorted collection will miraculously make its way to a recycling station. Jane was no different. From time to time "trash" would even make its way home where she could dispose of it properly. Nothing too crazy, just an empty water bottle here and a rinsed out paper cup from Starbucks there, random things she'd acquire over the course of a three-day trip. Jane was so passionate about protecting the environment that one houseguest decided it might be easier to pack a small bag of garbage inside her suitcase and fly home with it than sort it the way Jane had instructed.

Even though Jane was into organic food and I liked Chef Boyardee, we got along surprisingly well and quickly became good friends. Even after I caught her regifting a shirt I bought for her birthday. She made no apologies about it, either. That's what I liked about her, along with the fact that she could be super sweet, the kind of person who'd run, literally, two miles to the grocery store in a foot of snow to buy oranges when I got sick. When I began feeling down about the way things were going—more like not going—with Brent, Jane would write words of encouragement on Post-it notes and stick them on the bathroom mirror for me to find in the morning. And she was funny, too. Only Jane could make me laugh after Brent refused to take me to the airport because his favorite wrestling show was going to be on television. He gave me two choices. Either he could take me to the airport two hours early or I could call a cab. I did what any other flight attendant wouldn't do. I took a cab. Most of my colleagues will walk three miles uphill in a foot of snow to save a buck. That's how much I liked Brent. Plus, I didn't want to spend a second longer than absolutely necessary at an airport when I could be on the couch with him. And Hulk Hogan.

Jane had a killer figure that disappeared under the polyester tent she wore to work. Like me, Jane was still on probation, so her dress had yet to be altered. Since she was just two weeks behind me in seniority, we made a pact to do it together and then go out and celebrate our short hemlines, which, believe it or not, we looked forward to more than using our passes for the first time. That's how dowdy we looked compared to our more senior coworkers. Imagine our excitement when that day finally came, followed by shock when Jane showed the seamstress exactly where she wanted her hem to fall and the seamstress barked in broken English, "No—uniform!"

Unfazed, Jane said, matter-of-fact as can be, "Do it."

The woman shook her head violently. "Uniform—too short!"

After a good ten minutes of this we finally got our way, but we never did hear the end of it. Whenever we'd walk by the dry cleaning shop where the seamstress worked behind a sewing machine in the front window, she'd stop working on what she had in her hands and slowly shake her head at us. And every time, Jane would yell out, "Not too short!"

Turns out, we didn't go short enough, because one day while jogging the famous Venice boardwalk on a layover in California, Jane spotted the captain from her flight, a real ladies' man with Robert Redford hair and a reputation for dating flight attendants. He was headed her way on rollerblades.

"Hey!" Jane called out to him as he passed her by.

He came to a stop immediately, smiling at the brown-haired beauty wearing short shorts and a jog bra. "Well, hello, little lady. I'm Brad." He held out a hand.

She just looked at him. "I know who you are. I'm on your trip!"

Later on, she complained, "It's like they have no idea we have butts and boobs under those dresses!"

Even so, pilots loved Jane. This is because Jane believed in treating everyone fairly, which meant she always offered the cockpit food even if they weren't scheduled to eat on a leg. This is not the norm. It's an unwritten rule that flight attendants get first dibs on any leftovers from their cabin before offering anything to other members of the crew. Then, after every flight attendant has had an opportunity to eat, we *might* call the pilots to see if they're hungry. If they are, we'll offer an entrée. That's it. No extras. But Jane treated pilots like first-class passengers, offering up hot towels, appetizers, two different kinds of bread, and both dessert choices if she had them, which is why it came as no surprise when she broke up with a mountain climber from Denver and started dating a pilot she met on a flight from San Diego. Whenever she'd get an earful from another flight attendant for giving pilots "our" food, Jane would just say, "It's not *their* fault our union's negotiating skills suck." She had a point. On domestic routes crew meals were not in our contract.

At my airline before 9/11, flight attendants working domestic routes were catered "snack packs" instead of crew meals. These snack packs consisted of a cat-sized portion of canned tuna, a couple of crackers, a packet of mayo, a brownie, and the smallest apple ever grown on U.S. soil, all thrown inside a plastic drawstring bag. After 9/11, the not-so-filling snack packs were replaced with zilch, while pilots continued receiving the same crew meals they always had. Imagine working a twelve-hour day sustained only by white dinner rolls and soda while having to serve the cockpit a steak with veggies and a baked potato with all the accoutrements, and a slice of cheesecake on the side. Who wouldn't be resentful? Now, flight attendants have no choice but to bring food from home, which isn't always easy to do on a multiple-day trip, and which is why Jane's attitude toward pilots' food was so rare.

Jane was definitely unique, kind of like the house we lived in. It was in desperate need of a paint job and stood out from the other immaculate homes on the quiet tree-lined street in more ways than one. A cracked walkway led up to three lopsided steps and an aggressively overgrown bush blocked what otherwise would have been a lovely view into Jane's bedroom window, which would have been the sunroom if the house had not been illegally converted to add more rooms. All the homes in the neighborhood possessed the same floor plan, which might be why our elderly neighbor across the street spent the better part of his days staring at that very bush, which was all that stood between him and knowing what was *really* going on inside a house full of attractive women, an odd Russian cab driver, and a frequently barking border collie. Some days our dear neighbor would walk outside and pretend to collect the newspaper (his neighbor's), or take out the garbage (on noncollection days), or water the grass (that had already been watered), all in an effort to get a better look at us. We'd smile and wave. He'd turn around and walk inside. All the navy blue polyester and rolling bags in the world didn't seem to tip him off, and eventually he reported "the whorehouse" to police. When a couple of cops stopped by the house to check out the situation, it didn't escape my attention when a buff bald police officer placed a business card on our kitchen table and said, making direct eye contact with Tricia, a petite blonde with double Ds from Mississippi, "Feel free to call if the neighbor continues to harass you. Or if you need anything else."

The neighbor wasn't the only one who was confused. The cable guy's eyes about popped out of his head when I answered the front door wearing a short black silk robe with pink fuzzy slippers, my hair a tangled mess, and asked him to please, please, please try and be quiet because my roommates were still sleeping.

"We were working all night last night," I added. It was two o'clock in the afternoon. That's when Tricia came stumbling down the stairs wearing a silk eye mask on top of her head and a short, somewhat see-through nightie. I noticed a look of confusion followed by outright fear sweep across the repairman's face.

"No, no, no, we're flight attendants!" I exclaimed. The cable guy and I laughed.

Tricia, completely oblivious to the strange man standing in the middle of our living room with a bundle of cable wrapped over a shoulder, called out on her way to the kitchen, "After I grab a cup of coffee remind me to tell ya about the guy who tried to hide a gigantic package between his legs last night."

I swallowed hard, looked at the repairman and smiled innocently. "She's talking about luggage."

At least I hoped so, because out of all my roommates in the house, if anyone was going to talk about sex it was Tricia. Tricia went through men like most flight attendants go through first-class bottled water. Some she met at bars in Manhattan, others she either met on the airplane or through fellow coworkers whose boyfriends took one look and immediately wanted to set her up with their friends. Tricia was the kind of flight attendant that guys *specifically* looking to hook up with a flight attendant dreamed about. The kind of girl who wouldn't think twice about changing out of uniform in the lav after a flight to put on sexy lingerie and nothing else under a buttoned-up company-issued trench coat. She'd walk through the airport terminal greeting everyone who passed with a friendly hello, before exiting baggage claim and hopping into an expensive sports car with an attractive man behind the wheel. Not shy about discussing the details of these short-lived but hot and heavy romances, she'd frequently declare, "Y'all are not gonna believe what I did this weekend!" The only thing we truly wouldn't believe would be something that sounded believable. That's how crazy her life was. But it wasn't all good.

Whenever Tricia would utter the words "Oh my God, y'all," Jane would take a deep breath, roll her eyes, and quickly disappear. The tales were always elaborate and interesting, and in the beginning I loved listening to them. Take for instance the time she got into a car wreck and woke up in the street, her shoes stolen right off her feet. "Those were expensive shoes, too!" she cried, tears streaming. Never mind what had happened to whoever had been traveling in the car with her. Another time she left three large Nordstrom shopping bags on board a flight she'd worked from San Francisco. While waiting with a group of others for the employee bus she realized what she'd done and quickly ran back to the gate as fast as she could only to find the bags were missing. A handful of cabin cleaners denied ever having seen them. Two days later the bags were anonymously returned, but Tricia refused to ride the bus to the employee parking lot because she thought that ground personnel were talking about her. She may have been right because she began receiving death threats. It started happening around the same time she had to take out a restraining order on an old boyfriend who kept driving by our house.

"He's stalking me!" she screamed, running into the house late one night and waking up everyone. This sort of thing happened so often it got to the point where Tricia's very presence became overwhelming. The mere sight of her car parked in the drive was equivalent to a dark cloud looming over the house. It didn't matter if I'd had a layover in Tulsa, Oklahoma, or Bakersfield, California, as soon as I'd see that used silver Mercedes behind Yakov's yellow cab, I'd instantly want to fly back to wherever I'd just come from to avoid the stress.

Luckily each new man took Tricia away for a good two to three months at a time. They'd spend some time together at his apartment in the city or house in the Hamptons and life at the house would become peaceful once again. But like clockwork a big blowup would occur and Tricia would come storming back, dragging the ab machine none of us had ever seen her use behind her. To Jane's horror, she'd ditch the eyesore in the middle of the living room and leave it there collecting dust until the next guy swept her off her feet. And she'd start cooking up a storm. While the brownies and lemon bars cooled and a gigantic pot of vegetable stew simmered on the stove, she'd replay the breakup details over the phone in the living room with a glass of wine in one hand and an opened address book on her lap. Starting with the As, she'd torture us until the last and final Z. Tricia had a lot of friends.

"You're Tricia's roommate!" coworkers would say whenever I'd happen to mention her name in flight. "Oh my God, I love her! She's hilarious."

I'd just smile and nod. No one had a clue what it was like living with her.

Part of the problem was that Tricia had the most crash pad seniority. She was the queen bee. She got the largest bedroom in the house and the entire place was decorated with photographs of her draped all over friends from every corner of the world. Pots and pans, furniture and rugs, microwaves and air-conditioning units, everything belonged to her, either by purchase or by inheritance. Even the bed I slept on had once been hers. I bought it for twenty bucks—the same amount she had paid another flight attendant five years prior, back before it had a big green paint stain. Perhaps she had dated an artist. Because car magazines filled our mailbox when she dated the NASCAR guy; when the golf pro came on the scene, a full set of clubs took over the hall closet leaving absolutely no room for coats and jackets; and much to Jane's delight, gourmet cookbooks began to stack up on the kitchen counter after Tricia hooked up with a head chef at a five-star restaurant in the city.

It's not that I didn't like her, but I could only take her in small doses, which is why I almost died the day I got called out to work a trip with her. When I realized we weren't just going to be on the same airplane, but in the same cabin—business class—I wanted to slit my wrists and set myself on fire. Business class is the most junior position on the airplane for a reason. It's *a lot* of work. In coach there's not much to offer passengers, while in first class the passengers usually sleep through the service. But in business class passengers want to sample it all and then some. To prove this point a colleague once offered business-class passengers a silver-lined tray piled high with silver spoons.

"Would you care for a spoon?" he asked, and without saying a word passengers would reach for one. Two minutes later he walked back through the cabin and collected all the spoons. Next he put a box of Kleenex on a silver-lined tray and one by one passengers reached for a tissue. So while it was bad enough working with the most demanding passengers on the airplane *without* crew drama, I couldn't imagine dealing with such a high maintenance group of people with a coworker like Tricia.

To my surprise Tricia turned out to be a real joy to work with.

The service went off smoothly and Tricia proved herself to be one of the most professional, hardworking, and friendly flight attendants I'd ever encountered. And that's the moment I began to respect her. Passengers loved her, and I did, too! Honestly, Tricia and I had such a nice trip together that I would have "buddy bid" with her if she'd asked. She never did. But who would've thought? Not me, that's for sure. It just goes to show you never truly know someone until you've actually lived *and* worked with them first.

Strangely, I had the opposite experience with Dee Dee. Dee Dee was, in a word, cool. She wasn't a classic beauty, but she worked with what she had and always looked great. With a dark year-round tan and a trim build, she kept her black hair in the latest style and coordinated brightly colored sundresses with matching strappy sandals. Even though she was older than me, she had a youthfulness about her I'd never before seen in a woman her age. Dee Dee had been flying for seven years, so she had the most airline seniority in the house and always held the best international trips. I was in complete awe of her. If Dee Dee wasn't taking in a show in London or shopping for spices in Jamaica or buying clothes in Paris or eating Wiener schnitzel in Austria or relaxing on the beach in Brazil, she was rollerblading the boardwalks of Long Island or taking the train into Manhattan *before* her trips, which always departed late at night. The woman had more energy than all of us in the house combined. On top of that she commuted from Arizona, where she lived with her husband and a cat named Doug. The day before each trip Dee Dee drove an hour to the airport to hop on a flight to Chicago, where she'd connect to another flight to New York, landing after midnight. I never heard Dee Dee going up the stairs late at night to get to the attic, but Jane did, all the time. It was always a topic of conversation the following morning.

I'd never flown with Dee Dee before and I was excited about

getting assigned a reserve trip with her to London. We always had a good time hanging out in the crash pad together, so I assumed the trip would be just as much fun. On the flight over she kind of gave me what I thought was the cold shoulder. I was a little surprised, but I figured she was just catching up with her friends after a few days off—after all, these were flight attendants she'd flown with every month for years. And she did make sure to include me in their plans for our thirty-six-hour layover in London.

A few hours after landing, Dee Dee and I met up with some other crew members in the hotel bar, which offered 20 percent off to airline personnel and which therefore was packed with airline personnel. We'd just ordered beers and were snacking on vinegar chips when a handsome pilot I'd never seen before turned his attention on me. He had only one thing on his mind, I'm sure, but I didn't care. This was a first for me. Flattered, I decided to enjoy it, especially since the last time I'd spoken to Brent he'd made it clear that while he liked me "more than a lot," he still wanted to date other women. That hurt. This didn't. Anyway, my mother always wanted me to marry a pilot, not a personal trainer–lead guitarist for a cover band. Not that I had any crazy ideas about walking down the aisle with the adorable first officer who was now whispering something in my ear about taking a stroll outside where it might be a little quieter, but I did visualize us making the most of our flight benefits, heading off on exotic vacations on our days off.

"Don't you have a boyfriend?" Dee Dee asked out of nowhere.

All eyes were now on me. The pilot took a step back. Nervously, I laughed, "You mean the boyfriend who didn't call on my birthday because he was on a date with someone else?" I could have sworn I'd told her this already. Perhaps the booze had gone to her head or maybe the jet lag had made her forgetful, either way her block completely caught me by surprise.

I didn't go for a stroll with the pilot, but I did continue flirting with him. Dee Dee stood nearby, eavesdropping on our conversation, interjecting things that I'm sure would have been better left unsaid, since the rest of the crew was now cracking up. At one point we were discussing books and I mentioned something about feeling passionately about women's rights. That's when Dee Dee laughed and then said loudly enough for everyone in the bar to hear, "Didn't you used to work at Hooters?" All eyes were back on me. After that I decided to go to bed.

On the flight home I got an earful in the form of silence. Whenever I'd enter a galley, everyone would immediately stop talking and just smile. At first I thought Dee Dee and her friends just disliked pilots, and maybe new hires who were interested in pilots. I must have embarrassed her since I should have known better than to accept the advances of someone who worked on the wrong side of the cockpit door. But then a few weeks later a good-looking captain offered Dee Dee a ride home and she accepted. Excitedly, she rehashed the details of the twenty-minute drive, emphasizing the part where he tried to kiss her and she pushed him away. I realized then and there that she didn't dislike pilots, maybe only new hires who attracted pilots—in other words, me. Or maybe that's just me and my insecurities.

Besides the fact that they were both married, commuted to work, and lived in the attic together, Dee Dee and Paula had very little in common. We'd know when Paula was in town because a basket with knitting needles would appear next to the sofa, whether or not she was on a trip. Around the house Paula hung out in acid-washed jeans paired with ribbed turtlenecks in the winter or oversized T-shirts in the summer. Her auburn hair was always worn loose and wavy as she sat on the couch crocheting yet another scarf for another relative's birthday. Rarely did she wear makeup, which is why it was always a bit of a shock to see her dressed for work in uniform with her dark brown eyes lined in kohl and her lips painted a dark red, emphasized by hair that had been pulled back and held in place with a barrette. Even though Paula and Dee Dee were close in age, Paula seemed a lot older and wiser. But she was fun. Well, that is, when she was around, which tended to be hardly ever. In order to spend as much time at home with her two young sons, she'd fly to New York the morning her flight departed and work a high-time trip to get as many hours as possible in the shortest amount of time. As soon as the trip was over, she'd jump on the first flight home. It seemed exhausting. When I asked about juggling the whole wife, mother, flight attendant thing, she told me that if I could work a line of red-eye flights and act somewhat normal between trips, I could do anything, even run the PTA.

"What about your husband and kids, don't they mind that you're gone?" asked Jane who all of a sudden seemed overly worried about how this worked. Things were getting serious with the pilot, I presumed.

Paula laughed. "Of course they mind! But that's too bad. I need a little me time. Even our worst trip is a vacation from my regular life."

Like most flight attendants with children, Paula was a "slam clicker" on trips. As soon as she'd get to the hotel room she'd let the door slam-click shut behind her, never to reappear until pick-up the following morning. The next twenty-four hours were filled with bubble baths and room service, soap operas and books in bed, peace and quiet and waking up to the morning light instead of a husband who needed help finding his socks or the kids crying for breakfast early in the morning. Because of her job her husband couldn't take her for granted and the kids got to know their father in a way most never do.

"Trust me, Jane, they'll be grateful I have this job when they're older and we're flying around the world for free," added Paula.

When Jane wondered out loud if her boyfriend could be as

patient as Paula's husband, Paula, the nerdiest of us all, had this to say: "It's pretty amazing what men will put up with for a blow job." All of us laughed, even though Jane and I would later admit that neither one of us could imagine Paula doing something like that.

"It's the quiet ones you have to worry about," I told Jane when Paula was out of earshot. Before, I never really believed the saying, but now I knew it to be true.

The following day Jane looked at me mischievously. "She must do it a lot."

I didn't have to ask who she was talking about or what "it" meant. We'd both been traumatized by the revelation.

Like Paula, Grace was another roommate who was rarely around, not because she commuted or had kids, but because her boyfriend was in the military and stationed in Japan. Holed up in her room, she spent hours talking to him over the phone using discounted calling cards that seemed way too good to be true, even though she purchased packs of them at Costco. Grace began Skyping before I'd even heard of the word. She was on top of the latest means of communications and always trying to educate the rest of us in the house about things that seemed a little shady at the time, like using the computer as a phone. Grace had been dating her boyfriend for years. Sadly, they rarely saw each other. That was okay because she was strong, and whenever she began to feel weak, she read the Bible or distracted herself by taking the train to Koreatown to pick up treats she grew up on as a child that she would later force upon us.

"Don't knock it before you try it!" Grace once said, holding up a jar of something pink swimming in red liquid. None of us were up to trying it.

As much as Jane would have loved to have thrown away whatever it was Grace always brought home from her excursions into the city, she never did, not even when Tricia complained about needing extra room to house twenty Tupperware containers of vegetable soup. Paula, always the peacemaker, offered to reorganize the fridge to make it all fit after Dee Dee decided to get rid of the tomatoes, onions, and jalapenos she'd brought from Arizona by whipping up fresh pico de gallo for all of us to share. Whatever was left over she'd take to the crew working her trip later that night.

The most interesting thing about Grace was not that her childhood reminded me of the Broadway show *Miss Saigon*, but that that she worked for a different airline, one of our main competitors. After hours of comparing the two airlines, it soon became clear that, besides the fact that her airline served better snacks (cookies instead of pretzels, which she was kind enough to bring home by the case), everything was pretty much the same. Her passengers were always threatening to fly our airline, while our passengers wondered why they weren't flying hers. After one of my flights diverted to another airport because of bad weather in New York, one such passenger yelled out that next time he was going to fly my roommate's airline. A coworker walked over to his seat, opened his window shade, pointed to one of several airplanes parked on the tarmac beside us, and said, "Go ahead. There they are. Looks like they diverted, too." The man didn't say another word. That's when I realized it didn't matter who we worked for, we all had the same passengers. As well as the same cheaply made uniforms. Although I did find Grace's coat dress to be a little more flattering than ours. At one point I even considered offering to buy it from her, and then taking it to our favorite seamstress, who could switch out the buttons with ones that had my airline's logo on them. Besides the seamstress—"Uniform, wrong buttons!"—who would notice?

While I loved hanging out with Grace, Jane got on better with Agnes, which I couldn't understand because Agnes and I didn't exactly click. Then again, maybe I didn't try hard enough to make things click. When she spoke I could barely hear her. And when I did hear her I didn't always understand what she was saying.

Jane found her to be deep. I found her to be a little . . . well, different, considering she couldn't remember how to work the microwave and coffeepot no matter how many times I showed her. I don't think she knew how to work the oven or the fridge, either, because Agnes couldn't have weighed more than 110 pounds. The girl rarely ate. At five-feet-nine, she looked like a model, that's how willowy and pretty she was. Like Grace, Agnes had a strong connection to God, but unlike Grace she was quiet and pretty much only spoke when spoken to. With long strawberry-blond hair, light blue eyes, and fair skin, Agnes looked as angelic as she acted. On her days off she, too, would hole up in her bedroom, only she preferred the company of a good book to a phone or a computer. Rarely did she hang out with us, and when she did it never lasted long, because if we weren't bickering and gossiping, we were sharing things unfit for virginal ears.

Grace was the first one who noticed Agnes might be up to something. We were all sitting on the couch when Agnes tiptoed through the living room and into the kitchen, grabbed a loaf of bread, a container of mayo, and a couple of wrapped-up packages of deli meat, and without saying a word started for the stairs. Jane had seen her do this once before and wondered if there might be a connection between the sneaky sandwiches and the late-night hang-up calls we'd been getting for the last month. I thought the calls probably had more to do with Tricia's stalker, but Dee Dee wasn't so sure since the stalker and Tricia had recently made up and were trying to rekindle what they once had. Jane rolled her eyes. Paula brought up the empty baby stroller she'd noticed outside our front door the previous week. Dee Dee had seen it too, but figured it belonged to the neighbors who had young kids. Jane didn't think so—both boys were too old for a stroller. Anyway, she'd seen it behind the house next to the recycling bin and figured someone must have left it inside Yakov's cab. She was just happy to see he'd placed it near the right bin. Then she wondered why Yakov didn't use it to repair the broken washer since he had a tendency to do weird things like that. That's when Tricia ran through the front door and yelled out she had to get ready for a date, she was late. Paula worried about Tricia dating the stalker again, but Grace reminded Paula that Tricia had asked us to stop calling him the stalker, since his name was Steven. Jane made a face and Dee Dee started laughing. Paula offered to open another bottle of wine. When Agnes reappeared to put the secret sandwich ingredients back in the kitchen where it all belonged, Grace asked her what was up.

"Oh, uh . . . I was just hungry," she said, and disappeared back up the stairs.

It was an unwritten rule that in our crash pad no men were allowed to spend the night—well, no local guys. This rule was established by Jane after Grace ran into one Tricia's boyfriends in the kitchen early one morning. Grace didn't find it amusing to see him standing there in his tighty-whities. Jane was appalled to learn he had eaten her banana. Paula couldn't believe we were making a big fuss. Dee Dee was too tired from the red-eye from Buenos Aires to care. If anyone was involved in a long-distance relationship, it was perfectly fine to have the person over, even for a few nights. In that type of situation, it was safe to assume we probably knew him well (or at least, a lot about him) and there was little chance of his being a frequent visitor. Otherwise, no boys allowed. Not only because it wasn't safe to have strange men spending the night in a house full of women, but because the last thing we wanted to do was hear or see Tricia—I mean a roommate—having sex. So imagine our surprise when it turned out to be Agnes and not Tricia breaking the rules.

None of us knew how long it'd been going on, and we didn't want to know, either, because Agnes's stowaway boyfriend was creepy. And old. Twice her age, at least. Jane was the first one who saw him in person. She came home early from a trip that had been canceled and found him sitting on the sofa with his shoes on the table, watching a horse race and drinking Dee Dee's Diet Coke as if he owned the place. The worst part: he was there alone and unsupervised. Well, we thought that was the worst part until we found out more about him. When we confronted Agnes, we learned he was a single father with a gambling addiction who unofficially moved in with us after he lost his house. Agnes took care of his little girl, a precious child who called her Mommy, while he blew money she'd lent him at the racetrack. The dirty stroller, we realized, belonged to him. We were horrified to know how long he'd been around and not one of us had a clue. Agnes had wanted to have children for so long. When pressed as to why she would allow someone like him run her life, she admitted it had everything to do with the child. A few days after we banned him from the house, I spotted the stroller in a park two blocks away. I scanned the playground but never found him, and went straight home to warn my roommates to be on the lookout. Soon he started popping up on every trip Agnes worked. This went on for months, even though we're only allotted so many buddy passes for family and friends, until finally Agnes got suspended for abusing her flight privileges.

Agnes is the only person I'd ever met who could treat past abuse like an addiction and get away with it. A few therapy sessions later Agnes was back on the line and soon the boyfriend was trying to get back in her life, using his child to do so. When she realized the only way to make a change was to make a change, a big one, she transferred all the way to San Francisco (and, to my surprise, once she moved out we became good friends). We were all proud of her for finding herself and standing strong. We encouraged her not to regret what went down. To this day she will admit she's still trying to learn from that experience so that it wasn't a waste in her life.

We didn't have to look far to find another roommate to replace Agnes in the house. My mother moved in.

10

Flying Freak Show

DREAMS REALLY DO *come true*, I thought to myself after a male flight attendant walked on board and announced that the agent had told him Brad Pitt would be on our flight. (This was pre-Angelina.) I snuck into the lav to fluff my hair and refresh my makeup, just in case we made eye contact, not that I actually thought it would go anywhere from there. Then again, I had met a flight attendant who went on a date with Billy Idol and another who went out with Rod Stewart after becoming acquainted in flight. When I came out of the bathroom I noticed I wasn't alone, as all the other flight attendants looked ten times better than they did five minutes ago. The flight attendant who had made the exciting announcement now sat in a first-class seat cracking up and pointing at us, "Oh my God, look at you guys! I can't believe you fell for it!"

I *wish* I had fallen for it on another flight. During boarding I handed a grungy-looking guy in first class a glass of water. "Are you in a band?" I asked. There was no other way to explain the homeless attire. Turns out he was in a rock band, but not just any band: he was in my favorite band!

I looked at him funny. I'd never seen *this* guy before. "You must be new to the band."

"I'm the lead singer."

What he was, was a liar! Because the lead singer of the band I loved was hot. This guy with his scarecrow arms was not. At five-feet-seven I towered over the man. On television the lead singer looked tall and buff, always taking the stage shirtless, showing off a sexy six-pack. I highly doubted this guy on the plane had a two-pack under his thin hole-y T-shirt.

Back in the galley I decided to check the paperwork for his name. In a way I wish I hadn't. Because there it was, his name, printed on the thin paper that had been clipped to a compartment door housing all our glassware. I couldn't believe *that* was him! My rock 'n' roll fantasy.

Before I became a flight attendant, I didn't actually believe that dreams came true. Growing up in Dallas, a pretty big city with plenty of opportunities for a girl like me, never inspired me to think I could do anything extraordinary with my life. But once I moved to New York all that changed. I was living in one of the most exciting cities in the world and seeing things with my very own eyes that before only existed on television. Places like the Plaza Hotel, Central Park, the Empire State Building, Wall Street, Chinatown, Little Italy, which had always just seemed like movie backdrops. The world was at my fingertips and I had no idea what to do with it. I couldn't believe this was my life.

The celebrities were just the beginning of this realization. They were sitting in the same seat I had just sat in to eat the peanut butter and jelly sandwich I'd brought from home while waiting for the flight to board. My regular butt had touched the same fabric as many celebrity butts. I'll never forget the time I was deadheading on a flight home and the first-class flight attendant told me one of my favorite actresses had sat in my very seat after she won the Oscar last night. For whatever reason, that's the moment I believed I really could do anything with my life. Like, for example, become a photographer. So when I found out what the cute guy in the last row of business did for a living, I no longer wanted to date him. I wanted to work for him!

The guy was a well-known photographer, and there was clearly more to be had here than a night out on a town. On a whim, I offered to work for him for free for one day just so I could see what his life was really like, and surprisingly he agreed. This would have never happened to me working a regular job on the ground! Spending the day at his SoHo studio was one of the most exciting days of my life. All I did was water plants on his rooftop deck, order lunch for a group of grungy people I'm pretty sure were in a band, and file some papers, but the point is, I was there—me! Living a life so unattainable that I hadn't even bothered to dream about the possibility.

Just when I thought it couldn't get any better, we jumped on his motorcycle and took to the streets of Manhattan. He wanted to pick something up at his other studio. With my arms wrapped around him, we swerved in and out of traffic. With the wind whipping through my hair, I leaned back and looked up, taking in the magnificent buildings above. Along the way we stopped to give the grunge band's leftover gourmet lunch to a homeless lady the photographer knew by name. The experience was surreal. The best part may even be that I never heard from the photographer again. Sometimes it's best to leave a good thing alone. That day I had the time of my life, and I got to experience something I'll never forget. And if there's one thing flight attendants have it's a ton of these amazing moments.

My roommate Grace had her moment of a lifetime when Howard Stern called the house. Grace had an obsession with Howard that only got worse after she had him on a flight. Each morning she'd attempt to call his radio show, tying up the house phone for hours listening to a busy tone only to dial again. Then one day she finally got through and told him about the time she had him on a flight. They went on to dish about celebrities on the airplane. Grace wouldn't tell Howard her name, so he dubbed her "Loose-Lipped Meg," and soon there was an airplane buzzing in the background.

The following morning, the phone rang and when I picked up I heard the airplane buzz and then a very familiar voice asked if Loose-Lipped Meg was home. I told Howard to hold on and ran upstairs to wake up Grace. "Oh my God, it's Howard!"

"Who?" she asked, all groggy.

"Howard Stern!"

She bolted out of bed, ran to the phone, and after a quick introduction to his listeners, Howard asked, "So did you see the *New York Times* this morning?"

"No. Why?" squeaked Grace who must have known deep down in her heart this couldn't be good.

"They contacted Oprah. She's denying the story you told us about her yesterday."

"What!" Grace shrieked. Howard Stern. The *New York Times*. Oprah! Loose-Lipped Meg almost hit the linoleum kitchen floor. Yesterday she was just a lowly new hire and today she was the subject of a story running in the *New York Times*. Millions of people now knew who she was. Including Oprah. Who kinda-sorta was calling her a liar! This was bad, really bad.

Grace herself had not witnessed the incident (nor did I or anyone I know personally). But it was a pretty well-circulated rumor in flight attendant circles. The story is that Oprah boarded a flight and asked for an all-female cockpit crew, and then upon seeing an African-American flight attendant, asked to be served by her. The *New York Times* reporter felt Grace might be telling the truth since she had mentioned having Howard on board and discussed the conversation they had had. What sealed the deal for the reporter was when Howard Stern guessed the airline Loose-Lipped Meg worked for, the airline Meg denied working for with a nervous giggle, which was now printed in the *New*

York Times—airline name, giggle, and all. Oprah's people called the story ridiculous.

"What year did this happen?" asked Howard.

"Oh . . . umm . . . I'm not sure. 1995?"

"She could be telling the truth," his news anchor, Robin, chimed in. "Oprah's people stated she quit flying commercial in 1995."

Grace's world shrank that day. Luckily, she never did get in trouble for dishing the dirt on America's favorite daytime talk show host, but she did learn a very important lesson: keep your mouth shut. Flight attendants aren't allowed to talk about celebrities.

On the other hand, if we don't mention them by name, we're not really talking about them, right? So here's the galley gossip. He was one of the biggest pop stars of our time, and while he wouldn't breathe the air at 35,000 feet without wearing a face mask, he had no problem scarfing down two first-class meals. She has an A-list celebrity daughter and she once did three sets of sit-ups on the floor in the first row of first class. This actor known for having a thing for supermodels fell asleep with his hand down his pants in first class. A member of one of the most successful boy bands of the 1990s refused to buckle his belt while taxiing to the runway until the flight attendant threatened to have him removed from the flight. The comedian who got kicked off one of daytime TV's hottest talk shows asked the pilot not to make any more announcements in flight because her baby was sleeping. A beautiful A-list actress bit her toenails in business class. This same actress had once been married to the actor who cut his omelet into bite-size pieces with a knife and fork and then proceeded to eat it with his hands. Let's not forget the soulful singer who ordered the flight attendant not to talk to "her man" when all the flight attendant wanted to know was what he would like to drink. This long-haired singer of one of the most popular rock bands of the 1990s was way too old to be flirting with the captain's sixteen-year-old daughter, who was non-reving in first class. Two has-been R&B singers who are now divorced once exited the lavatory together looking extremely disheveled. Known as the sexiest woman in the world, she's also one of the nicest and most generous women in the world and tipped a gate agent $50 for letting her borrow a cell phone. The greatest R&B singer who ever lived was so afraid of flying he would only sit in the first row of first class. If that wasn't available he'd go on standby for another flight. This talk show icon left such a mess in first class that both passengers and flight attendants were shocked. A solo artist who once belonged to one of the most famous girl groups in the world lectured a flight attendant on the importance of being nice to his mother. A rapper who has changed his name several times over the years got caught checking out the flight attendant's you-know-what as she walked down the aisle. This young star sat in coach even though his movie was number one at the box office. A Canadian who shot to the top of the music charts with her scathing lyrics wouldn't allow a passenger in the window seat to pass by her in order to use the lavatory until quietly meditating with her first.

Once I had a cabin full of Victoria's Secret models and had no idea they were on my flight until one of my coworkers asked me how they were. Except for the fact that they ate lettuce without dressing and were super skinny and had smiles that practically wrapped around their face, they were just like anyone else traveling in first class on a red-eye flight. Many celebrities book full-fare business-class seats and then upgrade to first class, just like regular old passengers do. They, too, like a bargain. And when they don't get an upgrade, they freak out just like normal passengers. Although normal passengers don't often complain about being mobbed in coach when their upgrade doesn't go through.

On one flight to Los Angeles, my roommate Jane found herself non-reving in first class with an entire cabin full of Hollywood bigwigs. Jennifer Lopez, then a Fly Girl, sat in front of her with her first husband, the waiter, who sat directly across from Harvey Keitel. Harvey kept standing up in front of the cabin and stretching his legs. From time to time he'd stare intently at Jane. "I'm not sure if he was trying to figure out if I was someone important or if he wanted to ask me out!" We quickly came to the conclusion he wanted to ask her out. Between renting movies starring Jane's future boyfriend, we spent the next week trying to figure out how to contact him. Don't laugh. These things happen. And we weren't about to let a moment like this get away. Jane never did score a date with Harvey Keitel, but we sure had fun talking about it. This is why the job is so exciting. The possibilities are limitless. And just when you think you've experienced it all, something else wondrously amazing or far-out weird will happen.

Case in point, my mother started flying.

Large companies in any industry often engage in corporate upbeat talk about "being a family," when in reality they couldn't be any further from the kind. Then there are the rare corporations like Southwest Airlines that not only treat employees like family but actually employ married couples, parents, children, and even siblings. In 1989, Herb Kelleher, cofounder and CEO of Southwest Airlines, was quoted in *Texas Monthly* saying, "Some employees have been married to one employee, divorced, and then married to two, maybe three others." In 2006, Southwest was home to 763 married couples. My airline, on the other hand, traditionally had very strict antinepotism rules, but by the time I entered the flight academy in 1995, all that had changed. Even so, it was a pretty big deal when our instructors found out that a classmate's father had been a pilot for the same airline for more than twenty years. Two years later, in 1997, it was still a big deal when I pinned my mother's silver wings to her blue lapel at her graduation ceremony—not just because we were related but because I had the most seniority, which was pretty much unheard of at the time. That year we became one of two mother-daughter duos to be based in New York.

My mother had spent her entire life dreaming about becoming a flight attendant. I remember watching her over a bowl of Froot Loops at the kitchen table filling out applications to all the major carriers—American, Continental, Delta, Pan Am, TWA, United, Southwest—always tossing them out when they were complete. She realized she couldn't follow through if she had to transfer to another base and leave me and my sister behind. Eventually she gave up the dream and became a hairdresser. But when a few of her clients who happened to be flight attendants found out that my mother had always dreamed of flying, they each brought her an application from their airline. While flattered, my mother insisted that her time had come and gone—after all, she was in her late forties! The flight attendants told her to stop being silly.

Back in the 1960s stewardesses had to follow strict height, weight, and age requirements. According to Wikipedia, they had to be *at least* five-feet-two and weigh no more than 130 pounds. They also couldn't be married or have children. On top of that, mandatory retirement age was thirty-two. With that in mind it shouldn't be a surprise to learn that most stewardesses averaged eighteen months on the job. That's it.

Today the minimum age requirement to become a flight attendant is between eighteen and twenty-one. There is no maximum age restriction. As long as flight attendants can pass a yearly recurrent training program, and don't have any health or physical problems that would prevent them from flying, they can continue to work. Height requirements are for safety reasons only. Typically flight attendants range between five feet, three inches, and six feet, one inch. We must be tall enough to reach safety equipment stored overhead and short enough to avoid bumping our heads against the aircraft ceiling. (For this reason on some regional carriers using smaller aircraft equipment, maximum height requirement is five feet, ten inches.) In the 1990s weight requirements for flight attendants were dropped, but weight must be in proportion to height. If flight attendants cannot sit in the jump seat without an extended seat belt or fit through the emergency *window* exit, they cannot fly. Most foreign carriers still follow strict height, weight, and age requirements.

The benefits of hiring older people who have already had a career is they tend to appreciate what being a flight attendant is all about, and that shows on the job. Younger flight attendants who have never worked a regular 9-to-5 job have no idea how good they have it. Hiring more-experienced people also helps the airlines save money when it comes to paying for benefits and retirement. Once, while I was explaining this to a passenger who couldn't believe my mother was also a flight attendant, he informed me that he found it unsettling to stare at postmenopausal women pushing beverage carts for three hours. As if buying an airline ticket entitled him to eye candy. Of course, he wasn't much to look at, either. Another passenger wished the airlines would hire nicer, better-looking flight attendants like Virgin, because the last thing he wanted was to be scolded in flight by someone's grandmother or gay cousin. What's amazing is how often passengers complaining about flight attendants being old and ugly are old and ugly themselves.

I don't know what it is, but whenever it comes to flight attendants, people tend to forget that we have rights regardless of what we do for a living. What I find most unsettling is the number of passengers with ageist and sexist opinions about flight attendants who think it's okay to not just have these outdated opinions, but to express them to the very group of people they're talking about! I hate to be the bearer of bad news, but flight attendants are allowed to age and gain weight like the rest of society. One passenger had the nerve to complain about a "fat flight attendant" who ruined his flight because she kept waking him up whenever she passed down the aisle. I wanted to point out that if certain passengers weren't spilling out into the aisle (cough, cough), "fat" flight attendants wouldn't be knocking into them. Another passenger whacked me hard on the butt after she accused me of stepping on her toe. For the record, my height and weight are nicely proportional, but even I can't walk down the aisle in a straight line without swinging my body from side to side because of all the heads, legs and feet hanging out into the aisle.

My mother, like Linda, my old roommate from training, started flying when most people her age begin thinking of retiring. Her life went from turning yet another brunette a beautiful shade of blond with a bowl of bleach and a stack of foils to Vice President Al Gore saying hello to her in passing at JFK Airport outside of security. One day she was repairing another botched-up home cut and the next day a member of the band Air Supply is flirting with her in the first-class galley. On a bus from LaGuardia to Newark she shared family pictures with British reggae vocalist Maxi Priest's drummer. She was shocked to discover a well-known talk show host had hands that were so shaky she could barely lift her glass of wine. And she couldn't stop laughing when one of the most famous movie stars from the 1950s told one of her crew members—who had spent the entire flight bending over backward to please the difficult and demanding Hollywood star—"My dog likes you. I don't know why."

After a month on the job, my mother said to me, "Whenever you came home and told us about the crazy things that happened to you on the airplane I used to wonder if maybe you were exaggerating a little. Now I know you weren't."

With my mother on the line and living in my crash pad, my life went from weird to super weird. One day I walked into the house after a trip and Jane stopped me in the foyer with a nervous look on her face. "I don't know if I should tell you this or not, because if it were me I don't think I'd want to know—"

"Spill it!" I demanded, unzipping the back of my dress, eager to get out of my uniform as quickly as possible. After a flight I always smell like a mix of chocolate chip cookies, urine from the lav, and whatever I may have spilled—maybe an exploding bottle of champagne or an entire can of tomato juice. Customs and immigration in Vancouver once told me they could always tell when our flight had arrived because they could smell it as soon as the gate agents opened the aircraft door.

Jane took a deep breath. "Yakov can't decide who to ask out— you or your mother." I froze midzip.

It was bad enough that I'd had to pretend to be Yakov's wife in an emergency code enforcement situation, but to think he actually believed he had a shot was disturbing to say the least. On top of that he couldn't decide who he liked more, me or the woman who bore me. My mother, of course, claimed to find the situation to be just as sickening as I did, but based on the number of times she relayed the story to family and friends, blushing and giggling each time she recounted it, I think she may have been a little too flattered.

The dispatchers over at Kew Gardens Car Service weren't making it any easier. Whenever I'd call for a car, they'd ask in a yeah-baby kind of voice, "Is this the mother or the daughter?"

I'd close my eyes tightly, thinking to myself, gross, gross, gross, and then say, "The daughter," as matter-of-factly as I could. I didn't want to egg them on. They liked to tease.

Even worse was making the same distinction to a driver—in person! "Really, you can't tell?" I asked a new guy who refused to meet my glare in the rearview mirror.

Once a driver asked my mother how her date went the other night. At first she had no idea what he was talking about. When it finally dawned on her that he thought she was me, she made the executive decision to play along. "Great," she said, before closing her eyes and pretending to sleep.

"Why in the world would you do that?!" I cried over the laughter of my roommates.

"It was a long day. I didn't feel like talking."

"The next time I get into a cab I'm going to pretend I'm you and ask the driver out!" Then I one-upped it. "I'll also tell the lesbian doctor down the street that I'd love to grab a drink with her next time I'm in town."

My mother swore she wouldn't do it again. Then she added, "Just because the doctor lady asked me if I'd like to get a drink with her doesn't mean she wants to go on a date!"

Yeah, okay, whatever, Mom.

At work I couldn't decide which was stranger: Coming face-to-face with award-winners like Robert Redford or Leonardo DiCaprio or working across the aisle from my mother? Making direct eye contact with Goldie Hawn on one of my very first flights to Los Angeles or the time I needed the merlot from the other cart and accidentally yelled out "Mom!" in the middle of the business-class aisle?

"Don't call me 'Mom'!" my mother would demand before each flight we were scheduled to work together, as if I had actually *wanted* to cause a spectacle in flight. The reason my mother—I mean Ellen—didn't want me to call her 'Mom' had nothing to do with being professional and had everything to do with not looking "old." Ellen looked great for her age and the last thing she wanted was a planeful of passengers knowing she had such "an old child"—her words, not mine.

Although we only worked with each other a handful of times, Ellen was always quick to spill the beans. I could always tell whenever she'd shared our little secret because people would start looking at me with wide eyes and silly grins, their necks elongated to get a better view of the freak walking down the aisle. Whenever I'd confront her, she'd laugh it off and say, "Oh, it's just one person," only it was never just one person. One person would tell another person and so on and so on and so on.

"I can tell you told the guy in the last row," I said, giving my mother the evil eye.

"What was I supposed to do? He kept asking me to fix him up with the pretty flight attendant named Heather. I told him I'd put in a good word for him, but he wouldn't let it go. He's driving me crazy! And I was beginning to feel a little uncomfortable about it all. I thought it best he should know."

Not me. That's why my dates never found out the truth about Ellen whenever they'd stop by the crash pad to pick me up. To them she was my older roommate from Texas. There was no need to tell them her husband was also my father. Imagine running into a fetishist harboring both flight attendant and mother-daughter fantasies. Combine the two and you've got a serious pervert on your hands. Love was hard enough to find without worrying about that kind of stuff.

But for me, maybe the strangest thing of all was that on the airplane our roles switched and I became the overprotective one. When Ellen accidentally spilled a little water on a passenger's armrest, and the guy made a face like "What the hell is wrong with you?" I practically flew across the cabin.

I am not a confrontational person. But no one was going to treat my mother like that! It didn't matter how many frequent-flier miles the guy had or if he'd been an executive on the board of directors, I wasn't having it. Of course, I would have never reacted the same way if I'd been the one he had yelled at. I would have apologized over and over and then gone into the galley to curse him out with my coworkers. But this was my mother. It was different.

Ellen pushed me aside and whispered, "I can handle this!"

Of course she could. I didn't doubt it for a second. But I stood right there to make sure the guy didn't say anything disrespectful. Because that's my mama, dude!

Besides being overprotective, I wasn't always as patient with Ellen as I would have been with another coworker, and this always confused passengers who were unaware of the *Grey Gardens* situation happening on the airplane.

"Just pull on it!" I once demanded when my mother couldn't open one of the stuck business-class closets, before walking away to hand out mints in the cabin.

"That wasn't very nice," said a passenger waiting in line nearby for the lavatory.

"I don't like her very much," Ellen playfully growled. When the passenger looked concerned, my mother fessed up, "I can say things like that. She's my daughter."

Of course the look of concern immediately turned into one of freakish wonder.

Passengers weren't the only ones reacting oddly. We once had a captain make a silly announcement about it right after takeoff, and a ticket agent, who put two and two together when she noticed we looked a lot alike and had the same last name, made an announcement in the airport terminal. I'll never forget opening the jet bridge door and hearing over the PA: "Ladies and gentleman, I have some exciting news to share with you. Today on your flight . . ." No, no, no —she wouldn't! I thought to myself, but she did. She informed everyone in the gate area that a mother-daughter flight attendant team would be serving them on board their flight today. The response can only be compared to that of telling a bunch of kids that Mickey Mouse and Goofy will be on board handing out snacks. Don't get me wrong, working next to me in uniform made my mother proud. (And there were some perks, like the fact that I could always count on her to take a trip for me if I had a hot date.) But listening to the applause in the terminal that day, I wanted to bolt. It's just not cool to live and work with your mom!

What is cool is spotting someone you've had a crush on for a very long time on the airplane. For my mother that person was Keanu Reeves. She'd been in love with the movie star since he'd starred in the movie *Something's Gotta Give* as Diane Keaton's much younger doctor boyfriend. Imagine her surprise when he sat down across the aisle from her in business class on a six-hour flight she had been scheduled to deadhead on. She never spoke to him. She couldn't even look at him. But if she had wanted to she could have reached across the aisle and touched him. "Okay, I can retire now," she said after the flight.

My Keanu Reeves moment happened when I spotted the CEO at the watch company I used to work for, walking through the airport at LaGuardia. I had just gotten off a flight and made a beeline straight for him.

"Hi! Remember me? I used to work for you!" I said excitedly. I'd been waiting for this day for three years. He looked nervous. "I'm Heather Poole."

I could tell he had no idea who I was, and he confirmed this when he said, "I . . . uh . . . have to catch a flight."

"Okay, well, here's my number," I said, scribbling it on the back of a passenger's business card. "Maybe after you have a chance to relax you'll remember me."

Or maybe not. He never called. So I took matters into my own hands and called him. Being a flight attendant had given me confidence. I'd grown so accustomed to dealing with "important" people, or at least those who thought they were important, so I could handle myself in pretty much any situation, including dating the old boss. Anyway, I had nothing to lose.

I left the CEO a message, telling him I'd show him around New York City next time he came to town, even though he probably knew the city better than I did since his company had a show-room here. One year later, he returned my call. There was never any intimacy other than a little hand-holding and a kiss at the end of the night. But there were black town cars and first-row tickets to Broadway shows, nice dinners at the best restaurants, and plenty of good conversation that revolved mostly around where I'd been, where I was going next, and all the people I'd met in between. Basically I did the majority of the talking, which was fine by me because I like to talk. When he'd leave I wouldn't hear from him again for weeks, even months until he'd board a flight to New York, pull out his BlackBerry while sitting in first class waiting for the plane to depart and type, "What are you doing tonight?" Four hours later a black car would pick me up and whisk me into the city. He was a successful businessman who was fifteen years older than me, so we didn't have a lot in common, but what we did share was enough. We were living the dream. We were two lonely people who traveled.

11

Dating Pilots

I'**D NEVER DATE** a pilot. They're way too geeky!" said one of
my favorite pilots, right after I mentioned I had dated one back
before I'd become a flight attendant. Then, with a mischievous
grin, he added, "But I've dated flight attendants from every single
airline." I did not doubt it for a second.

Pilots are type A personalities. They're logical thinkers who
must remain calm, cool, and in control as they command the aircraft. There's no room for emotion when faced with a decision like
the one Captain Sully had to make when he ditched an aircraft
into the Hudson River. Flight attendants, on the other hand, are
nurturing and caring. The issues we deal with are rarely black
and white. So if opposites attract, it only makes sense that pilots
and flight attendants would wind up together. And maybe it isn't
a surprise to learn that pilots often marry nurses and teachers,
while flight attendants get involved with police officers and fire-
men.

There's a saying in the airline industry that you're not a real airline pilot unless you've been furloughed, gone on strike, and been divorced. I can't help but wonder how many pilots have flight attendants as ex-wives, since so many of them are brazen enough to try juggling more than one of us at the same time. It's not pretty when a pilot gets caught—and they almost always do. This is because flight attendants have a tendency to talk—a lot—and invariably we wind up talking about them. One lucky guy became the subject of jump-seat conversation when his wife and mistress were paired together to work a trip. Imagine how he must have felt when he pulled up that list of crew names! While his wife raved about her amazing husband, the girlfriend shared intimate details of her hot new man. Surrounded by passengers, a midflight fight broke out between the pissed-off mother of two and the young hot mistress who had no idea her perfect boyfriend wasn't so perfect after all. A different mile-high love triangle went down a little more peacefully when, instead of coming to blows, two flight attendants agreed to confront the wandering groin at the airport. They stood, side by side, arms crossed, at the top of the jet bridge just waiting for the bastard to walk off his flight. I wasn't there to see the end of it, but I'm sure the passengers seated in the surrounding gate area went home with quite an interesting story to share that day.

While not all pilots end up with flight attendants, many do tend to marry often. There are a few horror stories of embittered pilots who have made the galley gossip rounds. Take, for instance, the San Francisco–based pilot (I hear he's now deceased) who refused to speak to flight attendants at the end of his career. He made the first officer do all the talking for him. Later he went on to write about "gold-diggers" and the "lopsided" court system in a book, *The Predatory Female: A Field Guide to Dating and the Marriage-Divorce Industry*, after he wound up paying millions to a few "undeserving" ex-wives. I can't help but wonder how he may have died. Predatory female or pissed-off flight attendant? Or a combination of both? Then there's the story about a captain everyone hated from Eastern Airlines who got poisoned in flight and ended up in a hospital on his layover. The crew got called in for questioning upon returning back to base. As the story goes, he had recently divorced a flight attendant and was vocal about his hatred of all women. A friend of mine was working as purser on that flight and swore it wasn't her—she always passed off the job of feeding pilots to the most junior flight attendant on board.

Pilots and flight attendants usually love or hate each other— maybe a little too much since there's rarely an in-between. It's usually the latter for our more senior flight attendants who've been there, done that more times than they'll ever admit. They make it a point to take new hires under their wings and school them in the ways of pilots. One such flight attendant went so far as to write down a few tips in case I forgot:

Tip 1: Don't do it.
Tip 2: Don't do it.
Tip 3: Don't do it.
Tip 4: If you do mess up and do it, don't do it more than once.

A flight attendant who dates more than her fair share of pilots is referred to as a "Cockpit Connie," unless she's someone you really dislike, in which case she's an "air mattress." One can assume this kind of flight attendant is familiar with "touch and go." Pilots, on the other hand, get stereotyped as three things: womanizers, cheap bastards, and horrible dressers. Unfortunately, stereotypes come from a seed of truth and, because I ignored all four points on the list, I've dated them all, starting with Gary.

I met him at LaGuardia Airport back when I was still working for the watch company. My fourth flight ever was a trip to New

York. A girlfriend at work had scored super cheap tickets to visit her family over the weekend and invited me to come along with her. It was a quick three-day trip that landed late at night on day 1 and departed back to Dallas late in the afternoon on day 3, about two hours shy of the firework show over the city. While we were waiting for our return flight to board I thought it might be fun to ask a pilot to take a photograph with me. I would frame it and give it to my mother as a sort of gag gift for her birthday—she had a thing for men in uniform, which is one of the reasons she married my father, a retired lieutenant commander in the navy.

I had my camera out and ready to go when I locked eyes on three gray-haired pilots heading my way. With my girlfriend egging me on, I was just about to ask, but at the last minute I chickened out. They were too involved in a serious conversation to bother with my silly request. How could I have possibly known they were probably just discussing filing with the IRS after a third failed marriage? Right behind them, walking all alone, I spotted another one, and this one was young and cute and looking right at me. *Gulp.*

His name, it turned out, was Gary, and I'm pretty sure I saw him blush when I told him what I had in mind. Now if I had known my mother was going to react the way she did after she unwrapped the gold-framed photo on her birthday, I would never have stopped him to ask if he'd pose in a picture with me. And I certainly wouldn't have given him my phone number if I had thought my little joke would take on a life of its own, making its way into the homes of my grandparents, who displayed the photograph of a smiling tall, dark, and handsome pilot standing beside me with my big hair and exposed midriff on a bookshelf in the family room for all to see.

I knew nothing about the airline business at the time, so I paid no attention to the three gold stripes circling the wrists of Gary's uniform blazer. What I didn't know was that these signaled that he was a first officer, not a captain. Captains sit on the left-hand side, wear four stripes, and get first dibs on a choice of crew meal, almost always passing the vegetarian entrée off to the first officer. Pilots are never catered the same thing to eat on board a flight as a precaution against food poisoning. My colleagues and I were taught a lot of things in flight attendant training, but landing an aircraft wasn't one of them. This is why we aren't allowed to swap out cockpit meals for passenger meals if we run out of choices and a passenger doesn't get what he wants. If you go to use the first-class lav and catch a flight attendant eating what you think should have been your meal, don't get upset! Chances are that one of the pilots decided not to eat at the last minute.

Seniority for pilots works pretty much the same as it does for flight attendants. The big difference between pilots and flight attendants is a pilot can move up in rank. You can always tell how senior a pilot is based on the aircraft he's flying. The heavier the airplane, the bigger the paycheck, with the captain making substantially more per hour than a first officer. When there's an opening, the most senior first officer or captain will "move up." When a captain on a smaller plane is upgraded, the most senior first officer has a shot at becoming a captain. From time to time you'll find the first officer has more seniority than the captain. In these cases, the first officer has chosen quality of life over pay (a life off reserve). Now, if I had worked for an airline the day I met Gary, I would have known immediately that he was pretty low on the employee totem pole—he had three stripes and was working a flight that departed late in the afternoon on the Fourth of July.

When Gary walked away after our picture that day, I thought that was that, end of story. He lived in Florida and I lived in Texas. Where could it possibly go? I figured I'd never see him again, which is why I'd had the nerve to ask him for the photo in the first place! The last thing on my mind was to hook up.

But then I boarded my flight, plopped down into my seat,

glanced out the window, and saw a familiar-looking pilot looking up at the wing. "Oh no, he's our pilot."

"Wave!" my girlfriend exclaimed, leaning into me. I grabbed her hands and held them firmly down.

"Oh shit!" I exclaimed, sliding way down in my seat when he looked up.

An hour into the flight, just when I was starting to relax, a flight attendant holding a tray of food stopped at my row. "Gary asked me to bring you this. It's his crew meal," she said.

"How sweet!" my girlfriend squealed. Stunned, I just sat there. I'd really thought Gary hadn't seen my shocked face framed in the airplane window. My friend unlocked my tray and the flight attendant placed the first-class cheese lasagna on my table. It looked delicious.

"Umm . . . tell Gary I said thank you."

When I myself became a flight attendant, I reflected back on this moment many times and wondered what the heck Gary was thinking by sending the first-class flight attendant back to coach to serve me, a passenger he barely knew, a passenger wearing *a crop top on a plane*, a crew meal that should have been the flight attendants' by default.

I'm not sure which was more embarrassing, Gary's big-ball move or me ringing the call light after I finished eating so a flight attendant could take away the tray. Because unless it's an emergency or the seat belt sign is on or you're stuck by the window next to a sleeping passenger, you really shouldn't ring the call light. Flight attendants use a chime system to signal different emergency situations, and when we hear it, we assume it's an emergency. If we get a series of passengers who start using it to order drink refills, there's a cabin full of flight attendants wondering if they should grab a serving tray or a bottle of oxygen. If you can, it's always best to get up, stretch your legs, and walk to the back to say hi to the crew. Or just wait for a flight attendant to pass by—we're each required to walk through the cabin at least once every fifteen minutes. As for that flight attendant who came back to pick up the meal Gary had sent back after I did what I now would never do (*ding!*) she never once made me feel anything other than special. She handled it like a professional. Even so I'm positive I was galley gossip for the remainder of the flight.

Even though we'd exchanged numbers and I'd promised to mail him a copy of the photo after I got home, I was still pretty surprised when he called, and even more shocked when he asked me out. He had a layover in Dallas and wanted to know if I'd like to meet for a drink, since it'd probably be too late for dinner. But if I wanted dinner, he'd love to take me out, he quickly added. I'd never dated someone like Gary before. At the age of twenty-three I was only used to dating guys who had recently graduated from college, most of whom were still unsure of what they were going to do with their lives, not men in charge of aircrafts. I felt totally unworthy of his attention. I spent my days deciding which lugs went with which dials, mixing and matching different leather straps, while he spent his days flying passengers to their destinations. Handsome, smart, and sweet, he was a total catch. Too bad for my mother, he wasn't my type. At the time, you see, my type had a tendency to suck.

In hindsight, I realize the problem with Gary was that there was no problem with Gary. The man was perfect in every sense of the word. But I was twenty-three, and at that time in my life, there was one thing that I really couldn't handle. What bugged me wasn't that he had a four-year-old son or an ex-wife who lived not too far from his parents' house. Where he lived. No, what disturbed me were his clothes. I almost died when he showed up for our first date basically wearing his uniform. Because I knew he was on a layover, I let it slide—the first time. No doubt about it, Gary looked handsome standing in front of a cockpit door greeting passengers, but the uniform belt and uniform pants paired with a bright yellow T-shirt just didn't cut it on the dance floor.

It's an interesting topic, pilots and fashion. I'm not sure I can even use the two words in the same sentence since they go as well together as orange juice and toothpaste. Ask any group of flight attendants if they can spot a pilot in civilian "layover clothes" and they will emphatically say yes. Don't believe me? Next time you're at the airport look for the guy wearing Ray-Ban sunglasses. If he's also sporting pleated khakis with a powder blue golf shirt underneath a Members Only jacket, nine times out of ten his name is at the bottom of the non-rev standby list. Despite the reality, for so many women the word "pilot" conjures up images of dashing men in uniform. Think Richard Gere (*Officer and a Gentleman*), Tom Cruise (*Top Gun*), Leonardo DiCaprio (*The Aviator*), Andy Garcia (*When a Man Loves a Woman*), John Travolta (he owns a 707), and Jake Pavelka—ya know, Jake, the pilot from that television show *The Bachelor* who later went on to shake his groove thing on *Dancing with the Stars*. While he looked oh so dreamy dressed in a tux, I couldn't help but wonder as I watched the women fawning in their desperate quest for a rose if they would have even given him the time of day if they'd seen him in real life—say, passing through the lobby of a hotel in his layover clothes, holding a passenger's discarded day-old newspaper while sipping a discounted cup of coffee? Somehow I doubt it.

In the travel section of Barnes & Noble, I once met a guy named Bob. I didn't believe him when he told me he was a pilot. He looked too good to be a pilot! Not that Bob is conventionally handsome. He's kind of nerdy. But he knows how to rock the dark denim without the pilot's trademark running sneakers. When I asked Bob why so many pilots dressed terribly, he said it's because his coworkers spend too much time looking for tools in the Sears catalog and then accidentally stumble into its clothing section. "It's not so much that being a pilot causes one to be fashion-challenged, it's just that we tend to be better at things like engineering, checking the car's oil, fixing things around the house, and not asking for driving directions. This opposed to fashion design," he explained.

Too bad Bob wasn't around to help my roommate Jane's date, a 767 first officer, pick out something to wear on their first date. Hot Shot showed up dressed to impress wearing golf shoes, skin-tight acid-washed jeans, and a turquoise jacket.

"He looked like such a nerd," Jane cringed after the date. "I don't think I would have agreed to go out with him if he'd looked like that when he asked me out."

Thank God for first impressions. And uniforms.

They spent three weeks getting to know each other over the phone before their first date. They weren't intentionally taking it slow, but that's how long it took before they were finally able to coordinate their schedules. In the long run, this was a good thing since it helped that Jane was practically head over heels for the guy by the time they finally went out. Otherwise she might not have been able to overlook the off-duty fashion disaster, and he would have never made it to second base. Two months into the relationship Jane talked her man into donating the shoes and the jeans, along with a dozen or so obnoxious Christmas ties and half a closet full of college clothes, to Goodwill. Then she borrowed his credit card and went shopping. She may have purchased a few things for him, too, because after they broke up two years later Hot Shot was considered one of the best-dressed pilots in the system. Much to her dismay he had no problem scoring another flight attendant who got to enjoy the fruits of Jane's labor. But don't feel badly for Jane. She upgraded to an airbus captain.

Gary and I didn't date for long. In fact we didn't really "date." We went out a few times over the course of five months or so. But Gary turned into the better-looking but terribly dressed version of my mother when he began spending a lot of time talking to me about his job and why I should be doing it—or one somewhat similar to it. I never told him I'd interviewed with an airline before. Perhaps I wanted to block it from my mind. Instead I kept explaining to him that I wanted to do something more with my life than serve drinks and pick up trash. Every time I told him this I sounded snottier and more full of myself until I began to make my own self sick. I don't know why Gary put up with me. But he did, and that's when I started inventing reasons not to go out with him. When he didn't take the hint, I stopped calling him back.

A year after he disappeared from my life, I became a flight attendant with the same company Gary worked for. Needless to say after I graduated from flight attendant training I began thinking about him again. More than anything I wished I had handled things with him differently. All I could do was worry about running into him again! It was inevitable. It didn't matter if the airline I worked for was a big company with almost twenty thousand flight attendants or that flight attendants worked with different people all the time. The interesting thing about being a flight attendant is that while we may not see a person we've worked with for years after a trip, out of nowhere they'll pop up on the other side of the cart, as if no time had passed, other than that person gaining a little weight or losing a little hair. Just when we begin to feel comfortable and think that maybe, just maybe, the one we'd like to avoid has quit or retired or transferred to another base, his or her name will appear on a crew list. One minute we could be working with a flight attendant on the prowl, and the next time we see her she's the mother of three, sharing sippy-cup tips on the jump seat. Or even worse, one minute a pilot is dating a regular girl with a bad attitude on the ground, and the next time he speaks to her, she's wearing a matching uniform—but lying about it.

I had just moved into the crash pad with Georgia and Victor, the mankini-wearing, drugged-out landlord, when out of the blue Gary called to "check in and say hello." Too embarrassed by my past rants against the airline industry to tell him the truth—that at that moment I was laying over at a Holiday Inn not too far from the airport in Oklahoma City—I did the next best thing. I lied. I didn't want him to know I had just finished eating breakfast for dinner at a Denny's across the street by myself as I was the extra flight attendant on a trip and therefore on my own for the next three days, so I told him everything was great, life couldn't be better, and yes, I was in fact still working for the watch company. I went on and on about a life I no longer had or even wanted. I was on a roll, describing in detail things I hadn't done in over a year with people I no longer worked with, and Gary quietly listened. I don't remember how the conversation ended, but it's safe to assume that it did and when it did I was relieved. After that I dreaded flying the Miami run even more than I had before, which I didn't think was possible.

If I did find myself walking through the Miami airport, the most chaotic airport in the world and home of the most amazing people-watching on Earth, I did so briskly and never stopped for anything other than what was absolutely necessary. Rice and beans at La Carreta and a *café con leche* from Café Versailles. While I'd nervously wait in line for the most delicious Cuban takeout food, I'd scan the horizon for a familiar face, always scoping out what I could duck behind, maybe a magazine stand or group of passengers, in order to avoid an unwanted run-in. At some point I knew I'd have to face my fears, but I kept hoping that day would come later, not sooner. While I waited for the inevitable to happen I imagined all the different scenarios that could possibly occur—well, all but the one that actually did occur.

I had boarded a flight in Dallas with my crew. The plane was in the process of being catered and cleaned when I spotted a pair of aviator Ray-Bans on the galley counter. Naturally I picked them up, tried them on, and walked into the lav to check myself out in the mirror. As I stood with the door open, reapplying lipstick, I heard a familiar voice behind me say, "Excuse me. I think I left my sunglasses on board."

Oh boy. I swallowed hard and slowly turned around.

"I guess these are yours then." I took the shades off and handed them back to Gary. "Long time no see," I said, cringing as soon as the words were out of my mouth. I didn't know what else to say!

"W-what are you . . . when did you—"

"Last year." I didn't want him to know I had been lying the last time we spoke, so I did it again. I told him exactly what had happened, only I shaved off a few years. Then I did what any other flight attendant would do when a person dares to step onto the precious galley floor. I offered him a drink and prayed he'd go back to his seat, which turned out to be the left seat on a flight to Palm Springs. Gary had been upgraded to captain. I congratulated him and wished him the best.

"I can't tell you how odd it is to see you here, on an airplane, in uniform. You really look great!" he said.

I blushed. "Thanks. You do, too." He did. Even better than before.

When he took off his hat and scratched his head, I caught a glimpse of a young boy holding a bat and wearing a red jersey in a photograph tucked inside the clear plastic pocket on the underside of his cap, which is where single pilots keep their business cards and the others keep family photos. A way to distinguish one hat from another since they all look alike hanging on the back of the cockpit door during flight.

"So . . . why did we lose touch again?" he asked earnestly.

"Umm . . ." I didn't want to hurt his feelings, so I stared at the oven door for a count of three, as if seriously pondering the question, and then looked directly into his beautiful brown eyes and lied again. "I don't remember." What can I say? I was on a roll.

"Would you like to get together . . . again, sometime?" he asked. I couldn't believe it. I'd said terrible things about flight attendants, stopped calling him, become a flight attendant, and lied about it, and he still wanted to see me again.

Of course I said yes. Because I knew Gary was a great guy! I could only assume I'd grown up over the last three years. Surely I could appreciate all he had to offer this time around now that I was in a completely different place in life. Now that I was older and wiser and well traveled, I figured Gary and I had to have a lot more in common. So I scribbled my number across a beverage napkin and told him to call me for a second time.

Midway through round two of our first date, it was clear that we had a problem. Gary was, well, not very exciting. But he was thoughtful, in that he brought flowers and always opened doors. He was the kind of pilot that would grab crew bags out of the first-class closet and line them up on the jet bridge for a quick escape. But if I wasn't talking, we weren't talking—talk about stressful! At least with the CEO I could share funny stories, but if Gary hadn't already heard my funny stories, he'd heard of ones just like them. I knew he was a catch, so I tried not to let that deter me. But as he walked me to my hotel door at the end of the night I found myself dreading the kiss good night. Determined not to let a little thing like chemistry come between us, I kissed him anyway! I felt nothing. Really putting my all into it, I tried again. But we just weren't meant to be.

Years later, during a vacation in Puerto Vallarta, my mother turned to me and announced, "There's something I need to tell you." When my mother starts a conversation like this, what follows next is guaranteed to be frightening.

"Dad's dead?" I said half-jokingly.

"Worse." My mother covered her face with her hands and I could have sworn I heard her say something crazy like "I wrote Gary a letter."

"You did what?!"

"Right after you completed flight attendant training and moved to New York. You just seemed so sad and lonely. I was worried about you. I thought maybe if he knew you were a flight attendant he might call and offer to take you out."

I leaned back in my seat and adjusted the air vent so I could breath. I wanted to kill her. The fact that Gary had acted surprised to see me on the airplane and never even let on about the freaking letter just proved to me that he might be even crazier than my mother! Or one of the nicest guys in the world. Either way, it meant that he lied, too, kind of, so in a way we were even, sort of.

I haven't seen Gary since, but my mother has. Twice. The first time he was the captain on one of her flights. After years of staring at that stupid photograph, she recognized him right away. She almost died when he walked on board and stowed his bag in the first-class closet. The last thing she wanted to do was embarrass me, so she never told him who she was, but she does think he may have known based on the way he lingered around in the galley a lot during the flight. The second time she ran into him—a decade later!—he knew exactly who she was and told her so in the rear galley as she was setting up carts. After she was through telling me all about how great he was, and how he had nothing but nice things to say about me, and how he's moving to New York and is engaged to a girl who looks, based on a photograph, kind of like me, she exclaimed, "I swear, Heather, you'll never do better than him!" And she turned out to be right . . . at least as far as pilots were concerned.

12

Marry Me, Fly Free!

 EARLY ON IN my career, my roommate Tricia took me to a trendy bar in Manhattan, and a guy sporting Buddy Holly frames and electric blue Puma sneakers leaned over and asked what I did for a living.

"I'm a flight attendant," I yelled over the pulsing beat of the music, and then I took a sip of my apple martini.

Buddy Holly straightened himself up and walked away. I watched in shock as he crossed the room and made a play for another blonde. I guess she had a more respectable job, since he spent the rest of the night conversing with her.

"Asshole!" Tricia exclaimed. A group of guys who'd gathered around vying for her attention laughed. I pretended to care less, but, really, I was pissed! If I had told him that I was a watch designer, would it have made a difference? Probably.

Being a quick learner, I told the next guy I worked for an airline. That's it. End of story. When he pressed, I said I handled baggage. (Well, I do—during boarding!) Not only did he stick around, he bought me drinks. Unfortunately he turned out to be a FO-FO. This is what I call the first on, first off. FO-FOs are easy to spot. Like gate lice, they'll line up against the wall in front of the boarding door in the airport terminal, impatiently waiting to get on a flight before the flight attendants have even had a chance to do so themselves. They're also the ones that stand up before the seat belt sign is turned off in order to grab their bags out of the bin, crushing anyone who dares to get in their way as they sprint to the deplaning door. I hate to admit it, but I kind of like it when the captain slams on the breaks, sending a couple of FO-FOs stumbling down the aisle. Once I realized I was faced with a FO-FO, I did what any other flight attendant would do: I channeled my inner Buddy Holly guy and walked away, but not without politely excusing myself first.

People like Buddy have formed very strong opinions about flight attendants based on things we have zero control over, like a lack of drink choices or a used crossword puzzle inside the complimentary in flight airline magazine. Stuff like that can make some passengers nuts. Mix in a couple of hours with nothing to do but to sit and stew over the matter, and we've got a very unhappy passenger on our hands. And we're not the Royal British Guard. Sometimes, every once in a while, a passenger pushes us too far and we react. This usually happens around day 4 of flying several days in a row after having to deal with the same complaints over and over again. One frustrated flight attendant I know finally exclaimed, "This is an airplane, not a 7-Eleven!" after a passenger became irate that the airline didn't carry soy milk. Of course, it's always the passenger with the problem who will have to be reminded later on in flight that the seat belt sign is on. These are the same passengers who will then come to the false conclusion that we're picking on them. It never fails: whatever they ask for next, we won't have, which will lead them to the false conclusion that we're lying. It doesn't matter how many great flight attendants this passenger may encounter on future flights, from here on out, we're all liars and nothing we do or say will change that. If Buddy Holly was one of those, I guess I dodged a bullet.

The other danger of admitting you're a flight attendant to a potential date is finding one who is now more interested in your job than you. You'll be asking about them and all they'll want is to hear about the mile-high club. (To be fair, many people who are not trying to take me home also want to know about the mile-high club.) The not so sexy answer to this is that most people eager to join the club usually fail, because it's my job to stop it from happening as soon as I become aware of what's going on. This usually happens after an impatient passenger has complained about waiting in line to use the lav for a long period of time.

"Did you knock?" we'll ask. Nine times out of ten they'll ask us to do it for them. I always hate doing this because not everyone tying up the loo is having sex. Some people really just need extra time. Like the woman who cracked open the door as she sat on the commode and asked me to "fetch" her a magazine because she was going to be a while. Trust me: if someone is taking that long in the lav, most of the time it's just best to find another bathroom. Even if that means walking *all the way* to the back of the airplane. I'm talking to you, first class!

If there is something fishy going on inside the bathroom, flight attendants will order whomever is inside to come out (with their pants up), all the while praying they do as they're told. The last thing we want is to have to take matters into our own hands and unlock the door for them, thereby getting a glimpse of something we never wanted to see in the first place.

The first couple I ever caught exiting the lav together (in the middle of an afternoon flight, mind you) were both well known in the music industry back in the mid-1990s. Think R&B. The most shocking thing about it for me was that they didn't even attempt to hide it. Most people will take turns leaving the bathroom, mistakenly thinking that nobody waiting in line will notice the occupied sign immediately sliding back into place after one person exits. But not these two musical wonders. I guess when you perform on stage in front of thousands of adoring fans on a nightly basis, you don't mind doing what should have been the walk of shame back to your first-class seats. I couldn't believe it when the one with the killer voice didn't at least try to fix her hair first.

Over the years I've caught red-handed a few other passengers who were trying to join the prestigious club, but membership has been waning in the last ten years. Maybe this is because people are so stressed out by traveling today that doing it at 35,000 feet is the last thing on their minds. Or maybe passengers, like flight attendants, have gotten bigger or have become overly germaphobic. Or perhaps membership only *seems* to be on the decline because I now have enough seniority to hold something other than the red-eye flights, which tend to be popular with those looking to join the club.

One trend I've noticed (and, again, maybe it's the whole germaphobe thing) is that more and more mile-high members are avoiding the bathroom altogether, preferring to do the deed at their seat. They'll use a blanket to cover up, giggling and wiggling in the process, making a big public spectacle of themselves. As soon as one of us is clued in to what might be going on, we'll spread the word and each take turns slowly passing by their seat as we investigate the matter further. The couple will smile sheepishly, pretending they're not doing what they're oh-so-obviously doing. Or they might not even notice us at all until we stand at their row and loudly clear our throats. One flight attendant decided to make a couple's initiation into the club a little uncomfortable by continuously walking up and down the aisle with an illuminated flashlight. It's not actually illegal to engage in sexual activity on an airplane. But it is a federal offense not to comply with crew member instruction. What this means is if a flight attendant asks you to stop doing something, you need to stop doing it immediately or otherwise face the consequences, like authorities getting called to meet the flight.

Imagine being in jail and having to tell your cell mate what you're in for.

Not all passengers are looking to go all the way. A few are happy going just some of the way. I'm convinced that there's a female exhibitionist flying on the loose after walking in on a woman inside an unlocked lav. She just stood there, totally naked, with a leg up on the counter. I can't tell you how often people forget to lock the door, but normally they're still wearing most of their clothes and they're certainly not smiling when they're barged in on. Three months later, on a different route, I noticed a flustered passenger running from the direction of the bathroom back to his seat. After inquiring, he told me he'd walked in on a naked woman. Is it a coincidence that she also had a leg up in the air?

A friend of mine chose to ignore a passenger who massaged his seatmate's breast as he ordered lunch from a menu he held at chest level. What he didn't realize is we may not be able to see through things but we can certainly see over them. That's exactly what I told the man who tried to hide a pornographic magazine behind a safety briefing card. The two teenage girls snickering in the row behind him as they stood hovering over his shoulder were a dead giveaway. Later on in the flight I ran into the guy as he exited the lav, practically advertising what he'd been doing by carrying the same rolled-up magazine under his arm. Before I could avert my eyes from the disturbing evidence, he reached into a drawer of ice with what I hoped were clean hands and told me he worked as a producer on adult films. Handing me a business card, he wanted to know if I might be interested in getting involved in his next film—*Pearl*.

"What makes you think I'd be interested in doing something like that?!" I was shocked that he thought I was that kind of girl. Unable to make eye contact, but not wanting to seem overly prude, I busied myself with the cart and waited for an answer.

Smugly he smiled. "It pays five thousand dollars for a week's worth of work."

"That's it?" I asked. Not that it mattered.

Dangling what must have been the golden carrot, he added, "We're shooting it in Jamaica. Room and board is covered."

I've heard rumors of flight attendants getting involved in this sort of thing on the side, but rest assured, they do not remain employed for long. As you may have noticed, flight attendants talk, and as soon as an airline catches wind of something like a burgeoning adult film career, that flight attendant will be fired. And none of us is willing to risk losing our travel benefits! That's why most of us became flight attendants in the first place. Obviously Mr. Porn Producer had no idea that airline employees fly for free and get huge discounts on hotels and car rentals around the world—Jamaica included. And that's not all. Besides deals on airport food, cell phone service, luggage, amusement parks, and SkyMall gifts, we also get discounts on all kinds of crazy things like pet sitters, noise cancellation headsets, trucks, kitchen appliances, flowers, and memberships at gyms and superstores. There are even doctors who give special rates to crew, particularly dentists, dermatologists, and plastic surgeons—and I'm not talking about the ones in Brazil. All because we're free advertising and come into contact with a lot of people. Best of all, FedEx offers employees at my airline 75 percent off all our shipping needs, which comes in handy when we're overseas and need to ship something like a piece of furniture back to the States. Betcha a porn star working in Jamaica can't do that! Not to mention there's that little thing called longevity, as well as medical and retirement benefits. So while we may not make the big bucks for a week's worth of work, being a flight attendant does have its perks. And these perks certainly attract men.

Which brings me to the passes. I can always tell a man I'm dating is more interested in my travel perks than in me when he starts planning an extravagant trip on our first date to a place he's been dreaming about for years. This is equivalent to women talking marriage and babies with men they've just met. Talk about a great way to run someone off. What's worse is when a man tries to barter a room in his apartment for free flights. I've even had a woman jokingly ask if I'd be interested in polygamy just to get her hands on my passes. After we both stopped laughing, she inquired again. When people who are after my passes realize they've entered the point of no return and it's not looking good, they might come clean with their intentions. One guy informed me that his college roommate's mother had been a flight attendant, so he knew how the whole non-rev thing worked (wink wink). So as not to lose me, he then brought up how little I made as a flight attendant and said, "I can make it worth your while." I'm not selling passes, I'm looking for love! This is my cue to down my drink and walk out, never to look back again. Sometimes I'll even get the woe-is-me routine. One guy needed my passes because his sister was sick and she needed to see a doctor out of state. It's not hard to tell when a man wants me for me or if he's just looking to fly for free.

There's a popular phrase, MARRY ME, FLY FREE! I bought a T-shirt with that written across its back when I was working with Sun Jet. The phrase has since been changed to MARRY ME, FLY STANDBY! but I'm thinking MARRY ME, GET 20% OFF AT THE APPLE STORE might be a better promise. Let me put it to you this way, Bob, the stylish pilot, actually saves his standby passes for people he hates. Then he can gleefully relish when they get stranded in Senegal for ten days.

Buddy passes bring out the worst in strangers. I've had all kinds of people I didn't know hit me up for one: a mailman, a dental assistant, a lady working at a hardware store, a cabby with a wife still living in Pakistan, even a priest. Most people are surprised to learn that our buddy passes aren't free. In fact, nowadays a buddy pass costs almost as much as a full-fare ticket, because we have to pay taxes and fees on them. If I were to fly a friend on a buddy pass across the country in economy class, it would cost me nearly $200! And the money is automatically docked from my paycheck. That might not sound like a lot to some, but that's a new pair of work shoes for me. Anyway, would you trust a stranger to pay you back the money you need for the month's rent, food, and gas? Well, I'm no different, even if the stranger is a rabbi.

Flight attendants at my airline only get so many passes a year to distribute to family and friends. We don't just hand out tickets to anyone we want. We have to enter their names and Social Security numbers in a database. At my airline once a name is on the list it cannot be removed to make room for another name for twelve months. The only people who fly for free on a pass (or almost free, depending on the cabin they're sitting in and where they're going) are parents, spouses, and children under the age of eighteen, unless they're in college and then they can fly until they're twenty-one. Not even Grandma gets a break! And free applies only to coach seats on domestic flights, which are usually full, unless it's January, February, September, or October. Don't even think about traveling during a holiday or summer month. Even weekends are tough. If coach is full, even as an airline employee I have to pay to sit in first class. That's about eighty bucks on a cross-country flight, which, while really inexpensive in comparison to what a first-class ticket costs, adds up. Keep in mind most airline employees' midmonth check is about $500. We need that money to pay bills, not sip champagne.

Whether you're a flight attendant or one of our friends, there are rules to be followed when traveling standby. The biggest rule is not to bother the gate agents. They are there to help paying passengers, not standby passengers. Take a seat and patiently wait until your name is called—*hope* your name is called, would be a better way to describe it—before approaching the desk, but do know that won't happen until five minutes before the flight is to depart, which means by the time you hear your name only middle seats will be left and there will be no available space for your bag. Unless you're traveling with a small child, don't even think about trying to sit together. Or breaking the dress code while traveling on a pass. Shorts and flip-flops aren't allowed in coach, while jeans and sneakers cannot be worn in first or business. When standby passengers don't follow these rules, or try to argue about what they don't understand, the flight attendant who issued them the pass could lose his or her flying privileges for good. If you're a commuting flight attendant with no flying privileges, good luck!

Crazily enough, I've heard many times of spouses attempting to lay claim to the passes in a divorce settlement. In some cases courts have awarded it, but most airline policies won't allow it, regardless of court rulings. I heard a story about a flight attendant who requested her husband meet her in another country owing to a medical emergency. Because she had been living and working out of the country she used her flight benefits to get him there. When he landed, instead of finding an ailing wife, he was served with notice that she was filing for divorce. As soon as he flew back home she yanked his flying benefits. He couldn't fly back to South America on her passes to defend his property rights—or fight for the passes—because he couldn't afford the full-fare ticket.

When it became apparent I wasn't going to find what I was looking for in the cockpit or at a bar, I took my search for love online. Going by the name Skydoll, tag line "destination unknown," I quickly found my inbox swamped with emails from would-be suitors. It didn't take long to realize my profile—more specifically, my job—wasn't just attracting Mr. Wrong, but also Mr. Never-in-a-Million-Years. This doesn't seem to happen to pilots or male flight attendants. Or maybe it does and they just don't care, which is why you'll find so many of them posing in uniform in at least one of their profile pictures. One pilot turned out to be so successful at dating online he wound up getting hitched to a nurse and then starred in a nationwide Match.com television commercial with her. Female flight attendants, on the other hand, are a little less inclined to advertise the job because it turns out that a whole lot of guys have kinky ideas about the uniform. Don't believe me? Go to eBay and plug in two words: "flight attendant." There you'll find all kinds of airline paraphernalia, including used undergarments and work shoes worn by "a real flight attendant."

Genuine uniforms are not easy to come by. We are not allowed to give them away or even donate them to charity without first destroying any airline insignia on them. This way no one can impersonate us and do something crazy like, say, carry out a terrorist act! If a uniform item is stolen or goes missing, flight attendants are to file a police report, which is exactly what I did after I heard the door to my layover hotel room in Miami quietly shut and I awoke to find my closet door open and a uniform belt and vest missing. I'm not sure which disturbed me more; the fact that someone had come into my room while I slept or that someone wanted to wear my clothes.

A "full set" Japan Airlines vintage uniform (blouse, jacket, skirt, pumps, apron, nameplate, and stockings) can fetch as much as 280,000 yen (about $3,500), with well-worn items garnering premium prices. Female flight attendants from JAL are actually warned not to sell their outfits online to uniform fetish fans, and JAL requires flight attendants to return their uniforms at the end of their career. They even affix each one with a registration number inside, and it's been rumored that they might take it a step further and follow All Nippon Airways's footsteps by sewing microchips into uniform pieces. This all came about after some uniforms made their way into sex fetish clubs in Japan where people are willing to pay top dollar to live out a fantasy with an "entertainer" clad in an authentic airline uniform. Other than nurses, it's tough to think of another profession with as much dedicated pornography, which just reinforces the way people think of flight attendants. It's no wonder men have screwed up ideas about us—about me!

As soon as I realized how many men online were interested in me because of my job, I had no issue searching for hot jobs to date as well. Keywords like "doctor," "lawyer" and "PhD" resulted in quite a few amazing dates with many interesting men. I really hit it off with SexyErDoc who raved so often about how great my medical insurance was at one point I thought he might be more interested in my health-care plan than in me. And then it happened. The inevitable. On our third date he requested I put on the uniform.

"I'll show you mine if you show me yours," I teased. I thought we were joking. But when I got to his apartment and he answered the door wearing a stethoscope and only the top portion of his scrubs, I knew we had a problem. The skinny pantless legs still give me nightmares.

To be honest, the last thing flight attendants want to do on a day off is role-play like we're at work. Really, we don't get off on telling people what to do all the time. It's not fun having to remind passengers of the same things over and over again, like the electronic device policy before takeoff. Recently I had to tell sixteen passengers on a flight from Oklahoma to Chicago to turn their phones off, after having told them twice already! After a while it's kind of nice for someone else to be in control and take charge of a situation. I imagine a lot of doctors may feel the exact same way because CelebrityDoc didn't really seem all that interested in me until I told him off for yelling at a waitress who picked up his plate before he was finished. Everyone in the restaurant turned around to get a look at the ass across the table from me. I straightened myself up and in a quiet but stern voice told the doctor exactly how I felt about his poor behavior, but not without first demanding he apologize to the waitress or else have me make a scene as I stormed out. Surprisingly he did as he was told, and he did so rather jovially. The following morning he sent me a beautiful bouquet of flowers. I guess we all want someone else in charge some of the time.

Still, he was hardly the strangest. For example, I had no idea there were actually people out there who loved to worship flight attendant feet after a hard day at work until I met the podiatrist. He didn't tell me about his dirty little secret right away, but when he did it didn't bother me. What's the difference between that and butts or boobs? Nothing, that's what! Not to mention that, while I don't have big boobs, I do have nice feet. I couldn't believe I was dating a doctor who loved shoes and foot massages just as much as I did! It seemed like a match made in heaven. But after a while, it did get weird. I couldn't deal with the guy begging me to smash my pantyhosed feet into his contorted face after a long day at work every time I walked through the door. Everyone has their quirks, but that was just too much. Would you believe the podiatrist actually had the balls to ask me to refer my flight attendant friends to him after we broke up?

"You're crazy!" I told him, and slammed down the phone.

He called back, sweetening the deal by offering my friends 80 percent off orthotics! Well, that changed everything. I left his card tacked to the wall in flight operations.

Everything happens for a reason. I truly believe that. Because if not for the podiatrist, I might have actually mailed my work shoes off to an engineer I met on a flight. He told me he was a shoe cobbler on the side after he noticed my Mary Janes were in need of mending and he'd be willing to make them look as good as new for free.

"Pack them up and mail them to the address on my card," he said. He'd pay for shipping. Shoe cobbler, sure.

Eventually, I realized I might be better off meeting the man of my dreams on the plane instead of online. First class, business class, coach, I was an equal-opportunity dater. I didn't care where they were sitting, just as long as they were sitting with their seat belts fastened, even when the seat belt sign was not on. Hey, what's the big deal? I've seen enough TV to know that doctors date nurses, lawyers date court reporters, and the one with the corner office dates the one pouring the coffee. Where else was I going to meet men? On the airplane, flight attendants get to know people, *really* know them, when they're completely unaware of it. We see people when they're not dressed to impress or on their best behavior, and because we're in control of their safety and comfort, we know how they react at their most vulnerable.

They say you can tell a lot about people by the way they treat their mother. Turns out you can tell even more about them based on how they treat a flight attendant. Do they make eye contact? Do they say please and thank you? Are they polite when I run out of the beverage of their choice? Do they move the newspaper out of the way when I place a drink on their tray? Do they remove their earphones when I ask a question? Do they show respect to those who serve them? Do they show respect to the passengers seated around them? If the answer is yes, they're a winner! Major boyfriend potential.

"Whenever a passenger flirts with me, I just assume they want something for free: alcohol, headsets, whatever!" said a coworker after a super cute passenger slid me his number.

"Maybe they just want you," I suggested.

My coworker pushed his long blond bangs behind his ear and

sighed. "It would be nice to find a future ex-husband who could keep me in the lifestyle I'm unaccustomed to." When I laughed, he snapped his sassy fingers. "Gurrrl, I may be blond but I've got dark roots."

I pointed to my own dark roots. "I hear ya, sista!"

"And I'm not judging, sweetie."

Thank God for that.

But judge people do, including me, which is how I came to chat with a friendly lady on a flight from San Diego to New York. I knew she was nice based on the way she exclaimed "Happy Tuesday!" before I could welcome her on board, and I knew she was fun as soon as I spotted the hot pink hat on her head. Later on in flight she came to the back galley and asked for a glass of water. I brought up the hat.

"You know, you're the second person to compliment my hat today. A really nice guy standing in line at Starbucks said something to me about it and then he bought me a cup of coffee."

"Coffee? Oh, he liked you!" I said.

"Ya think? Oh no. I don't think so. Really?"

"Really. Listen, if there's one thing I know, besides uncomfortable seats and bad food, it's men. And strange men don't buy random women coffee at the airport. And they certainly don't notice cute hats. He just wanted to talk to you. Hey, is the guy on our flight?"

Pink Hat Lady wasn't sure, so she took a quick walk up the aisle to check. "He's in 22B."

"Wait here, I'm going to go analyze him for you." I picked up a plastic bag and walked to the front of the cabin, collecting garbage along the way.

Here's what I learned in five seconds about 22B. He had nice manners because when I asked if he'd like a refill, he said "No, thank you." Rarely does anyone say "please" and "thank you" anymore. He also made eye contact. A lot of passengers will just wave me away. This told me he had respect for people, regardless of what they did for a living. When he reached for his seatmate's empty cup to dispose of it for her since her arms were too short to reach, I knew he was kind and helpful. Most passengers will ignore one another, even if one of them is struggling with something—namely a bag. When I asked if he wanted me to dispose of what looked like top secret papers exploding out of his seat back pocket, he responded with something witty right back. A quick-witted and fun personality is always a plus in a man. The book he was reading had something to do with human anatomy. I assumed he was either a student, a professor, or a health professional.

"I like him," I told the Pink Hat Lady. "You two would make a good match."

She wasn't sure how to approach him, so I suggested that she walk over to him and thank him for the coffee this morning. Then I instructed her to tell him she'd like to reciprocate by buying him a beer or a snack, whichever he'd like. I was fairly certain he wouldn't take her up on the offer. I just wanted her to put the ball back in his court. Ten minutes later she came back to report that they were going to meet up in the terminal after the flight. A few weeks later I got a letter from her saying that they'd been emailing and had plans to visit each other. Just goes to show love really is in the air. And I was more than ever bound and determined to find it for myself!

13

Turbulence

THERE ARE FOUR types of turbulence: light, moderate, severe, and extreme. Light turbulence causes a slight, rapid, and somewhat rhythmic bumpiness without appreciable changes in altitude or attitude. Sometimes pilots refer to it as light chop. It's the kind that rocks babies to sleep, and even a few overworked flight attendants. The seat belt sign may be on, but flight attendants are still able to conduct the food service with little to no difficulty. Moderate turbulence is a little more intense. It causes rapid bumps or jolts without changes in aircraft altitude. Passengers will feel the strain of their seat belts. Unsecured objects in the galley may dislodge. Conducting a food service or checking for seat belt compliance is difficult. Severe turbulence causes large or abrupt changes in altitude. The aircraft may be momentarily out of control. Passengers are forced violently against their seats. Walking is impossible. If flight attendants haven't strapped into their jump seats already, we may not be able to do so and we'll have to grab the nearest available passenger seat. If there's not one open, we'll sit on a passenger—anyone will do. Make sure to hold on to us tightly. Extreme turbulence rarely happens, but when it does it will violently toss an aircraft about, making it practically impossible to control. Structural damage is possible.

There are probably a few nervous fliers who want to know just how rare extreme turbulence really is. I'll put it to you this way. Bob the stylish pilot has never experienced it in his twenty-six years of being a pilot for a major U.S. carrier, nor does he know any other pilot who has. I've been flying for sixteen years and I have yet to experience it myself. But once from New York to Los Angeles it became so bumpy on descent I had to hold on to a coworker who couldn't make it to her jump seat. A beverage cart fell over in galley. Soda, coffee, cups, napkins, and sugar spilled all over the floor. When it was over, the galley looked like a tornado had ripped through it. I had my arms wrapped so tightly around the flight attendant's waist that by the time we finally touched ground I could barely release my grip on her. My fingers were stiff and my colleague was bruised.

During another flight, one of my first flights I ever worked for Sun Jet, we encountered so much turbulence a passenger started screaming "I don't want to die!" This caused the others to start lighting up so they could have one last cigarette before we crashed. While cheap tickets attract passengers looking to save a buck, they don't always cover the cost of maintenance and upkeep, so the flickering side wall lights really set the mood. At one point even I began to feel like I was starring in my very own Stephen King horror movie at 35,000 feet. But because I was new and had never experienced any sort of turbulence before, I figured it had to be normal and did my best to put on a brave face for the passengers who watched my every move.

"Flight attendants take your seats!" the captain's voice boomed over the PA. Whenever you hear these five words it's probably going to be bad. I didn't have to run and buckle up because I had already done so.

From the front of the plane I could see some passengers clutching the armrests while others held hands across the aisle. With each dip

I heard moans and groans and even a few full-on screams, making a bad situation sound even worse. It's my job to keep the cabin calm, yet there's little I can do from my jump seat except reassure those sitting nearby that everything is going to be okay with a pleasant smile. But on that flight I wasn't so sure everything would be. It was so bumpy there was no way I could possibly get up to grab a bottle of halon and fight a fire if I had to!

"Put the cigarettes out!" I yelled from my jump seat. As soon as the words were out of my mouth I regretted saying them. The last thing I wanted was for someone to squash a lit cigarette into the flammable fabric covering the seat in front of them. Luckily, instead of doing as they were told, the smokers multiplied in number, puffing harder and faster as the lights blinked off and on and we jolted from side to side.

Later on, I learned two airplanes in front of us had aborted landing. That didn't deter our captain from attempting his approach into Love Field Airport. With thunder and lightning all around, he somehow managed to get the aircraft on the ground, but not without hitting the runway so hard it felt like the aircraft might split in half. As we taxied to the gate, passengers began jumping out of their seats and running toward the front door, screaming "Let me off this flight!" Problem was, there was nowhere for them to go. The airport was closed.

My coworker, a senior mama with only two years under her belt, firmly instructed me to keep the passengers back when the airplane came to a complete stop while she cracked the door open to allow a little fresh air inside to dissipate the smell of vomit. Although it was one of my first flights, even then a twenty-foot plunge in stormy weather didn't seem so bad compared to what we had to deal with now: an airplane full of sick and angry passengers on the verge of revolt. That's when the captain announced the unthinkable. He informed us over the PA that we had diverted to an airport a few minutes away from the one we were scheduled to land at, which meant that as soon as the storm passed we'd have to do it all over again!

Half the passengers had had enough and decided to abandon ship—er, plane, once the airport opened two hours later, leaving behind checked bags that would accompany us to DFW Airport. An agent had to escort them across the tarmac to the terminal while fighting to hold onto an umbrella blown inside out over their heads.

I didn't realize how serious our situation had truly been until I spotted the captain sitting in the cockpit staring straight ahead. His pale face isn't what scared me. What freaked me out was his white button-down shirt that was now drenched with sweat.

Although turbulence doesn't scare me, I have been frightened in the air more than once. I've experienced aborted landings and takeoffs and even landing gears that wouldn't go down, but that didn't scare me, either. I'm kind of embarrassed to tell you about my scariest flight of all time because nothing even happened. It was just a feeling of impending doom. I truly thought we were all going to die. I didn't get nervous until we began our descent into Los Angeles and I happened to look out the window and noticed we were unusually low over the ocean. It was 3:00 a.m. The thought of ditching an aircraft into the water totally freaks me out. For one I'm a horrible swimmer. But that's not what frightened me. What worried me was who in the world would be up and alert and ready to rescue an airplane full of passengers floating off the coast of California that early in the morning? Not to mention it was December. I figured if we plunged into that freezing cold water we'd only have a minute to stop hyperventilating from the "gasp reflex" and control our breathing. Maybe ten minutes of purposeful movement before our muscles went numb and unresponsive. About an hour before hypothermia would lead to unconsciousness. Maybe two hours before profound hypothermia caused death. The aircraft was equipped with slide rafts, but

I worried about the slides not inflating. And if they did inflate, would I be able to find the knife embedded on the raft used to cut the rope attached to the sinking aircraft? Not if I accidentally fell into the water and became blind from all the fuel contaminating the ocean.

And they hadn't taught us anything about sharks in flight attendant training! Oh, how I hoped I hadn't nicked my legs while shaving earlier that morning. Silently I began to pray, making promises to God I knew I couldn't keep. At some point I came to the conclusion that if I did become the victim of a late-night shark snack attack, it would be probably safe to assume my career as a flight attendant was over since there weren't any one-legged flight attendants that I knew of. Since then, I have in fact met a one-legged flight attendant. She has a prosthetic leg and has been flying with it for twenty-three years. Which just goes to show you should never lose hope, even when faced with a terrible situation. And that, dear reader, is the point I wanted to make. But I know you're more interested in how my scariest flight ever ended. To make a long story short, we landed without a problem. Later on, I found out the reason the landing felt "off" was because after a five-hour delay followed by a change in equipment, the baggage handlers forgot to load the bags, so the plane's weight and balance was off. According to a pilot not working the flight, we should have been flying higher, not lower, than usual that night I saw my life flash before my eyes, making my scariest flight ever one that couldn't possibly happen under the circumstances.

More than a million people travel by air every day, and yet only three people have died in the last twenty-eight years as a direct result of turbulence. According to the Federal Aviation Administration, from 1980 to 2008 there were 234 accidents involving turbulence, resulting in 298 serious injuries and 3 fatalities. Of the three fatalities, two passengers were not wearing their safety belt while the seat belt sign was illuminated. Of the 298 seriously injured, 184 involved were flight attendants. Each year approximately 58 passengers in the United States are injured from turbulence by not wearing their seat belts, while 10,000 passengers are allegedly injured by falling luggage.

During turbulence, there's such a difference between the front and the back of the aircraft that I've had to call a few pilots to let them know they needed to turn the seat belt sign on. We're rocking and rolling in the back, liquids spilling all over the place, and the pilots sometimes have no idea. Without the seat belt sign illuminated, I can't suggest to Mom and Dad that it might be a good idea to pick up their sleeping baby off the floor without completely offending them. I'm always amazed by the number of parents who are reluctant to sit a child up and strap them in for fear of waking them up when the seat belt sign comes on. I've even seen some pass newborn infants across the aisle to someone else or play a game of bouncy-bounce—up in the air! It's a wonder I haven't seen a baby turn into a football. What's worse are passengers who decide to stand up and get into overhead bins full of heavy luggage as soon as the seat belt sign turns on. Now, instead of just putting themselves at risk, they've included whoever else is seated nearby. I can't come to the rescue if I'm strapped in my jump seat. My priority is to keep from being injured so I can operate the exit doors in case of an emergency. It's because of this kind of behavior that one captain I know seldom turns the seat belt sign off. He claims he doesn't always know when it's going to be choppy and he believes it's too crowded in the aisles to keep it off. The guy has a point. Whenever flight attendants start bugging him about letting people get up, he'll remind them that passengers tend to ignore the sign anyway, and he has no desire to be a part of their lawsuit when they fall and get injured.

It's a fact that people love to sue airlines. A woman once sued because she lost her psychic powers after an in-flight videocassette tape fell out of an overhead bin and hit her on the head. Things shift in flight. Be careful when opening overhead bins. Another passenger sued the airline because his wife filed for divorce after he became impotent as a direct cause of a flight attendant rubbing his thigh with a paper towel after spilling a little coffee on him. Why so many passengers order hot beverages when it's bumpy is beyond me. In 2000 the *Los Angeles Times* reported a story about thirteen passengers who sued American Airlines after going through a rough patch of air turbulence that lasted twenty-eight seconds. The seat belt sign had not been turned on. No one involved in the lawsuit suffered physical injuries, but they did claim psychological trauma and demanded $2.25 million. The judge held the airline liable, and each person was awarded approximately $175,000. What I find most interesting about the case is two of the people named in the lawsuit are related to an Oscar Award–winning director. I can't help but wonder if that made an impact on the judge. I can certainly say the court ruling had an effect on me. So don't take it personally when I politely, but firmly, remind you the seat belt sign is on.

When the seat belt sign comes on, it's the flight attendants' job to make sure passengers are safely buckled up, but a lot of times it's too bumpy for us to do so. That doesn't stop a lot of us from trying. Former flight attendant Mary underwent several surgeries after being injured during four different turbulent flights. In 1978, and again in 1999, Mary herniated her lower disc after she hit the ceiling during clear air turbulence (CAT), which happens when bodies of air moving at wildly different speeds meet. CAT can happen unexpectedly, even when the seat belt sign is not on. After a turbulent flight in 2001 she had surgery on her back and left arm. In 2008 she underwent two hip surgeries. In 2003 my airline changed its injury on duty (IOD) policy. It was decided that in order to receive pay for an IOD the turbulence had to be considered severe. Because the turbulence during Mary's last flight was not considered severe enough, even though two other flight attendants were also injured, she had to use sick hours to cover time lost from work. After a year on the IOD list (even without IOD pay), a flight attendant loses medical coverage since we have to fly a certain number of hours to qualify for benefits. So after thirty-four years as a flight attendant Mary was forced to retire at the age of fifty-six because she didn't have health insurance. With retirement she qualified for retiree medical benefits.

Most injured flight attendants at my airline who find themselves in Mary's position aren't so lucky in that they are too young to qualify for retiree benefits. It's mind-boggling to me that I could be injured at work but the injury might not be classified as an IOD unless the captain loses control of the airplane or the airplane sustains structural damage. In either of those cases, the aircraft must be grounded and inspected. That's lost revenue for the airline. No captain wants to be held accountable for that! I'm sure you can see the writing on the wall. A friend of mine who works closely with airline management said he's never once seen a pilot label rough air as "severe turbulence." So if you see flight attendants sitting in our jump seats when it starts to get bumpy, we're just trying to make sure we're not going to be forced into early retirement!

If there's mild turbulence and a nervous passenger questions flight attendant Beth on how she tolerates it, she'll lighten the mood by telling them that in training we had to learn to walk on a tightrope to increase our balancing skills. Most of them actually believe her! Before my friend Vicki retired, she'd tell passengers she practiced her serving skills by jumping on a trampoline while holding a tray full of drinks. I'm probably the only person who believes her, but this is because I actually know her. In the past, I used to reassure fearful fliers that airplanes don't just break in half. But then Air France Flight 447 did exactly that in 2009. It's still unclear whether significant turbulence due to a series of storms in the area, a lightning strike, or something about frozen pilot tubes caused the airplane to "disappear." So now I just tell passengers to keep their seat belts fastened and everything will be A-OK. Depending on the type of rapport we may have, I might add a very unusual but quite interesting fact I've heard about dying on an airplane. More people have been killed falling off donkeys than by dying in an airplane crash.

What most nervous fliers don't realize is, turbulence is normal and it can occur even when the sky appears clear. If you are a nervous flier, don't be embarrassed to let the crew know during boarding. Flight attendants are trained professionals. If we know you're scared we'll go out of our way to be reassuring if the airplane does encounter a few bumps. I've gone so far as to sit in an empty seat beside someone and hold their hand. It's better not to wait until you're clutching the armrest for dear life and sweating profusely with each bump to let us know who you are. If there's time during boarding we might be able to introduce you to the cockpit. Pilots are better able to calm nerves by letting passengers know what to expect in terms of when it will happen, why it happens, and for how long it's scheduled to last. Aircraft fishtail during turbulence, making the back of the airplane much bumpier than the front, so one good trick is to book a seat as close to the cockpit as possible. If that's not possible, get to the airport early so an agent can switch your seat to a more desirable location. Airlines block the best seats for frequent fliers. Frequent fliers use miles to upgrade and a lot of times their upgrades don't go through until the last minute, so be patient with the agent if they ask you to have a seat in the terminal. If that doesn't work, tell a flight attendant what's wrong and we'll try to move you. Also, don't forget to count the number of rows from your seat to the closest exit door or window. If something does happen and it's dark, you'll be able to feel your way to safety.

While passengers dread turbulence, what leaves flight attendants shaking are in-flight confrontations. It's a really big deal for us to walk off a flight or even have a passenger removed. Really, we do not enjoy rocking the boat—or in this case, the plane—but sometimes we have to. There's no calling the cops or the fire department or an ambulance at 35,000 feet, which is why we always try to take care of potential problems on the ground.

Does it come as a surprise to learn intoxicated passengers have a tendency to turn into trouble after a few too many? The reason they seem tipsier in the air than on the ground is because of lower oxygen levels in the blood. The same amount of alcohol goes a lot further at 35,000 feet. While rarely a threat to the safety of the aircraft, unless of course they're threatening to shoot the flight crew with a 9mm handgun like one drunken passenger did on a flight from Cuba, they do have a tendency to wreak havoc. I'm positive this is one reason why it's against FAA regulations for an airline to board someone who appears to be intoxicated. If an airline gets caught knowingly doing so, they will be issued a fine.

It's not hard to spot inebriated passengers when they walk on board and announce, "Let's party and have some drinks!" Those we know to keep an eye on. It's the quiet ones we have to worry about, the ones who ask for a cup of ice, and that's it. That's a big red flag that there might be a little something-something hidden somewhere. Like bartenders, we're responsible if anything bad happens to passengers who've had a few too many drinks after they leave our flight. That's why we don't allow passengers to bring their own booze on board, why we don't automatically serve free drinks when there's a delay, and why we'll cut people off if we feel they've had enough.

It's not always possible for a few of us to keep tabs on so many of you, so some people do squeak by. For instance, after serving a very large first-class passenger not *that* many Jack and Cokes, we couldn't stop him from coming into the galley and eating leftover shrimp tails (i.e., garbage) he picked off used passenger meal trays we were stacking back inside the carts after the dinner service. Then there was the elderly woman who drank four vodkas within an hour after takeoff. I had no idea my coworker had just served the sweet old lady a double when she flagged me down and asked for "two of those cute little bottles." Once we realized our mistake, it was too late. Our crazy little granny with the thick Irish accent was attempting to christen the entire coach cabin with water from the lav on her dripping hands. When one of my colleagues tried to talk her into taking a seat (near the back of the cabin so we could keep an eye on her), she screamed something I will not repeat about my colleague being gay. I don't know what surprised me more, Granny's potty mouth or the fact that my coworker didn't have the gay mafia waiting for her after our flight. I also always love the passengers who use their seat back pocket and/or that of their neighbor, as a barf bag. And the ones who lock themselves inside the one and only first-class lavatory —and never come out.

One hot young thing, determined to talk a couple of male passengers into buying her drinks, once made the rounds on a flight overseas until one of my coworkers confronted the underage girl in the galley. The girl responded by punching my colleague in the face. Now, if that had been me I don't know what I would have done, but my Puerto Rican coworker, a petite young thing herself, didn't skip a beat. I can't tell you what happened next, but I will say I just stood there stunned because girlfriend had just messed with the wrong flight attendant.

But my all-time favorite was the sharply dressed man who took a seat in the exit row after staggering onto the airplane with an open container of alcohol. Of all the seats the guy could sit in . . . I asked him to hand it over, but instead of doing as told, he guzzled it down and burped in my face. Then he wanted to argue about why he couldn't bring his own booze on board. As I was reminding him that most businesses do not allow open containers of liquor, he passed out, head smack against the tray table.

Drunk passengers aren't the only problem. In San Francisco, an agent was called to remove a passenger who was so out of it during boarding that she couldn't even find her seat, let alone walk down the aisle without assistance from some lucky passenger who just happened to be standing in line behind her. The whacky behavior, I'm sure, had something to do with sleeping pills, since we were on a red-eye flight headed back to New York. But because passengers have to be conscious (and wearing shoes) when they come on board, the woman was taken off and rebooked on the next flight the following morning—that is, assuming she found her shoes. Smart passengers will wait until after takeoff before using sleeping aides. Flight attendants appreciate this because there's always a chance there will be a mechanical issue and we'll have to go back to the gate and deplane. It's hard enough waking someone who has chased down two Ambien with a shot of whatever they were drinking at the airport bar without having to explain to them where they are, again, and why they have to get off the airplane—again. If the backpacker who fell asleep during boarding hadn't missed the captain's announcement about the three-hour delay, he wouldn't have been so confused when he finally came to and noticed we were at the gate—wow, so early! He assumed we had landed. I'm the one who had to break it to him at the aircraft door that we never even took off. Sighing, he went back to his seat and popped another pill. Flight attendants are capable of doing a lot of things, but during an emergency evacuation, there's no way we're going to be able to drag half a plane full of disoriented, limp noodles by the ankles through a smoke-filled cabin and down the slide. Hard to believe, I know.

And then there are the limp noodles who eventually turn cold and gray and, well . . . if anyone asks, they're just "resting." I say this because no one officially dies on an airplane, no matter how dead they actually are. When a person passes away they're still considered "incapacitated" until a doctor makes an official pronouncement. Thirty years ago, my friend Vicki, who had never had a passenger die during one of her flights, noticed a man who was clearly asleep (wink wink). So as not to distress the rest of the passengers, she placed a gin and tonic and an opened bag of nuts on his tray table. Knowing Vicki the way I do, she probably chatted him up a few times for appearances. Depending on who's asking, she'll even swear she saw him take a sip of that drink. That's her story and she's *still* sticking to it.

Not everyone is as smooth as Vicki. During descent on a Sun Jet flight, one of my coworkers noticed a passenger with his seat all the way back. She asked him to put it up and quickly discovered he, well, couldn't. Without hesitating, she dragged his lifeless body into the aisle, hiked up her tight skirt, straddled him in a way that would have made any living man envious, and started doing CPR. When paramedics came on board to take him off, she was still going at it. She couldn't stop. Paramedics had to pull her off. Later on she got in trouble for not being in her jump seat during landing, an FAA regulation.

My only close call with death happened on one of my first international trips. I don't remember where we were flying to but, man oh man, the food looked delicious, so much better than it did on the domestic routes. In hindsight I realize I was probably just hungry as I was fairly new and broke at the time. But back then I honestly couldn't imagine anyone wanting to miss out on something that looked so good, which is why I confidently tapped a sleeping woman on the shoulder to wake her up. When that didn't work, I rubbed her arm. Then I lifted her hand and let it fall—that is, flop—down on her lap. *Uh-oh.* Nervously I glanced at my coworker. Based on the way his eyes were bugging out of his head, I knew he was thinking exactly what I was thinking. Silently he grabbed her by both arms and gave her a good shake. No response. Our facial expressions must have said it all, because that's when the woman sitting next to her jumped up and started screaming, "Oh my God! Oh my God! Oh my God!"

We checked for a pulse. We checked for breathing. We cleared the row of passengers and were just about to get her body flat on the ground when out of nowhere her husband, who unbeknown to us had been seated a few rows back, appeared and jabbed her in the neck with a knuckle—at least that's what it looked like he did. At once her eyes popped open and upon seeing us all hovering over her she began to giggle uncontrollably. My heart was beating so fast I thought I might have a heart attack myself. It's not every day you're serving drinks and then have a dead lady on your hands. Nor is it every day you have a dead lady come back to life, then have to go right back to serving drinks—with a smile. Right then and there, I swore I'd never bother another sleeping passenger again! In coach, that is. I didn't care how dead they looked.

Most passengers prefer sleeping to eating, if they're already asleep that is—until they come to and realize what they wanted to eat is no longer available. I've been scolded for waking passengers up. And I've been scolded for *not* waking them up. In coach, I'll leave sleepers alone. The food, if there's any on board, is not worth waking up for. But in first and business class it's a different story. Not because the food is all that, but because they've paid a lot of money for a seat and have unrealistic expectations about the service. Now, if I'm the one taking meal preferences after takeoff, I'll play it safe and gently touch their arm so later on, when they wake up and become upset because there's nothing good left to eat, I can at least say that I tried. That said, I wasn't quite sure what to do when I came upon one guy snoozing in business class. His black T-shirt had me confused because it had the word AWAKE printed in big, bold, white letters right across his chest. Pen and paper in hand, I stood there a good minute contemplating whether or not this was a personal message worn specifically for this moment so he wouldn't miss out on the chicken or beef. And it's because of that stupid shirt I came to the incorrect conclusion the guy had a sense of humor.

"Can't you see I'm sleeping!" he yelled.

"I'm sorry, it's just, well, normally I don't wake people up, but your shirt . . ."

He turned all the way around in the big, cushy, leather seat so I could read the back. Turns out, AWAKE was not a comment on his state of consciousness on the airplane but the title of a movie I'd never heard of.

Most flight attendants love when passengers fall asleep, as a quiet cabin is a happy cabin. The exception to this rule is when a passenger falls asleep on the floor in the middle of the aisle. That can only mean one thing: medical emergency. Imagine my surprise when I walked out of the business class galley with a couple of drinks on a silver linen-lined tray and noticed that every single passenger on my side of the cabin had turned all the way around in their seat and was now staring at me. No one moved a muscle. No one said a word. There were just fourteen pairs of eyes wide open. That's when I noticed the woman on the floor. As I ran to her side, I ordered another flight attendant to page for a doctor.

When it comes to medical emergencies, I've been pretty lucky in that there have always been a few medical professionals on board willing to volunteer their services. Whether they're a group of doctors on their way to a medical convention or a couple of flight attendants who once worked in nursing or as EMTs, there's usually someone, besides me, who can help. But this time I wasn't so lucky. No one rang their call light. I asked the flight attendant to try again, and again, as some medical professionals will wait a few seconds in hopes that someone else will respond so they won't have to.

Thank God, I thought, when I heard not one, but two call lights ring. The man in the button-down shirt across the aisle turned out *not* to be a doctor, dammit! He wanted to know if he could get another gin and tonic. The woman sitting in first class also turned out not to be in the medical field, but just a concerned passenger, which would have been nice if what she cared about hadn't been whether whatever was going on in the back would affect her connecting flight! In the meantime the unconscious woman came to, passed out again, and then came to again—and thankfully stayed that way. I learned she was an up-and-coming fashion designer who hadn't eaten all week, so I handed her a wheat roll and went back to work. The most disturbing thing for me was not one person who had witnessed the event inquired about her well-being. They were more concerned about drink refills and whose tray I would take away first since they'd all been waiting a long time and needed to get back to work.

Although I dread medical emergencies, I'll take one any day over a New York–Miami flight. Demanding, ballbusting, ick, hellacious, unfrigginbelievable, avoid, and the F word are a few of the words my coworkers use to describe the route. Lycratubetop and Sickcall deserve an honorable mention. It's one of the most, if not *the most*, difficult routes in the system. Flight attendant Sherly needs Prosac, Valium, and a shot of vodka after just *thinking* about working the trip. The problem stems from combining passengers possessing two completely different yet very strong personalities. Mix them with the most junior flight attendants inside a confined space for two and a half hours, and you better believe there's going to be drama!

I make it a point to avoid the route altogether, but if I do get the city pairing on reserve, I try my best not to smile during boarding. It's essential to set the tone for the flight. I don't want anyone to come to the (correct) conclusion that I'm the one they can walk all over. These passengers seem to come with the mindset of whoever yells the loudest wins. They think the nice one is the weak link, as well as the ticket to free booze, and depending on how badly they've abused the crew, sometimes they're right. One New York–based crew fought back by refusing to work after passengers booed them in the terminal for arriving late to the gate. It wasn't the crew's fault their inbound flight had been delayed taking off from wherever they had flown in from, causing a domino effect for flights using the same equipment (and crew) later on in the day. Passengers sometimes mistakenly think there are extra airplanes lying around the airport waiting to be had when a situation like this occurs, but there aren't, and the best you can do is just go with the flow and try to relax. Instead, this particular group of obnoxious passengers caused the crew to deem the environment too hostile to work. They walked off the airplane and refused to go back to work, forcing the airline to call out reserves to staff the trip, delaying the flight even longer. And that's just one New York–Miami flight.

Still, New York and Florida aren't the only states with a reputation. Thanks to Eagle County Airport, the gateway to Vail, Colorado, has a bad rap, too. In fact the New York–Vail route is so bad a friend of mine will take Miami any day and every day over that crowd, "the worst bunch of selfish A-holes in the world," she says. This from a girl I'd never before heard curse! But I know how she feels. It's a route where every single person sitting in coach truly believes she (or he) should be in first class. And they're irked about it, too, from the moment they step on board wearing Chewbacca boots and carrying Louis Vuitton luggage to the time the plane touches ground and they're calling their drivers and ordering the nannies to gather their belongings. PETA would have a field day if they took one of these flights. The full-length furs are out of control! I'll never forget the lady who called me over and then silently turned her back to me. It took a few seconds before I realized she expected me to help her take off her mink coat. Because the tiny closet in first class isn't big enough to house more than a handful of these furry monstrosities, and because nobody is willing to stow them inside an overhead bin, they wind up on laps of sulking owners who are upset about the inconvenience. They take it out on me by *not* ordering a drink because there's not enough room to get their tray table down. Life is really tough sometimes.

The thing about problem passengers that bothers me the most is they always seem to have problems (thus, the name). When problem passengers are on board they'll take up all our time, as if they're the only passengers on board. Usually they make themselves known right away, either by having to be told several times to turn off an electronic device before takeoff or by complaining about a passenger who has reclined his seat right after takeoff.

A quick aside here on reclining: anti-recliners need to understand that all passengers are allowed to recline their seats, even during the meal service. (Although I've heard there are some foreign carriers that do require the seats to be put back up during the meal service.) Of course, recliners should be mindful of the way in which they recline. We see laptops get damaged all the time by speedy recliners who whip back and break the computer screen leaning against their chair. And if you're an anti-recliner, do not block the recliner with your knees or threaten to punch him in the face if he reclines one more time. This is not acceptable behavior on or off an airplane. As for those seat-blocking devices that attach to the tray table and keep the seat in front from leaning back, leave them at home. We will confiscate them. Flight attendants hear more complaints about recliners from anti-recliners than anything else. A woman wearing Coke-bottle glasses called me over to show me she could not put down her tray table because of the seat in front of her. I suggested that perhaps if she removed the very large fanny pack from around her waist it might go down. By the way she looked at me, you'd think I was the crazy one. And don't even get me started on the big guy who had the nerve to complain about a recliner even though his own seat was reclined!

As far as bad passengers go, Tony Last-Name-Starts-with-a-D (not Danza) is by far the worst I've ever encountered in my fifteen years of flying. I should have known he'd be a problem the moment he stepped on board, considering he was the first person to walk on the plane and he wasn't even sitting in first class. Even though all the overhead bins were empty, he wanted to stow his rolling bag in the first-class closet and became angry when I wouldn't allow him to do so. It's against FAA rules to stack bags in the closet and it was already filled with my crew bag and a passenger's wheelchair the agent had brought down earlier. I tried to explain this to him but he wasn't having it. He stormed off and threw his bag inside a first-class bin. I asked him to take it down and find another bin in coach closer to his seat. Even though it's first come, first served when it comes to overhead space, first-class bins are only for first-class passengers, who, incidentally, get boarded first. He knew that, but he got pissed off about it anyway. We were off to a great start. For the rest of the flight it was one thing after another, starting with my insufficient explanation about our twenty-minute weather delay on the ground to the alcoholic drink he wasn't allowed to finish because we were on descent and about to land. As I passed him on my way to my jump seat, he reached out and grabbed my wrist roughly.

"I want your name!"

I gave it to him. I even spelled it out for him. Then I went up to the front to grab the list of passenger names, which comes in handy during times like this. All I'd done was what the airlines hired me to do, so I wasn't worried. But it was his word against mine, and because I didn't trust him I wanted to write my own letter to explain how it really went down.

Well, life happens and sometimes we just forget to write those letters we had every intention of writing. What doesn't usually happen is that we run into the very person we had planned on

writing about a week later in a totally different city, just as he is
cutting the line to talk to the gate agent. I wasn't on the clock, so
I wasn't wearing anything navy, flammable, or polyester. That
day I was just a regular (standby) passenger trying to get home,
which is probably why Lance didn't recognize me when we first
locked eyes. But I must have looked familiar because he actually
smiled at me. Too stunned to do anything else I smiled back, but
just barely.

I don't know how to explain what happened next. I've said it
before and I'll say it again, I'm not a confrontational person—I'm
not! But something weird happened to me that day. My feet suddenly began to move my body toward Lance. As if in a movie, he
shifted to face me, and if you didn't know us you might mistake
us for long lost-friends, or even worse, lovers. Before I knew it I
was almost upon him and that's when I heard the dreaded words
come out of my mouth.

"Ya write that letter yet, Lance?" And my feet kept walking,
while my heart pounded double-time and my brain wondered
what the heck my mouth had done! I regretted it as soon as I had
said it. I really did.

He sounded more like a volcanic eruption than a human being,
"FUUUUUUUUUUUCK YOOOOUUUUUU—YOU—YOU—YOU—
YOU!"

The agent pulled me off the flight. Three managers were called
to the gate to take care of the disturbance—me! At least that's
how the agent had made it seem. Lance wanted my job, and every
single person traveling through the terminal that day knew it. I
probably would have gotten into pretty big trouble if Lance had
been able to calm down at some point, but I had pushed him
over the edge and there was no coming back. Even the managers
seemed a little taken back by his behavior. Eager to put an end to
it, one of them assured him they'd take care of me and then sent
him on his miserable way. As for me, my punishment was having

to fly back to New York via Newark because the last flights to LaGuardia and JFK had just departed with Lance and without me. Flying into Newark Airport is pure torture for flight attendants living in Queens because of the amount of time and cash it takes to get home, which means in the end Lance kind of won.

Or maybe I won, because the lesson learned by far outweighed the two and a half hours lost and the sixty bucks spent making the trek back home. Problem passengers are problem passengers and nothing is going to change that. We can't take nasty passenger behavior personally and truly, for every jerk there's a plane full of wonderful passengers. So when a similar situation occurred the following week, I considered it a test of my new-found knowledge.

It was my last leg of the day and I had been assigned to dead-head to New York out of Miami in first class. No sooner had I taken my seat when the agent came down to tell me a first-class passenger had checked in at the last minute so she had to switch my seat to one in coach, an aisle in the bulkhead row. I collected my things and moved a few rows back.

"I wanted to sit there! Why does she get to sit there? She's an employee!" whined a voice a few rows behind me.

"I'm so sorry," said a working flight attendant leaning in close to me, "But a passenger is really upset that you're sitting here. Would you mind switching seats?"

I had no problem switching seats. But it had been a really long day, I was exhausted after working a ten-hour shift, and he was still complaining in that annoying voice about why the airline would treat an employee better than a passenger. As I bent over to collect my things for a second time, I might have mumbled, "What a jerk."

"What did you say?!" said the voice. Oh God. I stayed low, pretending to be still collecting my things. "Did you just call me a jerk?"

I didn't know how he had heard it or why he seemed to think that the other flight attendant had said it. Slumping down in my seat, I stayed that way while the flight attendant tried to calm him down. When that didn't work, the flight attendant went to get the captain who came back and tried to rationalize with the guy, who then made the major mistake of calling the captain a fucking idiot. This is a great way to get kicked off a plane, and that is exactly what happened. Five days later, I kid you not, the exact same passenger wound up sitting in the row directly behind mine on a flight from Chicago. I kept my head down and didn't dare ask if he'd written a letter yet. I never wanted to have to fly back through Newark again! As I said, lesson learned. Confrontation avoided for a turbulent-free flight.

There's No Respect Flying Domestic

Working to Seattle today. When I get back tomorrow night I'm taking you out to celebrate. Happy Birthday!

Love, Jane

P.S. Enjoy your day off with Yakov! ☺
P.S.S. I'm evil, I know. Sorry.

FOUND THE YELLOW Post-it note stuck to the mirror in the bathroom. It was noon. I had just woken up. Based on the deafening silence, I had the house all to myself. Normally I would have been thrilled, but today wasn't just any day. It was my birthday. I wanted to cry. I'd been doing a lot of reflecting and analyzing in the weeks leading up to the big cake-eating event, and I'd come to the conclusion that life sucked. I had no life. No friends. Not even a steady boyfriend! I was spending my twenty-sixth birthday all alone in Queens, New York, with my cab driver landlord and his border collie who didn't want anything to do with me regardless of how many of Jane's organic dog treats I offered her.

By the way, did I mention Yakov had moved in? As in *into* the house with us. Oh yeah, out of the dungeon and into the front room where Jane used to live before Tricia got engaged and moved out to be with the man she always dreamed of. We were in the process of reshuffling bedrooms so those with the most crash pad seniority could occupy the best rooms when we discovered that Yakov had installed not one, but three deadbolt locks on the bedroom door, not so quietly claiming the tiny space for himself. It happened so quickly Jane didn't even have time to post the ROOMMATE WANTED—NO DRAMA PLEASE! sign up on the bulletin board in flight operations at LaGuardia Airport. If that wasn't bizarre enough, Yakov then hung white paper over the front window so we couldn't see in. More disturbing than that was the XL brown terry cloth robe I found hanging in the coat closet right next to my wool work coat.

"Whose is this?" I asked, holding up the ratty thing. Jane covered her mouth with both hands and that's when I knew. Immediately I dropped it on the floor.

"I'll get the Lysol," offered Jane. That's what friends are for.

So while my ex-roommate Tricia spent her days planning a lavish wedding in the Hamptons to a pint-sized bazillionaire she'd met on a flight, I spent my birthday doing laundry and eating a can of chicken noodle soup. All alone. In a house I shared living space with five other women and a plus-sized Russian Hugh Hefner wannabe in Queens. Why didn't I pick up a trip? That way I could have been miserable and angry about having to fly on my birthday instead of feeling lonely and depressed while not working on my birthday. Feeling down in the dumps, I did what any other single girl in her midtwenties would do. I called my mother.

"What do you mean you have no life?" my mother exclaimed

over the phone from Dallas. I could hear my sister laughing in the background. "Didn't you just fly in from Paris this morning?!"

She had a point. Which reminded me I had a jar of Nutella chocolate and a day-old flakey croissant from Paris still inside my unpacked bag. As well as a forgotten bottle of El Yucateco hot sauce and six packages of $5 birth control pills I had bought on a whim the week before during a three-hour sit in Mexico City. Happy birthday to me.

People with regular jobs aren't very understanding when flight attendants complain about their lives. Our bad days automatically sound good if we're able to toss in words like Paris, Buenos Aires, Rome, and Madrid into random sentences on a regular basis. Even if we don't fly to those kinds of places, people automatically assume that we do. Sadly the majority of flight attendants get stuck working cities like Dallas, Dulles, and Denver instead. Not that there's anything wrong with Dallas, Dulles, or Denver. It's just that when we're flying to one of the three Ds, we won't have to advise passengers how to inflate the life vest because those cities, like most domestic cities, aren't located over or near water.

Seniority is everything at an airline and those who have it take full advantage of it by flying international routes, making the rest of us suffer in their glamorous wake. I don't blame them. One day I, too, hope to have enough years under my thin blue belt to work all the best trips and make junior flight attendants (and some passengers) cry by not retiring when *they* think I should. Why retire when all I'll have to do is work two five-day trips to Narita each month? Gardening is nice, but so is eating sushi with real wasabi and shopping in the Ginza district! Until then you'll find me laying over in St. Louis with nothing to do except browse the Hustler store or go to Denny's for the early-bird, super-bird special. Both establishments are located directly across the street from our airport layover hotel, right next to a cemetery that, if I'm desperate enough, doubles as a running path.

Whenever I tell anyone where I'm going or where I've been, I can see the disappointment in their eyes. There's no respect flying domestic! It's like comparing Walmart to Barneys. My friend Melanie can tell international flight attendants from domestic ones based on the shopping bag hanging off the back of their roll-aboard alone—Harrods versus Trader Joe's. No one wants to hear about my layover in Orange County spent eating fish tacos and wandering around a high-end mall when my roommate Dee Dee is talking about lying on a beach that has its own Barry Manilow song.

Hey, I get it, because I feel the same way about foreign-based flight attendants. Their lives can't be all that much different from mine, yet they seem so much more exciting and glamorous, even when they end up on the opposite side of the same hotel pool. Perhaps it's the accent that makes the grass seem so much greener. Maybe it's the uniform. Because something tells me the Air France flight attendants aren't wearing skirts made in China or pants made in Poland with blazers made in Guatemala, which explains why my navy blues don't always match up and why I look like one of the Bad News Bears whenever I'm surrounded by my stylish foreign counterparts. For a while I wondered if the airline I work for, an equal-opportunity employer, wanted our uniform pieces designed by every country we flew to.

The first time I came into contact with a foreign-based crew was at the Milford Plaza Hotel in New York City. Located in the heart of Times Square, it's the kind of place tourists stay when they're on a budget. Today the going rate is $109 a night, but something tells me it wasn't all that much more than that when I first started flying and my airline housed crews with layovers more than twelve hours there. Crews with less time stayed closer to the airport on the wrong side of town. The Milford had tiny rooms, dark hallways, and a restaurant located on the street level that served up a very questionable pastrami on rye. Basically, it wasn't the kind of hotel I would have ever imagined an overseas airline would choose to house its beautiful flight attendants, who wear gorgeous silk saris in soft shades of orange, yellow, and pink. But they did. And I could not stop staring at them! I was sitting in the lobby waiting on a pilot I can barely remember to take me out on a date I wish I could forget when I spotted a group of women huddled off to the side of the check-in counter giggling. I had no idea they were flight attendants until a lanky, brown-skinned guy with an overgrown mustache and wearing a pilot's uniform two sizes too big walked over to the group and handed each woman a room key. Immediately questions began to fill my head. *How long are they here for? Are they allowed to go out alone? How long are they allowed to work? What will life be like once they go back to their normal lives after having seen the world?*

The women took turns whispering a three-digit number as the others scribbled it down on the back of paper-covered key cards. As I watched them waiting for the elevator, another crew walked in, an army of matching flight attendants, all with sleek black hair pulled back to expose luminous pale skin and blood red lips. Thirty sensible low heels clickity-clacked single-file to the desk. Each woman pulled a black roll-aboard exactly like mine at home, along with a gigantic hard-case Samsonite on wheels. More questions filled my head. I could have sat there all day watching the parade of different crews from around the world, but unfortunately my date didn't show up late and he had no desire to stick around the lobby. Not when there was a sports bar serving cold beer on tap with spicy chicken wings and greasy potato skins within walking distance.

Not every pilot is so quick to turn away from the international allure. Jane's latest boyfriend, an Airbus captain based out of Miami, proved to be one of them. I ran into him at our layover hotel in São Paulo as I was on my way out to grab a quick lunch before pick-up. He walked through the revolving doors trailing behind a crew of ten tired-looking flight attendants and two pilots with tennis rackets strapped to their backs. Immediately I recognized Jane's future fiancé from a framed photograph she kept in her room on the bedside table: the two of them arm-in-arm, helmets in hand, on top of a mountain with dirt bikes on the ground behind them. He had to be a good two feet taller than her.

"What do you have planned for your layover?" I asked, just to be nice, after officially introducing myself for the first time.

One of the other pilots, the youngest-looking one, spun around and slapped him hard on the back, a thin gold wedding band wrapped around his ring finger. "He's coming with me to check out the Finn Air flight attendants! I hear they lay out topless."

"Oh really," I said, and that's all I said. The future father of Jane's children blushed.

Thirty minutes later I was peering through the glass doors leading out to the sun deck, under strict orders from New York to go up to the rooftop deck and check out the situation *now*! I was happy to report back to Jane over the phone that there were only four attractive blondes lounging around the pool in string bikinis, all eight nipples barely covered, but hidden nonetheless. As I stood in the doorway, I couldn't help but wonder if the buff, bronzed dude getting out of the pool might be a Finn Air pilot dreaming about a soon-to-be bikini-clad American me!

"If I made as much money as passengers thought I made, worked as little as my neighbors thought I did, or had as much fun on layovers as my friends think I do, I'd have one helluva of a job!" exclaimed one of my friends after he heard me trying to explain what it's like, *really* like, to work for an airline without enough seniority to hold the good trips.

If you meet a flight attendant and you're wondering if he or she works international routes, don't bother asking. Those who do will make it known ten minutes into a conversation. Or the moment they walk into flight operations and find themselves surrounded by lowly junior flight attendants like me. It starts out innocently enough, I'll give them that, but very quickly it becomes quite unbearable. It goes something like this:

"Anyone working to Paris?"

"Nope. Tokyo. Again."

"I thought you did the Caribbean?"

"Thought I'd try something new. Have you been to the new layover hotel in Delhi?"

"No, but I hear the one in Frankfurt is wonderful!"

The rest of us will silently print out our itineraries, and then, sooner rather than later, make our way down to a gate where a small jet is departing to a city like Jacksonville, which now sounds even less glamorous than it did before sign-in. If I sound jealous it's probably because I am. How could I not be?!

What most international flight attendants don't realize is we know who they are—they don't have to rub it in. Their age and uniform size is the first thing that gives it away. So do the number of bags they're carrying. All that shopping requires extra luggage, making them look more like glamorous homeless people than flight attendants. One senior mama travels to London with a lunch bag, a computer bag, a tote bag, and two roll-aboards: one for clothes and the other for a full-size espresso machine. All for just a twenty-four-hour layover! In the morning she likes to make coffee in her room for the entire crew because the hotel only provides electric teapots for their guests. At the airport, the pilots have to help her up the metal stairs after the van drops us off on the tarmac underneath the belly of the plane at London's Heathrow Airport.

Junior flight attendants normally get stuck with the short hops on single-aisle aircraft. An aircraft with two aisles means your crew is either on reserve or has quite a bit of seniority with the airline. The size of the aircraft is the second clue you might be on an international flight (the first and most obvious being the flight's listed destination). Longer flights require bigger planes and, in many cases, an extra pilot, so when one takes a break there are always two in the cockpit. Bigger planes equate to nicer flights for a flight attendant. Not just because they're more comfortable for passengers, which makes for far less complaining and a lot more snoring, but because flight attendants have extra places to hide out if someone does become difficult. Because longer flights almost always result in longer trips for passengers, there's a lot more overpacking taking place. This means their luggage will get checked. After all, if they have to wait around baggage claim for one suitcase, they might as well wait around for all their bags, which is why they walk on board empty-handed and looking, dare I say it, happy! A stress-free boarding will do that. Trust me, there's nothing more worrisome for passengers (and flight attendants) than overhead bin space—or lack thereof. But when passengers check their luggage, as most international passengers do, flights get off to a good start. Flights that start off well usually go well. Passengers will actually thank us for a great trip as they deplane.

Domestic flights rarely start out as nicely as the international ones do. With passengers arguing over where to stow belongings, the first impression of the flight crew is usually negative, and before long, nobody on board is smiling, including the flight attendants. Airline employees will do anything to keep from being cited with a late departure and subsequently fined. Someone has to take the blame and if that person is written up too many times he or she won't have a job for long. We end up barking orders over the PA about stepping into the rows while stowing bags so others can get by and we can depart on time. The rule is that an agent can't shut the aircraft door until all bins are closed and all passengers seated, so when the overhead bins seem full, instead of smiling and making small talk, my colleagues and I have to frantically move bags around to magically create more space for the last few passengers. Otherwise the agent is going to try to put the blame on the crew.

"Hey, that's my bag!" I often hear.

"I'm just going to move your bag right . . . over . . . here," I'll say, struggling to get it into a nearby bin without dropping it on another passenger's head.

"If I wanted my bag in that bin, I would have put it there!" Here's my question: Would you rather have your bag in a particular overhead bin or get to your destination or connecting flight on time?

"Are you going to bring my bag to me when we land?!" one man spit when I pointed to an empty bin three rows behind his seat after he flagged me down to inform me there was no place to stow his bag. Based on the frequent-flier bag tag attached to the handle of his suitcase, I knew that he knew the answer, but some people just need a punching bag. Unfortunately, that often ends up being me!

"I want your name," growled a tweenager after I refused to remove another passenger's bag in order to make room for hers. What I want is to know what happened to respect! If not for me, how 'bout for the passenger who got on board first?

"When are you guys going to make these bins bigger?" shouted a passenger, struggling to basically push a square into a circle.

"We expanded the bins last year," I informed him, while moving things around so that his suitcase would fit. "So passengers started bringing on bigger bags."

And that's the truth! They went from eighteen to twenty-one inches in length.

Based on my limited international experience, I'm pretty sure international flight attendants spend a lot less time saying, "I'm sorry." After all, beyond the luggage situation, they get the tools they need to make passengers happy—and then some. I'm talking blankets, pillows, headsets, movies, breakfast, lunch, dinner, snacks—sometimes all on the same flight! Did I happen to mention there's alcohol? Free alcohol. Doubles! In coach! Well, at least to Europe there is. And it's the good stuff, real champagne, not sparkling wine. On top of that, first-class and business-class passengers receive newspapers, amenity kits, and, on some airlines, silk pajamas and slippers. Is it any wonder that international passengers seem happier?

Happy people tend to have good flights. That's a fact. So my theory is that domestic travel isn't as bad as some people would love to make it out to be—it's just that they're starting off on the wrong foot. But for whatever reason, I've notice a real uptick in unhappy—and outspoken—passengers in the last few years. And that's why I am sorry, sorry I have to say sorry all the time for things that don't even make sense. Like having too many middle seats. I've even apologized because we needed to get rid of the last row.

"But then the second to last row would become the last row and then we'd have to get rid of that, too," I chuckled, trying to make light of the situation. The passenger did not find me the least bit amusing.

In a magazine I read years ago, a bigwig working for an international Asian carrier was quoted stating, "Passengers wouldn't dare yell at a flight attendant wearing a dress." It felt like a snide remark directed toward flight attendants in the United States who prefer to wear pants. Instead, it just demonstrated that he hadn't spent much time with U.S. passengers, who are nondiscriminating. They are happy to yell both at flight attendants wearing dresses and passengers wearing dresses.

Of course, yelling tends to work best when you speak the same language, which is another advantage that international flights have. On domestic routes, we hear any and all complaints loud and clear. On international flights, there's often a language barrier, which means there are fewer problems on board. Sure, international routes are staffed with flight attendants who speak the destination language, but at my airline, it's only one per cabin. If you can't tell the flight attendant who doesn't speak your language that you'd like to speak to the one who does, the flight will continue on as peacefully as it had been.

At most airlines "speakers" wear the country's flag of the language they speak on their name tags. If there were a flag for Jive, I'd channel my inner Barbara Billingsley from the movie *Airplane* and wear that. If I could, I'd also attempt Yoda-Speak, just as a way to get the attention of passengers when I'm trying to prepare the cabin for takeoff or landing. Unfortunately (or maybe it's fortunately) for the passengers stuck on my side of the cabin, my gold-plated name tag is a flagless one. Once, a passenger tried to rip me a new one because I didn't speak Spanish (I think). I knew just enough "airplane Spanish" to say, "No com-pren-DAY!" as I handed him a glass of *naranja*, no ice (what's the word for ice?) and smiled real big. It's easier to keep smiling when you have no idea what they're yelling.

Even when international passengers do speak English, accents can occasionally lead to an awkward moment or two. One passenger asked my friend Vicki for a "cock," pointing at his throat. He got exactly what he wanted, a Coke, served with a smile. "Your cock, sir." But I must have said, "Excuse me?" five times to a passenger who wanted "penis cake" before I realized she was trying to say peanut cake. After I apologized, I informed her we didn't serve either—just to cover all my bases. There's an urban legend of sorts about a passenger from India who rang the call light and then, pointing to the button above his head featuring a stick figure, complained about fingering the flight attendant numerous times because his wife was a vegetable and he was a vegetable, too. Turns out he had ordered a vegetarian meal.

And miscommunication isn't limited to passengers! One time a coworker accidentally skipped a row while we were serving drinks. The passengers started chanting and making weird hand gestures at him—er, us! Because I was on the other side of the cart. A voodoo curse, I presumed. I'd heard stories from other flight attendants who worked the Haiti route about this kind of thing happening. To say I was scared is an understatement. The Haitian speaker working my flight that day wasn't surprised to hear what had happened, because in Haiti, she said, there were a lot of witch people. She started telling me about witch people who wore witch clothes and lived in witch neighborhoods and sent their kids to witch schools.

It wasn't until the passengers were deplaning that the Haitian speaker leaned over and whispered in my ear, "Here come some witch people." That's when I noticed a well-dressed couple making their way up the aisle. They did not look like witches, unless of course they were good witches. And then it dawned on me: on top of an accent, my colleague had a lisp that made her *r*'s sound like *w*'s. Our thirty-minute conversation about "witch people" had really been about *rich* people! Even so, I was nervous—I had no idea what kind of a curse might have been put on me. All that chanting still gives me nightmares.

What might give you nightmares is a story about the time I sat in the cockpit on a flight from New York to Caracas sometime around 1999. Over the radio, I heard an air traffic controller say something in a thick accent that for the life of me I could not make out. The captain picked up what looked like a CB radio handset, answered back in English, and then adjusted a few knobs before turning his attention back to me and the conversation we were having before the interruption.

"How do you understand what they're saying?" I asked.

"I don't." He smiled genuinely and added, "I've been flying this route long enough to know what to do." Something in the tone of his deep voice and the look in his droopy hound-dog eyes made me believe him. To this day I still have no idea if he was kidding around or not.

The other area of life where communication issues can cause, well, issues is when meeting attractive foreign men. Some may disagree, but I believe it's important to understand what your partner is saying. Life is hard enough without assuming he's talking to his Dutch female friends about you while you're sitting right there at a beachside table with them. When this happens it's probably not a good idea to drink too much wine and then try to imitate their accents or, worse, pretend you know what they're saying after they refuse to let you in on the conversation and then tell them off! I beg you, please, learn from my mistakes. Sign up for a foreign-language class ASAP or stick to dating English-speaking men.

The other tricky part about dating internationally is the time difference! Imagine landing in an amazing city you don't get to visit often if at all, because you're too junior to hold the trip, and not taking full advantage of it—and your date—has to offer. To be honest, it doesn't matter where the man lives—California can be just as tough as Europe! One man from Los Angeles was adamant about picking me up the moment I called to tell him I'd arrived. It was nine in the morning when we landed in California and I'd been awake since three o'clock his time. When I suggested meeting later on so I could take a nap before meeting him on his boat, he assumed I wasn't all that into him and left without me. He never called back. But when I gave in to another man from San Francisco, my lack of enthusiasm for everything but a bed (without him in it) on a Napa Valley wine tour was a turnoff, and our first date quickly became our last. Overseas it's ten times worse.

The real advantage that domestic flight attendants have, in my opinion, is sleep. Can you imagine working an eleven-hour flight to Brazil, laying over for eleven hours, and then working the trip back, not once seeing the light of day for thirty-three hours? That's what it's like for a lot of flight attendants these days. Personally, I think it should be illegal to have layovers shorter than our duty days. As far as I know, this does not happen with overseas carriers. It's one reason why foreign-based flight attendants look so much better than us! They get more sleep. Still, I know U.S.-based flight attendants who actually enjoy working these horrendous trips because of all the days off. I have no idea how they cross several time zones in a single day, several times a week, without feeling like they were hit by a Mack truck. But there are a lot of flight attendants who can do it, and not all of them turn to the wine-Ambien-caffeine cycle in order to accomplish it.

Not everyone loves to fly international trips. Some flight attendants don't do jet lag well. I'm talking about me, of course. Even if I'd get more days off each month, what's the point if I end up spending those extra days off recuperating from the last trip? It doesn't matter how much water or coffee I drink, the kinds of food I eat, the amount of melatonin I take, or how long I nap, I'm dragging after a long-haul, red-eye flight. When you work flights like that, a lot of time is spent on the ground adjusting sleep patterns. Some flight attendants will wake up early the day their trip departs so they can take a nap before they have to stay awake all night. For me it's easier to become a vampire by staying up all night so I can sleep all day, but what kind of life is that?

Those of us on reserve can't prepare for an international trip the way line holders do, because we have no idea what time our next trip will depart. I've been brushing my teeth and getting ready for bed when crew schedule called me out for an 11:45 p.m. departure to London. That's a tough one to stay awake for, especially working in a dark cabin for eight hours straight! "Resting" one eye at a time during flight helps, as long as the other eye doesn't accidentally decide to join in. Before I became a flight attendant, I never drank coffee. Now, depending on my trip, I drink it by the gallon. One of my biggest pet peeves is when passengers get angry with flight attendants talking too loudly in the galley during a night flight. First of all, the galley is my work space. There's nowhere else for me to go! Second, how else am I supposed to stay awake? Sipping weak coffee and whispering in the dark sure ain't gonna do it.

On flights longer than eight hours, flight attendants get what is called a "crew rest," a nap that is scheduled based on crew seniority. Junior flight attendants almost always get stuck with the first shift. I don't know about you, but right after takeoff is when I'm the least tired. It doesn't help matters that most of our airplanes don't have crew bunks like the foreign carriers do. A lot of times we sleep in passenger seats that have been blocked off for crew in the last row of coach. I've never felt comfortable sleeping in front of passengers while wearing my uniform, even when I'm allowed to do so. I imagine they're staring at me and thinking, look at that lazy flight attendant with her mouth wide open! While it might look like I'm sleeping on the job sitting upright and leaning into the window in a passenger seat, I'm probably just lying there with my eyes closed counting the number of times the toilet flushes. This explains the dark circles around my eyes and the delayed reactions to passenger requests when my nap is over.

YOU: Can I get something to drink, please?
ME: (*blink, blink, swallow*) Sure.
YOU: (*whispering to seatmate*) What a bitch!

I'm not a bitch, I swear! I'm just tired.

It also can be expensive to fly international routes! True, the flight attendants may make more money per hour, but it's impossible not to spend that extra cash on layovers that are longer, with more expensive things to do. This isn't so much a concern for senior flight attendants making the big bucks. In Lima, Peru, my crew invited me to go to lunch with them, but not without first making it clear that they liked to enjoy their layovers and did so by first ordering a $60 ceviche appetizer. If I wasn't up for it (i.e., couldn't afford it), they didn't want me to go. Well, I went anyway. And I'm glad I did, because the ceviche turned out to be the best I've ever had. But I couldn't afford to order anything else and wound up hitting a bodega for cheap rotisserie chicken on my way back to the hotel. In Paris, the crews like to drink French wine. Expensive French wine. Before meeting my crew in the lobby, I went to find an ATM machine so I could take out some money. I figured $50 would do. I almost had a nervous breakdown when I accidentally extracted my entire life savings! Here's a tip: know the local currency rate before you enter your PIN and press ENTER. A thousand dollars might not sound like much to some, but that's all I had, and now I was walking around with it in my purse! At night! In a foreign city! A few glasses of red wine later, I calmed down, but not before the wine had convinced me to put a pretty good dent in it. Now I had to pick up another trip just so I could afford to pay the rent. A domestic layover with nothing to do didn't sound like such a bad idea after all.

I had just sat down with my birthday Nutella and croissant for a solo pity party when Yakov walked in to the room to announce that he was getting married. But first he had to travel to Russia to find a wife. How's that gonna work out with all of us here? I wondered. It turned out to be something I didn't have to worry about, because Yakov gave us five days to move out. What he forgot to mention was that on day 3, a family from Russia would be moving in.

That week I saw thirteen real estate agents before I found a guy willing to work with a flight attendant. They're all afraid we're going to move into a place and sublet it to a million different people. That's because we do. This explains why no one cared that I had $3,000 in cash to throw down on the first decent place I found. At least not until I let it slip that the person I'd be sharing the apartment with was not just another flight attendant but my mother. "She's married to my father, who makes really good money," I assured him, so he wouldn't think we couldn't afford the place based on our crappy salaries. I guess that did the trick because he agreed to show me a one-bedroom apartment in Forest Hills that had a "cute little balcony." In Texas we call it a fire escape. Not that it even matters. What mattered is that now I had to work high time—or international trips—to afford it!

15

I'll Never Quit!

IT'S ONE THING to get down on your hands and knees to crawl inside a dirty food cart in an attempt to find something, anything—half a cashew!—to eat after the captain announces a two-hour air traffic control hold in flight due to bad weather on the ground after you've already flown five and a half hours across country. True story. It's quite another thing to collect a mountain of leftover Saran-wrapped sandwiches piled so high in your arms that you can actually rest your chin on top. Simply because you *might* get hungry later on. Flight attendants are a lot like survivalists. We've learned from experience to plan for the unexpected. We're like raccoons, scavenging to survive.

"Hey, guys, look what I saved for us!" I exclaimed in front of the cockpit door. In my arms I held two hundred gourmet sandwiches.

After a very long pause, one of the pilots, the more handsome of the two, asked, "Why?"

Why? He had to be joking. Now it was I who looked at him strangely. "In case we get hungry on the layover." Duh. For the life of me I could not figure out why they weren't more excited about the sandwiches! Most of the pilots I had encountered up to this point were just as bad as the flight attendants, if not worse, when it came to leftover airplane food.

The problem with these two ungrateful pilots was this. They were employed by bazillionaire Mark Cuban, owner of the Dallas Mavericks basketball team. We were on board Mark's GV, a fourteen-passenger Gulfstream jet. To put it in perspective, at the time Oprah also owned a private Gulfstream jet. Because of this plane he bought online, Mark made it into the *Guinness Book of World Records* for largest electronic transaction ever made. And there I was, in my own black slacks and red silk blouse, in need of a serious sandwich intervention on board a $41 million private jet.

The pilot sitting in the right seat, the nicer of the two, with five kids at home and a tendency to wish people a blessed day, finally spoke up. "You know you get a per diem, right?"

Per diem? What did that have to do with anything? At my airline, the per diem was about $1.50 an hour. It wasn't enough to buy airport food, let alone room service, much less pay the monthly rent after purchasing a few pairs of DKNY opaque tights. Sure, designer hose are a little pricey for a girl on a budget, but they were the only ones I knew of that didn't snag each time my leg rubbed against an aisle seat, so by spending money I was actually saving money. At least that's what I kept telling myself.

"Seventy-five dollars a day," he said, snapping me back to reality.

"Wait . . . what? Oh my God—oops, sorry!—say that again!" I wanted to make sure I heard that right.

At that moment, the clouds parted, light came streaming down into the cockpit upon his bald head, and I could have sworn I heard angels singing in the background as he spoke. I almost dropped all two hundred sandwiches on the floor. Holy moly, hallelujah, it truly was a blessed day!

At my airline, it would have taken half a month to make what the Mark Cuban gig paid for two days of work. At my airline, I never would have dreamed of laying over anywhere for longer than thirty-six hours. Now I had three days off between two easy workdays. At $75 a pop, that totaled to a tremendous amount of food I could eat, and would eat, just because I could. All I had to do was keep track of my receipts.

That night, I agreed to meet the pilots for dinner at the hotel restaurant. As luck would have it the restaurant turned out to be a Benihana steakhouse. Things were looking up. I went a little crazy and ordered the shrimp and chicken combo, as well as a spicy tuna roll appetizer. Why not? For the first time in my flight attendant life, I could afford it. I even paid the extra fee for fried rice instead of white rice. Talk about living it up! To top it off I asked the waitress to bring me a Japanese beer, Sapporo. The big one.

Afterward, when the pilots made a beeline back to their rooms to call the wives and kids, I took a quick stroll across the street to a health food store I'd spotted earlier in the day. I placed a case of protein bars on the counter. Name a flight attendant who couldn't use twenty-four grams of protein covered in yogurt? I'd need one in the morning. Back in the hotel room, I spotted a bottle of Evian water provided by the hotel in my room sitting on the dresser next to the television. After staring at it longingly for a good five minutes, I realized I didn't have to lean over the sink and slurp water out of the tap. I could actually break the plastic seal and guzzle it down without having to worry about paying the five-dollar charge or running out to a convenience store to find the same brand in the same size before checkout. I'll never forget how freeing it felt to crack the seal on the plastic cap. Water never tasted so good.

Without thinking, I picked up the remote and ordered a movie in my room the old-fashioned way. I pressed MENU, scrolled through a list of titles, chose a classic chick flick, and pushed OKAY. I can't tell you how nice it was to skip spending twenty minutes unscrewing cable cords, crisscrossing the lines and then screwing them back in in a lame attempt to score free cable without getting electrocuted. Life didn't get much better than this.

So how did I come to be lying on a king-size bed in a nice D.C. hotel, propped up against the fluffy white pillows watching the movie *Serendipity* starring John Cusack with the curtains drawn all the way back to reveal way off in the distance a beautiful view of a big white building, possibly the White House? (I wasn't sure.) It's kind of a strange story. I got the job through Mark's brother, Brian, whom I had met on an online dating website a year earlier. Let the record state I never went out with Brian. Let the record also state that I think Brian had a crush on my sister, who was also using the same online matchmaking site, which may have had a little something to do with getting the job. Then again, Brian is a really nice guy, so he may have just been doing what he does best, connecting people, creating opportunity.

For his birthday Brian wanted to borrow Mark's jet to fly friends and family to Vegas for the weekend, and because he knew what I did for a living he offered me the job. I didn't have any private jet training, but apparently I didn't need it since the plane only seated fourteen passengers and I would be listed as one on the official paperwork, a passenger who also could serve drinks. I didn't ask. I just went with it.

I wish I could say that working on a private jet was a dream come true, but the truth is, I never dared to dream so big. The plane looked like something out of a movie. It was so breathtaking I had to photograph it from every angle—twice. Just so I wouldn't forget every single light beige leather with dark wood grain detail. Who knew if I'd ever be given this opportunity again? Four oversized leather swiveling chairs faced each other in front of the cockpit—snap! A long leather couch with decorative throw pillows spanned the length of the cabin—snap, snap! A large wooden boardroom table at the back of the plane between four more of those first-class swiveling chairs—snap, snap, snap!

On the walls were a couple of television screens. I'd been instructed to have each one tuned into a specific sports television station before Mark boarded the plane. The bathroom really impressed me the most. It was roomy, and the gold sink fixtures added a special touch. Never in my life had I seen such a cushy seat on a toilet. Like Goldilocks I was tempted to sit on it just to see what it felt like—snap, snap, snap, snap!

While the galley looked impressive at first, with its crystal wine goblets housed behind clear panes of glass, I quickly learned the space was not flight-attendant-friendly. The dorm-room-size refrigerator was too small to house the cold lobster and shrimp party trays. Pouring water into the coffee machine proved to be the biggest challenge. It was mounted on the wall so high above my head that I had no idea if I was even pouring water inside. Hence all the half pots of brewed coffee during flight. I'd thought working the first-class 737 galley with its lack of counter space was bad, but this was ten times worse! But what the galley lacked in comfort, my jump seat more than made up for. Secluded behind a wall, it felt a world away from everything else, like my own private closet. To see what was going on during the flight, I'd have to stand up and step around the corner to check on everyone. Well, that is, if I could remember to do so, because with one push of a button a small video monitor popped out of my chair. There were dozens of channels to choose from!

I had decorated the plane with a Happy Birthday sign I had created at home with colorful markers, poster board, and a deck of cards and fake poker chips. I twisted red and black streamers together and taped them to the wall. As the guests boarded, I handed out birthday hats and party blowers. A little cheesy, I know, but I considered Brian a friend. I guess I felt overly grateful to have the job. The flight from Dallas to Vegas was a short one. A few cups of black coffee and a couple of rum and Cokes, and before I knew it we were on the ground parked at the end of the tarmac next to a dozen other private jets. Some were bigger, most were smaller. The most memorable thing about the trip happened next. When the airplane door opened, a red carpet was laid down at the bottom of the short flight of metal steps. "Welcome to Vegas," it read in black script, two lucky dice decorating the left-hand corner.

After everyone else deplaned, the pilots and I straightened up the airplane and then jumped into a rental car waiting for us at the end of the red carpet. That has to be the very best thing about flying private. There's no traipsing through the airport, no going through security (at least not before 9/11), and no waiting around for an airport shuttle, because when you land, a valet at the airport parks your car next to the plane with the trunk and driver's door open, the key in the ignition, the engine purring. For the first time in my life, I felt like a celebrity, not the hired help.

The plan was to work to Vegas on a Friday night and then head back to Dallas Sunday afternoon, so I figured I could stay out late after we got in and try my luck at the slots in the casino at our hotel. Imagine my surprise when I got a call early the following morning that startled me out of bed.

"Hello?" I mumbled into the wrong end of the phone.

"Plans have changed," said a pilot. I had no idea which one it was. "Mark wants to see the team play today, so we're going to leave in an hour."

An hour! I threw back the covers and jumped out of bed.

"It's just going to be Mark on board today. Go ahead and call catering from your room. The number is on the menu I gave you yesterday. Meet us down in the lobby. We'll fly back to Vegas after the game."

Corporate flight attendants normally keep notes on regular passengers so they know what to order from catering when they're on board. Nothing makes a passenger feel more special than a flight attendant who not only remembers their name but also what they like to eat and drink. Since I really didn't know Mark that well, or at all, I had no idea what he might like. That's why I decided to order a little bit of everything! They say a way to a man's heart is through his stomach. I prayed the same could be said for obtaining a permanent position on his plane.

Only once in my life had I ever served just one passenger on board a commercial flight. His name was Robert Redford and he sat all alone in first class on a late-night flight to New York. Business class and coach were totally full. That was my lucky day because I was the one and only flight attendant working in his cabin. My partner had been repositioned because of the light load up front. We're taught in training that the service isn't officially done until all cabins are completely finished, so as much as I would have loved to hover over Bob and dream about running my fingers through his beautiful thick blond hair, I knew I also had to offer my assistance in the back. Because all he wanted on a five-and-a-half-hour flight was a Diet Coke, just one, the least I could do was run through coach real quick with a pickup bag a few times. I'm only sharing this with you because even though I only had one customer to look after, there's always something else to do, at least on a commercial flight.

Robert Redford and Mark Cuban have a few things in common. Besides being extremely nice and maybe even a little shy, they both made me very nervous because they were way too easy to please. I'm not used to that. Mark, like Robert, only wanted a Diet Coke. That's it. Keep in mind that I have a lot of experience serving Diet Coke. You might find it interesting to learn that it's the most annoying beverage a flight attendant can pour for a passenger in flight, because in the time it takes us to fill one cup, we could have served an entire row of passengers. For some reason the fizz at 35,000 feet doesn't go down as quickly as it does for other sodas, so flight attendants end up standing in the aisle just waiting to pour a little more . . . and a little more . . . and a little more . . . until passengers sitting nearby become impatient and begin shouting out drink orders I can never remember.

"Just one second," I'll say, still pouring a little more . . . and a little more until finally I just hand them the can. I've actually had nightmares about frantically trying to finish a never-ending Diet Coke beverage service before landing. Who would have guessed that working on a private jet and serving a single Diet Coke to one passenger would turn out to be even more difficult?

Mark sat at the boardroom table watching television or reading a magazine. Each time I got up to check on him, he'd look right at me, smile and say, "I'm fine." The two words were out of his mouth before I could even take three steps in his direction.

"Oh. Okay," I said and quickly retreated back into my private corner.

Talk about awkward. I couldn't walk by him or even near him without him knowing I was checking up on him since there was no one else on board and he sat all the way in the back. To be honest I couldn't even figure out why I was there. I couldn't stop wondering what I was supposed to be doing because there had to be something other than nothing! That's when I started getting nervous. Did he have some sort of bell to ring when he wanted to get my attention? Would he just call out my name? How would I know if he needed something when I couldn't see him? Would he just wait until he saw me again or would he get up and serve himself? Oh lord, I didn't want that to happen!

"Really, I'm fine." Smile.

"Just checking . . ."

Soon I began fixating on the glass. Should I collect it as soon as he finished his drink or wait until he pushed it out of the way? I really didn't want to screw this up before I even began. On a commercial flight, there would have been nothing to think about. I'd walk down the aisle, pick it up, and ask the passenger if he'd like a refill. But Mark wouldn't even allow me to get that far.

"Still good."

"Okey-dokey." Oh my God I did not just say that! What is wrong with me?

I'll tell you what was wrong with me. The harder I tried to relax, the worse I became. It was no use trying to get comfortable on that sleek, luxurious plane. I'd grown too accustomed to people constantly wanting something from me. To be honest, I don't think Mark felt entirely at ease with my popping up every five seconds, either. So what should have been a wonderful experience turned out to be kind of weird—thanks to me.

We never did make it back to Vegas that night. I drove to my parents' house and sat around catching up for two, there, four hours—however long it takes to play a basketball game—until it was time to head back. When I got back to the airport, Mark called to tell us he'd changed his mind about going back that night. The flight was canceled. I assumed it had something to do with his team losing the game. Both pilots were thrilled—they both lived in Dallas. I overheard them telling their wives they'd be home for the night, but then they'd have to head out again the next day to pick up the rest of the gang.

"But what about all the catering I ordered for the flight?" You can take a girl off of a commercial airline, but you can't take the commercial airline out of the girl.

"Take it with you," said the first officer. I'm pretty sure my eyes gleamed with joy. While the captain loosened his tie and rolled his eyes (okay, so I may have imagined that last part), the FO actually helped me load it all into the backseat of my car. And that's how my family came to eat Mark Cuban's dinner. My mother and father thought it was delicious. My sister couldn't believe I had brought it home!

At first it might seem like flying private is the way to go, especially when you're a flight attendant and you board a flight early in the morning to find a pilot vacuuming the floor with a full-size Hoover. I had to pinch myself to make sure I wasn't dreaming. He seemed to be doing a really good job, too. I'd never seen anything like it.

Note to self: Marry a corporate pilot.

After I picked my jaw up off the floor, I came to realize the pilots really do it all, from ordering fuel and loading bags to stocking magazines and hiring flight attendants. I've heard of some pilots even acting as flight attendants on some corporate flights. I'd love to see that! I have no idea what their pay is like compared to other pilots, but I do know that corporate flight attendants are paid a whole heck of a lot more per trip than most flight attendants who work commercial. The thing is, most are not guaranteed a certain number of hours each month, whereas commercial flight attendants can count on a monthly average base salary of seventy-five hours. I'd choose security over salary any day. And many corporate flight attendants don't even have health insurance unless they pay for it on their own. The worst part about working corporate for both pilots and flight attendants is that it's like they're on reserve without the hope of ever holding off. When Mark says it's time to go, his pilots have to go, even if that means taking Mark and his friends on a joy ride at three in the morning. It doesn't matter what might be going on at home. Birthdays, anniversaries, recitals, all must be pushed aside. Might be why I sensed a little tension when I called one of the pilots on his cell to confirm the departure time of our trip the next day.

"Twelve o'clock!" he snapped. Then he whispered, "Don't call me at home!" and hung up.

Guess who didn't eat. For the record, I didn't eat, either. I made the executive decision to not order catering for the crew.

Note to self: Do not marry a corporate pilot.

Originally I was only supposed to work the one trip to Vegas, but when Mark's usual flight attendant couldn't make the trip to D.C., and the pilots couldn't find anyone in Dallas to use as a backup, the pilot who told me not to call him at home called me at home and asked if I could fill in.

"Let me check my schedule . . ." I held my breath as I sat on the phone pretending to look at a calendar. I figured I'd make him sweat a little before letting him know, hell, yeah, I could do it! I already had the days off.

The best part? They offered to fly to New York to pick me up!

Some airlines do not allow flight attendants to work second jobs, regardless of what that job may be. Mine, thankfully, is not one of them. But flight attendants at my airline, as well as most other airlines, are not permitted to work for another carrier. I figured if push came to shove I could argue that Mark Cuban couldn't be classified as a carrier, being he was a man—who happened to have a plane.

After I prepared the plane for our trip to D.C., I saw four of the tallest men I'd ever seen walking toward it. Years ago I had Magic Johnson on a commercial flight. He's one of the nicest passengers on Earth. I watched him sign hundreds of autographs at the Long Beach airport baggage claim after our flight to Los Angeles made an unscheduled landing there. He was the very last person to collect his bags and leave. But even though I'm one of Magic's biggest fans, I'm not that into basketball. So I had no idea what the Final Four was all about or who any of the really tall men were that were now walking up the stairs. I later learned their names were Dirk Nowitzki, Steve Nash, Michael Finley, and I forget who the fourth one was (sorry!). For a quick second I thought about setting my sister up with the short one. At six feet, Nash looked little compared to the other two guys. Thank goodness I never felt comfortable enough to suggest it because while my sister is pretty, she's not Elizabeth Hurley! Which is who I saw cuddled up next to him at a basketball game on television a few weeks later. When I greeted Dirk, the youngest and tallest of the men, the top of my head came to his . . . hips. Not every flight attendant can say they've spoken to a passenger's crotch. Talk about awkward. It was either that or risk getting a crick in my neck, which could have interfered with my real job, and I wasn't about to risk that! And all of the guys had humongous feet. Their shoes looked like they weighed twenty pounds each. In a way they reminded me of those circus clowns that drive the tiny cars, except instead of cars, we were on the Barbie jet and I was the tiny flight attendant. It's nice feeling petite.

What surprised me the most about these four gigantic men were their manners. They really impressed me! Seriously, it goes down in the books as the most polite flight I've ever worked in fifteen years. I've never been treated with so much respect. They were all "please" and "thank you," "yes, ma'am" and "no, ma'am," which kind of took me by surprise considering I was only about three years older than them. Perhaps it was being called "ma'am" that made me feel maternal toward them, because when they fell asleep during the flight I turned out the lights and covered them with blankets, extra long blankets. I kind of wish I'd taken one of them home as a souvenir—a blanket, I mean, not a player!

I only worked two flights for Mark. That's it. But it was the most memorable time of my flying career. Would you believe that those two amazing trips to Vegas and D.C. totaled to six individual legs over the course of just two months? By far my favorite flight was the first trip, second leg—the one from Dallas to Vegas, without any passengers. We had to go there to pick up his brother Brian and friends and bring them back. On that flight it felt like I owned the plane. I lay across the sofa and flipped through a few magazines. After I caught up on my basketball reading, I sat in Mark's favorite chair, watched TV, and drank a Diet Coke. It's really nice being Mark Cuban. I even peeked inside his extremely organized snack drawer and wondered if he would notice a missing candy bar. (FYI, the candy bar was still there after I left!) Now I know most of you probably already know that Mark lives a good life. But that day, my life didn't feel too shabby, either, thanks to him! It wouldn't be right to thank Mark without also thanking Brian for being single in Dallas at the same time as me. On that note I should also thank Match.com, and my sister who went behind my back and signed me up for the online service in the first place. Just goes to show anything can happen if you just take a chance!

Meanwhile, back in the real world of commercial aviation, life was getting better. I now had five years seniority under my belt and because the airline had been on a hiring craze for the last three years I was officially off reserve and able to hold a pretty decent line—757 transcontinental flights. Once a flight attendant can hold a trip like that, it's the only flight we're going to work until a senior mama retires and we can hold something even better, like a 767 transcontinental flight or a trip to Europe. Doesn't matter how long it takes, or how many times we fly to the same city month after month, year after year: a good trip is a good trip until we can hold a better trip. For me that route was New York–Vancouver.

I'd been flying to Vancouver pretty much every month for a year and a half. I didn't care that our layover hotel was located an hour away from Vancouver by public bus because there was plenty to do and see in Richmond, British Columbia. A lot of flight attendants who can hold a regular line establish routines at layover hotels frequented often. In Vancouver, mine included a workout at a gym that had allowed me to purchase a half-priced, monthly membership. That's where I had met the Mongolian guy who looked just like Ricky Martin, except cuter. He worked for a Canadian airline, but on the ground. We went out a few times and things started getting hot and heavy until we decided to go to Whistler for a romantic weekend away. That's where we realized we had absolutely nothing in common and actually kind of hated each other. I always say if you're not sure how you feel about someone, go on vacation together. It will make or break a relationship. I didn't kick the Mongolian down the mountain, no matter how tempting it may have been. Instead we drove back to the airport in silence. Still, the scenery was so beautiful it was worth every miserable minute spent sitting next to him.

When a coworker asked me to trade trips with her, I agreed. Not because I wanted to fly to Seattle, but because she was a friend and she wanted to work with her husband who was also a flight attendant on my crew to Vancouver. Seattle is worth the same amount of hours as Vancouver, so I wouldn't lose any flight pay. It also departed at the same exact time, the crack of dawn, so it would be an easy trip to work. Morning flights are a piece of cake. Passengers are too tired to stir up any real trouble. Most fall asleep on takeoff and don't wake up until an hour before landing. Afternoon flights are a little more difficult because passengers bring on board the stress of their day. Dinner flights are the worst because they drink like fish and then spend a good amount of time getting up and down to use the lav. This makes the job more difficult because when the seat belt sign comes on, nobody wants to return to his or her seat. Worse is when we're in the aisle working and they ask if they can "squeeze by real quick." Very few people can physically fit between a cart and a row of passengers. Luckily, I'm pretty darn quick when it comes to steadying hot pots of coffee. If I ask passengers to wait a few seconds so I can finish serving a row, they'll stand right behind me, and I mean right behind me, as in on top of me, so that each time I reach down to take something out of the cart, my butt rubs up against them. After the third time I'll ask them to take a few steps back. They never look happy at this request.

The first passenger to preboard our flight to Seattle that morning was wearing dark, wraparound, Stevie Wonder glasses. "She's going to need help getting to her seat," said the agent standing next to her for support. "She's blind."

"Color-blind," the woman corrected.

I'm not a touchy-feely person, so when I go to help a passenger who needs assistance I'll grab a bag instead of a baby or an elbow instead of a hand. Something came over me that day, because I placed her Louis Vuitton purse over my shoulder and took five warm wrinkled fingers in mine.

"My name is Heather and I'll be one of your flight attendants in first class. You're sitting in 6B. It's the last row in first class, an aisle seat."

"I was supposed to fly to Vancouver today but the flight was oversold, so now I'm being rerouted through Seattle," she told me, giving my hand a good squeeze for someone so frail. I was just about to tell her that I was supposed to be on that flight, too, but then thought better of it. She wouldn't care. And at the rate we were moving, we wouldn't get to her seat for another five minutes, so I didn't want to distract her from the task at hand.

"Only two more rows to go," I said coaxing her on.

"You're sensitive. You go out of your way to do what's right. You've surrounded yourself with a good circle of friends. Be careful, darling, you trust too easily. Someone you know will betray you."

I stumbled on a snag in the carpet, but quickly regained my footing before falling face first and taking my new friend along with me. I made a mental note to write it up later. "Are you some sort of psychic?"

"No, not a psychic, but I do have the gift and I enjoy giving it away."

At row 6, I placed her designer bag under the seat for her and then moved the seat belts out of the way so she could sit down. "What else can you tell me?"

"Let's see. You completely changed your life. Ten years ago you were going down one path and then, out of nowhere, you chose a completely different path, a whole other life. You left someone behind, someone you cared for deeply."

Brent! My on-off (mostly off) college boyfriend. I hadn't seen him since we got stuck our Costa Rica fiasco. We were traveling on my passes, but the flight was full so we couldn't get on. I was freaking out because I had flight attendant recurrent training the following morning, so without thinking twice I purchased two last-minute, one-way tickets to Panama for $150 each. There we would have enough time (forty-five minutes) to connect to a flight back to Miami using my passes. I should have known something was up when I spotted the armed military guys following us around the airport terminal in Panama. They even waited outside the chocolate shop for us before trailing behind us to the gate. But it wasn't until we were safe and sound on U.S. soil going through customs and immigration that I realized someone might be in trouble. Red lights began to blink as a siren went off. An officer yelled, "Up against the wall!" I remember turning around and looking for the guilty party, only to find out that someone was me.

"Me?" I asked just to make sure, because surely it couldn't be me. I was a flight attendant! I showed him my crew ID to prove it. We were detained while they checked our luggage with a fine-toothed comb. That was three years ago. There wasn't a day that went by when I didn't think about him.

The old lady with the Stevie Wonder glasses patted my hand reassuringly. "Oh darling, he wasn't worth your time. You're much better off without him."

I nodded, even though she couldn't see me—in color. I believed her. "Thank you," I said, trying to hold back the tears. My mascara wasn't waterproof and I didn't want to have to redo my makeup before takeoff.

"You about ready to board?" asked the agent standing between the cockpit and first class.

"Almost!" I called out, wedging myself between the bulkhead wall and the last row of first class and reaching between the seats for the woman's hand before it was too late. "Tell me more. What about my future? Can you tell me about that?"

"That, my dear, is rather interesting." Leaning toward me she whispered, "Most people are afraid of the truth. Of what lies ahead. I don't know why. The truth is all we have." I could see my distorted reflection in the black frames vigorously nodding back at me. "Now, listen closely. I've been fortunate enough to hold the hands of many famous people. The thing that sets them apart from everyone else is their powerful life force. I can honestly say that I feel the same thing when I hold your hand. You're very creative. You're going to do great things." She patted my hand twice. "You have a message. Your name will be well known."

"I'm going to send them down now!" said the agent, who hadn't bothered to wait for my reply.

I called back, "Okay!"

Now I was confused. I had no idea what the heck the psychic passenger was talking about. Maybe she really was just a regular old crazy lady dripping in jewels and carrying very expensive luggage. But then it came to me. I could feel my heart beating wildly.

"I'm an actress! Well, really, I've only been doing extra work, but—"

"No. That's not it."

The first few passengers began walking on board. I tried to squat down so they couldn't see me. "That's got to be it. I've been taking acting lessons."

"I said, that's not it."

"But I've been getting really lucky. Last week I got a line in a movie and——"

"You're a writer. Tic Tac?" she asked, shaking the little plastic box at me.

A writer? I held my hand out and let a few green mints drop into my palm. "I don't know about that. I'm not a good writer."

Pointing a crooked finger at me, she stated, "That is not for you to decide. It is not your business to determine how good you are. That is for the world to decide!"

There was one more thing I needed to know about before the rest of the passengers made it on board. One really important thing. "What about love? Will I ever find it?"

"You'll know soon enough."

A passenger seated a few rows up turned around in his seat and asked, "Can you take my jacket, miss?"

I smiled at the man and said, "Oh, sure. I'll be there in just a minute." When he turned all the way back around, I whispered between the seats, "How soon? This month? This year?"

She took my hand in hers and squeezed. "I predict a proposal three months after the New Year."

Three months after the New Year? But that was soon! The sooner the better, I told myself. Quickly I did the math in my head and gasped. Eight months! I did the math again, just to make sure I got that right. It was still eight months away. The UN guy. It had to be the guy who worked at the United Nations. I'd just met him online. We'd already had two dates and I really liked him a lot.

"Darling, take a deep breath. All great loves come from friendship. You must remain patient. Let it grow. Your life is about to completely change." She yawned and closed her eyes, and didn't open them again until we landed in Seattle.

I didn't really believe in psychics, or even nonpsychics who just had the gift, but on my layover I could not get our conversation out of my head. I took a brisk walk down to Pike Place Market to wander around and get a little fresh air. I ordered a latte and then found a place to sit outside the coffee shop. Normally I enjoy people watching, but that day, pen over paper, I decided that if I was supposed to be a writer I should probably start writing. Problem was, I didn't have anything to write about! For a split second I thought about writing about my job, but that would be boring. Who would want to read about that? That's when the idea hit me: a dark comedy about a serial killer flight attendant. I decided to call it *Stewardeath*.

The last thing the psychic had told me was my life would completely change. Boy, did it ever. Thirty days after she walked on board my flight, something horrible happened. On September 11, 2001, I landed in Zurich early in the morning. I was on vacation. After a short nap, followed by a quick shower, I sat on the end of the hotel bed with wet hair and turned on the television. With a hairbrush resting on my thigh, I watched in horror as the second plane crashed into the World Trade Center. I did not move from that spot for hours. Being so far away only made it worse. I didn't care that at that moment Switzerland was probably the safest place on Earth. All I wanted to do was go home.

Even though I'd been told by an airline representative not to bother going to the airport as a standby passenger, I went anyway so I could get my name on the list. I guess others had the same idea because I wound up being number nine-hundred-and-something on the list. I could have bought a full-fare ticket in coach for $8,000 that would have guaranteed a departure on the twenty-first if I weren't broke from having to pay a hotel every night and an overpriced espresso and croissant at the airport each morning. After two weeks of checking in and out of a Swiss hotel and lugging my bags on and off a train to get to the airport and then back to the hotel every day, I finally made it back to the United States. I landed at an airport in Texas because my flight to Chicago had been canceled. Instead of continuing on to New York, I decided to stay with my parents for a while. I had the time off because my route, the flight I'd flown for almost two years, New York–Vancouver, had been wiped off my schedule for the month, never to return again because it was an unprofitable route that catered to cruise lines. I was lucky because I got a little time off that most of my colleagues did not. They had to go right back to work. Of course, there were a few that quit, like my friend and ex-roommate Jane, who was now married and pregnant, but the majority of flight attendants I knew soldiered on. I can't even imagine what it must have been like to fly in the days right after.

I returned to work less than a month after so many people lost their lives. As I stepped out of the Kew Gardens cab in front of my apartment building in Queens, the smell in the air was strange and unexplainable. It lingered for months. The black soot that accumulated on our windowsill in the apartment had to be cleaned off every day. A pile of cardboard moving boxes sat on the curb, waiting to be loaded into a truck. Every morning they were there, the same boxes with different shipping addresses written on the label, different neighbors dispersing to different faraway cities. When I noticed a few of them were headed for Japan, I felt sad knowing the opera singer I'd never met other than a quick hello in the elevator would no longer be filling our hallway with beautiful music. As people left New York in droves and the odd smell refused to dissipate, my colleagues and I went back to work, back on the airplanes. And while we did so, memorials for coworkers who had lost their lives were set up in Operations.

During one memorable flight into New York, we were low over the city, and all the passengers were glued to the windows on one side of the aircraft to get a good look out the window at where the World Trade Center had once been. A dark hole on the ground was the only thing left. It smoldered for far too long. I wondered if the pilots were tipping the wing of the airplane in its direction in respect to what had happened.

Flying had changed. We were all scared. Conversation on the jump seat only seemed to be about one thing. During takeoff, one flight attendant sitting beside me asked, "What are you going to do if something happens?"

I had a few ideas of what I *could* do, but I didn't know exactly what I *would* do, if, in fact, it came to that. God, how many times did I pray sitting on the jump seat during takeoff that it wouldn't come to that? And if it did, I prayed it would happen before we finished the service because I didn't want to have to do all that work and then die.

"Here's what I'm going to do," said the voice beside me. I was so busy thinking about dying that I had forgotten he was there. He motioned to the insert of soda sitting on the linoleum floor beside the jump seat, an FAA no-no. Grabbing a can of Pepsi, he made quick and aggressive throwing motions. "Bam! Bam! Bam!"

"You're going to kill them with Pepsi?" I asked.

"It's better than nothing!"

Every flight attendant I met had some sort of plan, and each plan was more original and ingenious than the next. Broken wine bottles, hot coffee, and seat cushions became some of the weapons we could use. One flight attendant carried packets of salt and pepper to rub in their eyes. My weapon of choice also became a can of soda. But I wouldn't be throwing it. I would place it inside a long sock that I would swing over my head like a lasso if anyone tried any funny business on one of my flights. I kept the sock and a can of soda hidden in the seat back pocket behind the last row of seats in whichever cabin I happened to be working that day.

Meanwhile, flight attendants and passengers came together like the rest of the world did. We were a team and everyone offered their support. There were times, only a few, when questionable things would happen. Like the time the dark-skinned man kept going in and out of the bathroom with a McDonald's bag. It felt like he might be doing a "test run" to let others know how we would react if someone decided later on to hide a bomb housed in a McDonald's bag in the bathroom. After we reported the guy, every suit from every agency on Earth met our flight at the gate in Los Angeles. After speaking to him for an hour, they didn't arrest him, but we later learned that he had purchased a one-way ticket with cash. His passport had also just been issued to him. Was it also a coincidence that he would soon be going to school in Florida? Maybe. Maybe not. On that same flight there were three other Middle Eastern men, musicians who walked on board with three guitars. They kept switching seats in flight. We moved their instruments from the first-class closet behind the cockpit to the one located nearest the rear of the plane. Just to be safe. There were other times when passengers did things to obviously take advantage of the situation. An elderly gentleman from the Middle East sat in the first row of coach and kept his Koran and book about weapons displayed on his tray table for all to see. We ignored him, and his evil glare, as it was all too aggressive to be taken seriously. Plus, we knew there was a lawsuit just waiting to happen.

Even now, ten years later, whenever I hear about any accident involving an aircraft I'm taken back to that day in September. Most people don't have to think about it every time they go to work the way I do. From the moment I step out of my shoes to go through airport security until the aircraft slides into the gate, I think about what happened to those planes. They were my planes. My coworkers. My passengers.

After 9/11 many flight attendants lost their jobs. The ones who stayed took pay cuts, watched days grow longer while layovers grew shorter, and began working flights staffed with FAA minimum crew. Things we took for granted, like pillows, blankets, and even a few airlines, slowly began to disappear. At yearly recurrent training we were taught something new: karate. We talked about throwing hot coffee at lunging terrorists along with other things I'm not at liberty to discuss.

If passengers weren't afraid to fly, they could no longer afford to do so, so the airlines had to drastically lower ticket prices. A one-way ticket could now be had for the same price as a pair of designer jeans. In July 2011 my airline advertised a fare from Los Angeles to Las Vegas for $46. That's about the same price it costs to take a cab from JFK Airport to Manhattan. Because airlines are determined to fill every seat by offering rock-bottom airfare specials, commuters have a difficult time getting to work. I've seen flight attendants trying to get to work come to blows over who's next in line for the one and only jump seat on a flight. In an effort to stay in business, free food in coach was the first thing to go. Airlines no longer had to pay for the food, or the food's weight in fuel, or the caterers who delivered the food to the aircraft, or the extra flight attendants required to serve the food.

Slowly but surely people returned to the skies. First-class closets were taken away and replaced with extra passenger seats. Ticket prices stayed low, and everyone and their grandmother could afford to fly, many times a year. In the past it was during the summer that our flights were filled with kids, but after 9/11 our strictly summer passengers turned into year-round passengers. There's no longer a busiest season of the year—it's now a constant. Frequent fliers multiplied, so the airlines had to create a VIP top tier to separate the million milers from the three million milers. Flights were booked full and the lines at security grew. Passengers began losing their patience, not just with airport security but with one another. No longer did they remain seated on the plane when it arrived at the gate so those with tight connections could deplane first and not miss their flights. It didn't take long before I started having flashbacks to an earlier time. It was like working at Sun Jet all over again, but now I had to dodge insults *and* keep a watchful eye on the cabin for up to fourteen hours on the job after an eight-hour layover at an airport hotel.

These days when passengers complain about "bad service," I take it personally. There's only so much I can do with the tools I've been provided. I work hard, harder than ever before, to do a job I still take pride in. The reality is that passengers are not getting bad service, they're getting limited service—à la carte service. I'm still serving passengers the same way I was taught fifteen years ago. The only difference is, we charge $7 for a small bottle of wine and $10 for a turkey sandwich with chips in coach. My career changed to meet the demands of the flying public—cheap tickets. But now everyone seems to have buyer's remorse, including my husband, who is a frequent flier who travels more than a hundred thousand miles each year for business. When we first met he used to joke around about hitting the jackpot: an unlimited amount of travel passes. Nine years later he prefers to pay for tickets.

And speaking of my husband—four months after the psychic made her crazy prediction he walked on board my flight to Los Angeles. I didn't notice him right away. But as I pulled the salad cart to the front of the cabin, I spotted the best-looking deli sandwich I'd ever seen sitting on a tray table. I couldn't believe a business-class passenger had brought his own food.

"That looks good," I said, passing him by.

"Want a bite?"

Oh boy, did I ever! But I declined since I was, well, working. I appreciated his kindness and handed him an extra bottle of water as a thank-you. Normally we're only catered one per passenger, but the load was surprisingly light for one that departed two days before New Year's Eve. Then again, it was only four months after 9/11.

At the time 10J wasn't my type. As you might remember, my type had a tendency to suck. For one, he was shorter than I preferred, even though he was (just barely) taller than me. And bald. Okay, so he shaved his head—the point is, he had no hair and I liked hair, lots of it! But he was nice. And cute for a guy who wore jeans and a T-shirt and didn't look at all like he belonged in business class.

What I liked about him was this. The guy knew how to share—and with a flight attendant no less! This is not normal behavior on an airplane, which is how I knew he was special. I've had thousands of passengers borrow pens and never give them back. Some have taken newspapers or magazines lying on top of my crew bag. One even stole an egg McMuffin right out of my jump seat and thought nothing of it once he realized who the rightful owner was! Even if 10J hadn't offered me a bite of his sandwich, I still would have pegged him as someone I could be interested in because that sandwich alone told me he was a man with a plan, a man who knew how to take care of himself, even in business class!

I come across a lot of helplessness in the premium cabins. I once had a passenger refuse a meal tray because his turkey sausage was touching his scrambled eggs. Another passenger, a famous singer, had me run for several cups of tea because there were "black thingies" (tea leaves) floating in the hot water. And then there was the woman who wanted me to discard a single cube of ice from her glass of club soda because she had asked for three cubes, not four. Although at least she wasn't one of the ones who complain about their ice being too cold (seriously!). And in addition to saying "please" and "thank you," 10J also made eye contact whenever I addressed him. But he didn't flirt. I don't like flirters because I assume if they flirt with me they probably flirt with everyone else. That or they're about to ask me to send an extra dessert to a friend in coach who didn't get an upgrade.

It didn't go unnoticed that instead of taking advantage of the call light, 10J actually got out of his seat and stepped into the galley to ask for a cup of coffee. When he did so I immediately stopped talking to my coworkers about the guy I was dating at the time, but because he had overheard some of what I had said, he wanted to know more. I told him. Why not? The flight was light and there was nothing else to do. Plus, he was a straight guy and I needed a straight man's opinion on some questionable behavior.

"I don't care how many guys you date—one or five. If they're not treating you like you're number one you shouldn't date them, and he's not treating you like you're number one," said 10J, after I asked him if he thought I was acting paranoid.

And that's when the bell rang in my head. It didn't quite alert me that he was The One, because surely The One couldn't be short and bald. Not that there's anything wrong with frequent-flying, short, bald guys. It's just that's not what I had imagined for myself when I dreamed of walking down the aisle toward the nameless, faceless, groom that day five years earlier when Georgia mentioned the wedding I never did get an official invitation to. Anyway, I realized 10J was right. I deserved more, a lot more than a guy with a sexy British accent who dressed in fine tailored suits and couldn't be bothered to wrap my Christmas gift—or remember we had plans. Those wise words in the galley, coupled with the fact that after 9/11 I just wanted to settle down, get married, and have kids in three years with someone who shined with goodness, made me want to give 10J a chance—if he asked. And thank God he did!

I agreed to go out with 10J, but I was worried that I might be unduly influenced by the psychic. At the three-month mark I told him not to ask me to marry him in an attempt to slow things down. I didn't want to make something happen that wasn't supposed to happen just because I had a crazy idea in my head. I might have even subconsciously tried to sabotage things on our second date, when I laid my cards on the candlelit table at an Italian restaurant fifteen minutes from the Los Angeles airport. Besides telling him exactly what I wanted in a life partner, I informed him that while I didn't want to work my you-know-what off, I wouldn't quit my job—EVER! No matter what. I was shocked that he stuck around. And even though I bought a wedding dress four months into our relationship, it was only because I really liked the dress, not because I was in love with him. Who knew when or if I'd find another one like it!

But a year and eight months after we met, we walked down the aisle in Carmel, California, overlooking the Pacific Ocean at sunset. As far as I know we still hold the record for the cheapest wedding ever held in the history of the Highlands Inn. There were only twenty-four guests, including the photographer, and you better believe I packed my beautiful wedding gown that was on sale (and discontinued) for $199 inside my crew bag.

My life completely changed again two years after the wedding when four different pregnancy tests came back negative, positive, negative, and positive again—all in the same day. Flight attendants are allowed to work the first few months of their pregnancy, but I chose to go out on a maternity leave the very next day. Although radiation has not been proven to harm an unborn fetus, I wasn't taking any chances by flying seventy hours a month! Or even thirty hours a month. Flight attendants who do choose to work while pregnant are allowed to drop trips, no questions asked, whenever they like. At twenty-eight weeks they're forced to go out on maternity. The best thing about working while pregnant is getting to wear a maternity uniform top. It's a button-up dark blue "jacket" with capped sleeves and pleated flares under the bosom. It looks like a great big pleated belly skirt. One look and it deters passengers from asking for help lifting their luggage. This explains why one flight attendant I know who is no longer pregnant continues to wear it.

It was around this time that my mind turned to mush. As my pregnancy went on, I could no longer stand the thought of rewriting the serial killer flight attendant book after every agency and publishing house on earth rejected it—four times. (One agent who is famous for being snarky wrote on the bottom of my manuscript that she was now afraid of all flight attendants and that she hoped to never see me on any of her flights.) Writing a book requires a working brain, as well as time, lots of it, which was something I didn't have, trying to juggle motherhood and a flying career. So I put my book on hold and decided to create a blog. A blog post, I figured, only requires me to use half my brain and the baby to nap on a day off.

I got my first paycheck for writing a blog about flight attendant life in 2008, seven years after I met the psychic. In 2010 an editor at HarperCollins contacted me after reading one of my blog posts and then asked if I'd be willing to write a book. So far none of my friends have betrayed me, but that doesn't mean I don't sleep with one eye open. And just like I promised my husband on our second date, I'm still flying—and the stories just keep getting better, like the elderly woman in business class who yelled at me for talking too loudly to another passenger, then asked me to help her get her bra on later in flight, and then—well. You'll have to read about that in the next book!

Acknowledgments

I'd like to thank . . .

THE HUSBAND who walked on board my flight and sat on my side of the cabin and then actually stuck around after realizing what he'd gotten himself into. Without him none of this would be worth it.

MY FAMILY. Love and support is everything in life. I'm more than blessed. Of course a special shout-out goes to MY MOTHER. Without her this book wouldn't exist, and something tells me a book about marketing/sales/psychology wouldn't have been half as much fun.

MY IN-LAWS, who eagerly lent a helping hand during many long and tortuous reserve months. They say it takes a village to raise a child. Well, they were right. Thank goodness we're all part of the same village.

JANETT AGUILAR, CHRISTOPHER BAILEY, SHERLY CADET, DIEDRE CHRISTENSEN, JOHN GONZALES, BETH HENRY, VICKI HOWELL, FLORENCE HUE, IVORY KING, GRETA KOVAC, STEPHEN KRAUSS, MELANIE MCCARTHY, SEAN MORAN, KRISTEN NAVARRO, NICHOLAS ORTIZ, LENA SKINNER, DUSTY MIRLY STEEDMAN, KIM TOLIDO, and ANH

NGA WITTEN are just a few of the many flight attendants who have inspired me over the years with funny stories and words of wisdom. Many thanks are owed to them for sharing their thoughts as well as snippets of their lives with the rest of the world. As for my go-to guy for all things pilot, BOB NADELBERG, thank you for always answering my questions quickly regardless of how trivial they may seem.

CADY COMBS, who witnessed many of the events in this book and still encouraged me to write about them, even when she probably shouldn't have. You're the best friend a girl could ever ask for!

MARGO CANDELA, PAULA GILL, and ANNE VAN. I have no idea why they answered a desperate pregnant woman's online plea to create a women's writing group in Los Angeles, but I'm certainly glad they did for they pulled me through a difficult phase in my writing life without once complaining about reading Skydoll one more time. On that note, think you can read it again?

Last but definitely not least, a debt of gratitude is owed to STEPHANIE MEYERS, editor extraordinaire at HarperCollins. I truly consider myself the luckiest writer in the world to have had her by my side over the past two years, supporting me every step of the way.

ADAM ALMEIDA

About the Author

HEATHER POOLE lives in Los Angeles and *still* commutes to New York.